NATIVE SOUTH

NATIVE SOUTHERNERS
Indigenous History
from Origins to Removal

GREGORY D. SMITHERS

UNIVERSITY OF OKLAHOMA PRESS : NORMAN

Library of Congress Cataloging-in-Publication Data

Names: Smithers, Gregory D., 1974– author.
Title: Native southerners : indigenous history from origins to removal /
    Gregory D. Smithers.
Description: Norman : University of Oklahoma Press, [2019] | Includes
    bibliographical references and index.
Identifiers: LCCN 2018032849 | ISBN 978-0-8061-6228-7 (pbk. : alk. paper)
Subjects: LCSH: Indians of North America—Southern States—History.
Classification: LCC E78.S65 S57 2019 | DDC 975.004/97—dc23
LC record available at https://lccn.loc.gov/2018032849

CONTENTS

ILLUSTRATIONS

TABLE

ACKNOWLEDGMENTS

There are many amazing people and fine institutions that I'd like to thank for helping me write this book. I must begin, however, by acknowledging my ongoing indebtedness to the incredibly knowledgeable archivists and librarians at the Library of Congress; the American Philosophical Society; the Bodleian Library, Oxford University; the John C. Pace Library, University of West Florida; the David M. Rubenstein Rare Book & Manuscript Library, Duke University; the Georgia State Department of Archives and History; the Huntington Library; the National Archives of Great Britain; the National Archives of Scotland; the National Archives in Washington, D.C.; the Newberry Library in Chicago; the South Caroliniana Library, University of South Carolina; the Southern Historical Collection at the University of North Carolina, Chapel Hill; the Virginia Historical Society; the Western History Collection at the University of Oklahoma, Norman; and the William L. Clements Library, Manuscripts Division, University of Michigan, Ann Arbor.

The field of Native American history is as vibrant and thought-provoking as it has ever been. I continue to learn new things from my colleagues all the time. The work of scholars such as Andrew Denson, Angela Pulley Hudson, Kristofer Ray, Andrew Frank, Tyler Boulware, Julie Reed, Kelly Fayard, Alan Gallay, Robbie Ethridge, Paul Kelton, Katherine Osburn, Jace Weaver, and many other wonderful people continues to deepen our knowledge of the Native South. For the sake of brevity I wanted to offer my particular thanks to Kathleen DuVal, a historian I've looked up to and admired since graduate school. Kathleen's deep knowledge of the Native South and her generous spirit helped me to transform this project into a book.

I'd also like to thank Richard Godbeer, the Director of the Humanities Research Center at Virginia Commonwealth University, for providing financial support to complete the research contained in this book. Thanks also to John Kneebone, Chair of the History Department at VCU, for his support.

I must acknowledge the wonderful team at the University of Oklahoma Press for their professionalism and dedication to bringing this book to fruition. Thanks to Emily Schuster and Bonnie Lovell for skillfully and efficiently getting the book through copyediting. I'm especially grateful to Alessandra Tamulevich, an encouraging and insightful editor whom I can't thank enough for her ongoing support.

Finally, I conclude as I always do by thanking the three most important people in my life: Brooke, Gwyneth, and Simone.

NATIVE SOUTHERNERS

INTRODUCTION

Stories matter. Stories tell us about our ancestors, about ourselves, and about our communities. Storytelling is a gateway to meaning; stories help us to understand our individual and collective experiences, and they add layers of meaning to a sense of place, or home. In short, stories inform our worldviews and our identities.[1]

Appreciating the importance of storytelling—of not only speaking, but listening—is critical to understanding the histories of Native Southerners. For thousands of years, Native Southerners have told stories around their sacred fires in family and kinship settings. Lumbees, Catawbas, Waccamaws, Calusas, Cuseetas, Cherokees, Tuscaroras, Apalachees, Yamasees, Seminoles, Creeks, Yuchis, Nottoways, Chickasaws, Choctaws, Occaneechis, Haliwa-Saponis, Biloxi-Chitimachas, and scores of other Native communities have refined narratives of origins and belonging through oral communication, dance, song, pictoglyphs, and the development of systems of writing to communicate stories and give renewed meaning to a sense of place, belief systems, and communal life.[2]

Central to traditions of storytelling in the Native South—as in other parts of North America—is an understanding of origins. This is as true for Indigenous people in the southeastern United States today as it was for Native Southerners forced into diaspora in the trans-Mississippi West by the American government during the early nineteenth century. For well over two centuries, Euroamericans have continued the Western intellectual pursuit of "scientifically" understanding Native American identities by pinpointing where Native people came from. Studies of Indigenous linguistic traits, cultural characteristics, skull proportions, color and blood quantum, and DNA markers have all punctuated this pursuit for knowledge (and colonial power) over Native American people. As historian Alexander Ewen (Purepecha) argues, the "science" associated with understanding Indigenous origins and identities has been influenced by the colonizer's racial "dogma."[3]

What happens to our understanding of Native Southerners—of their origins, their history, and their contemporary communities in both the southeastern United States and throughout North America and beyond—when we deploy Indigenous storytelling and worldviews to interrogate the hubris of Western "science," the possessiveness of settler colonialism, and the divisiveness of racism (and the misogyny and violence that often informs it)?

What happens to our understanding of Indigenous identities when we listen to the stories of Native Southerners like Kathi Smith Littlejohn, a Cherokee woman born in North Carolina in 1950? In the mid-1990s, Littlejohn sat down with Cherokee folklorist Barbara Duncan to recount "some Cherokee legends." The tales that Littlejohn shared with Duncan were published in a book titled *Living Stories of the Cherokee*. Duncan's title was well chosen, as the narratives she published highlight the ways in which Cherokees—like other Native Southerners—shaped, and were shaped by, stories about origins, Indigenous traditions and medicine, tales about the ghosts of ancestors haunting the contemporary colonial landscape, and many others.

Littlejohn told Duncan that Cherokees have always viewed storytelling as a critically important facet of life. The stories Cherokees tell aim to give meaning to a collective sense of identity. According to Littlejohn, the antiquity of these stories, and the manner in which Cherokees preserved them, made them special. The ancient Cherokee forebears "didn't have books," Littlejohn declared, nor did they "go to school." So, she explained,

> They needed legends to teach people
> About different animals
> With stories
> And how things came to be
> And about the rules that everybody was supposed to go by
> So they would treat each other with a lot of respect
> And take care of one another
> That's why we have legends.[4]

I relate Littlejohn's story not to give primacy to Cherokee storytelling in the Native South but to highlight why stories matter to all Native Southerners. This book, then, is about the Native people of southeastern North America. It's a story about the forebears of Native Southerners who've descended from different ethnic, racial, and linguistic traditions—such as Muscogean, Southern Iroquoian, Siouan, and Caddoan peoples. It's also a story of Native life that's illuminated by the work of archaeologists, anthropologists, sociologists, historians, and geneticists. The research of scholars in these fields for too long objectified (and, in fact, colonized) Indigenous people. This has inspired new critical approaches to Indigenous studies, approaches that seek to refocus attention on Native words and actions in conversation with both colonists and other Indigenous people. This book is part of that critical tradition. It therefore aims to provide a chronicle of historical events analyzed through the oral and cultural traditions of Native Southerners and the written archives bequeathed to posterity by European colonists and their Native counterparts.[5]

When the Indigenous people of southeastern North America—or Turtle Island, as they knew the continent—first encountered Europeans and Africans during the early sixteenth century, Native peoples lived in communities with well-established social and political hierarchies. Native Southerners also enjoyed rich cultural and ritual lives and built societies whose architecture warranted the label of "monumental." By the 1540s, the people of the Native South had built complex, prosperous, and culturally enriching societies. The meaning of this wealth and cultural complexity, however, was not fully appreciated by the first Europeans to travel through the Native South. When Hernando de Soto, the Spanish explorer and conquistador, journeyed through Indigenous communities in the Southeast between 1539 and 1543, he expressed disappointment that the mountains of gold he hoped to discover did not materialize. De Soto, like many other Europeans, didn't find the type of wealth he was so eager to discover.

Given this early European focus on wealth extraction, de Soto's early perceptions of Native Southerners and their natural resources reminds us of the limits of European observations about Indigenous societies during the sixteenth, seventeenth, and eighteenth centuries and why it's important to engage with Native American sources—oral traditions, ceremonies, and archaeology—to reconstruct a fuller picture of life in the Native South in the centuries prior to the removal era of the 1820s and 1830s.[6]

The goal of this book is to introduce readers to the societies, cultures, and people who made and remade the Native South. While the book concludes with what's become known as the Trail of Tears, it's important to keep in mind that the United States government's forced removal of 70,000 to 100,000 Indigenous people from eastern North America did not eliminate Native Southerners from the Southeast.[7] Native Southerners remain in the Southeast today—having navigated the removal era, the American Civil War, Jim Crow segregation, and widespread bigotry—just as their kin continue to carve out lives in diaspora. My goal is to therefore present readers with stories by and about Native Southerners that will appeal to a wide cross-section of readers. Through these stories it's my hope that this book will inspire further interest in, inquiry into, and collaboration with, the people and places who brought (and continue to bring) the Native South to life.

First, though, a simple but important question: where is the Native South? The geographical scope of the Southeastern culture zone remains a point of disagreement among scholars. This is particularly true of the northern and eastern limits of the region. Scholars often contend that present-day Louisiana constitutes the southwestern boundary of the Native South, but given the exchange economies among the Native peoples in that region of North America it's useful to consider modern-day Louisiana and eastern Texas as a vibrant southwestern borderland connected to the Native South and that allows us to focus on the histories of smaller polities (or *petite nations,* as the French called them) like the Caddo, Natchez, and other Native polities in this region.[8] Scholars also disagree about the northern and eastern boundaries of the Native South. Some consider modern states such as Missouri, Illinois, and Iowa as part of the northern borderlands, while others stop at modern-day Tennessee and Kentucky. The eastern border regions include southern and southwestern Virginia and lands down the Atlantic coastline to what we know today as Florida.[9]

These broad-brushed geographical definitions of the Native South do not do justice to shifting borders and borderland regions that Native Southerners debated, fought over, and called home over many hundreds, indeed thousands, of years. These boundaries, regions, and borderlands changed over time because of climate change, warfare, alterations in socioeconomic and agricultural practices, and the arrival of Europeans and Africans after 1492. For example, during the period of the Mississippian chiefdoms (ca. 700 and 1600), archaeologists and anthropologists observe social, cultural, and linguistic differences among Native polities and classify communities among the South Appalachian Mississippians, Middle Mississippians, Caddoan Mississippians, and the Plaquemine in the Lower Mississippi Valley.[10]

Scholars identified these regional distinctions in the hope of illuminating similarities and differences among Indigenous polities in the Native South prior to the invasion of Europeans and sustained contact with both Europeans and Africans. It's important to remember, however, that Native Americans in the Southeast did not live in static societies characterized by unchanging cultures. In fact, Native Southerners migrated and intermarried, adapted and innovated, and traded and warred both before and after the arrival of Europeans.[11] As a result, the boundaries of their towns and villages shifted over time, the borderlands of their hunting grounds were contested, and the stories that Indigenous Southerners told about themselves evolved with each new generation.

In the chapters that follow, the Indigenous peoples who called these different regions of the Native South home and nurtured identities that connected them to a sense of place and community come into focus. Indeed, the stories that helped Native Southerners nurture communal identities remained at the core of their efforts to assert legal and political sovereignty— that is, communal ownership and authority—over their homelands in the face of European and Euroamerican invasion and colonialism during the eighteenth and nineteenth centuries.[12]

In general terms, though, the book builds on the Smithsonian Institution's National Museum of the American Indian (NMAI) geographical framework and defines the Native South as extending from its western boundary in present-day Louisiana, Arkansas, and the southeastern corner of Missouri. The northern boundary (through which trade networks extended into and beyond the Ohio and Illinois River valleys) extended eastward through modern-day Tennessee, the southern sections of Kentucky, portions of West Virginia, and southwestern, central, and southern and southwestern Virginia—the latter being homelands and/or hunting grounds of the Nottoways and Meherrins east of the fall line, the Occaneechis and Saponis in the Piedmont, and the Cherokees in southwestern Virginia. It should be noted, however, that while the book pays some attention to the Indigenous peoples of Virginia, I follow the general contours of anthropologist Raymond Fogelson's conceptualization in defining what is today Virginia as a northeastern borderland of the Native South (a conceptualization that places members of the Powhatan chiefdom, the Rappahonnock, Monacan,

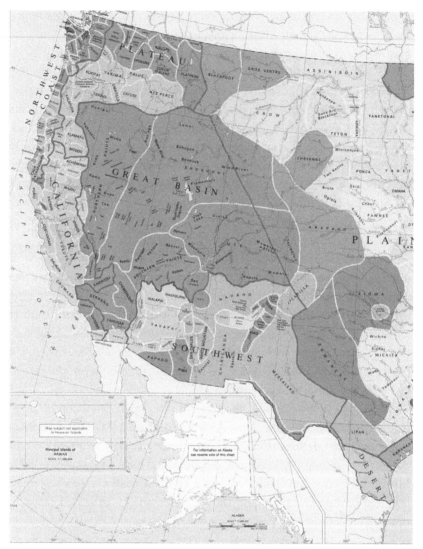

William C. Sturtevant's map of Indian tribes, cultures, and languages (1967). *Library of Congress, Geography and Map Division, Washington, D.C.*

Manahoac, and tribes of the Shenandoah River in the Eastern or Northeastern culture zones). That said, the eastern border of the Native South extends south through what are today the Carolinas, the Georgia coast, and Florida, and then westward along the Gulf Coast.[13]

My analysis therefore situates the Indigenous people of the Virginia and

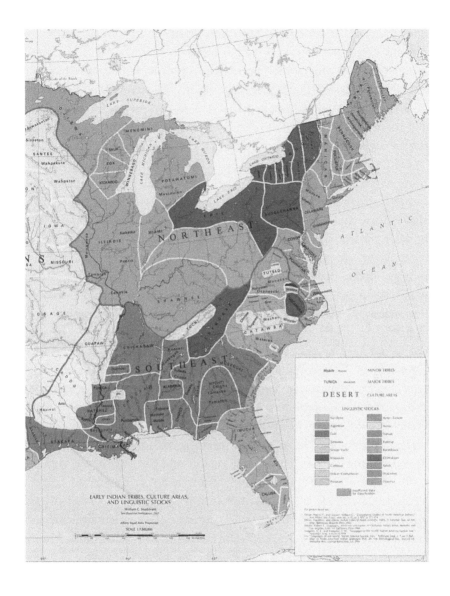

EARLY INDIAN TRIBES, CULTURE AREAS,
AND LINGUISTIC STOCKS

William C. Sturtevant
Smithsonian Institution, 1967

Albers Equal Area Projection
SCALE 1:7,500,000

Maryland Tidewater region in the Eastern Woodlands. Anthropologists and archaeologists divide the lands east of the Mississippi River in what is today the United States among the Southern, Eastern, and Northeastern Woodlands. Some scholars simplify these regional designations, referring to the Northeastern and Southern Woodland regions.[14] Nonetheless, these designations refer not only to the ecologies of the Eastern Woodlands—characterized by deciduous forests, southeastern pine-oak and hardwood forests—and the geographical distribution of Native populations, but they also define social and cultural characteristics.[15] The term "Woodland," for instance, refers to cultural and social developments in pottery, burial mounds, and agriculture.[16] As we'll see in chapter 2, these developments have aided archaeologists in distinguishing among the Mississippian chiefdoms.

While geography—notably the fall line—made regular trade between the tribes of the Chesapeake and the people of the Native South difficult, the Indigenous peoples of the Southeast did have contact with people from outside their culture zone. For example, trade, diplomacy, and occasionally warfare, between the Iroquoian-speaking Cherokees and Nottoways punctuated the relations of these polities during the eighteenth century. Similarly, colonial records indicate that Indigenous warriors from the Northern Woodlands, whom the people of the Native South referred to as the "Northwards," routinely attacked towns and villages throughout the Native South.[17]

In the Southern, Eastern, and Northern Woodland regions, however, chiefs and headmen engaged in diplomacy and trade with their Native counterparts. This proved particularly true throughout the Southern and Northern Woodlands, with overland trade routes and the Tennessee, Ohio, and Wabash Rivers opening vast networks of Native exchange. Native Southerners worked hard to keep the white path of peace open to traders and diplomats from other tribes, thereby drawing outsiders into the reciprocal responsibilities designed to promote balance and harmony in the world.[18]

By the time Spanish, French, and ultimately British colonialism became a regular part of life in the Native South, Indigenous people had already established networks of diplomacy and exchange. During the sixteenth and early seventeenth centuries, the Beloved Men and Women of the Native South, or those elders who sought out the "white path" of peace in diplomatic dealings with foreigners and worked to ensure peace and harmony in their respective towns, were often well traveled, and well practiced at the intricacies of diplomatic and trade relations.[19]

Chronologically, this book introduces readers to an enormous time frame. The book begins with a brief assessment of the "origins" debate before transitioning to what archaeologists and anthropologists refer to as the Paleo-Indian and Archaic periods (between ca. 10,000 to 3,000 years ago). The book's narrative then moves on to the Early, Middle, and Late

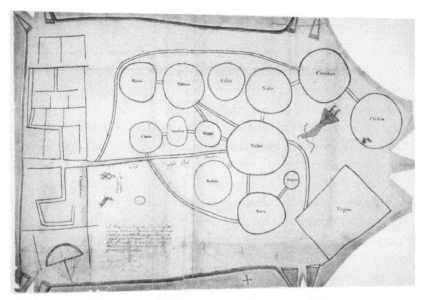

Chickasaw deerskin map, ca. 1725. *National Archives of Great Britain.*

Woodland periods (between ca. 3,000 and 500 years ago) before culminating with the "post-contact" period, or the centuries between European encounters with the Americas in the fifteenth century and the infamous era of removal during the 1820s and 1830s. This sweeping chronology will make it possible to highlight change (and continuity) over time, a particular focus of historians, while also introducing readers to the different cultural and linguistic groups in the Native South and the identities nurtured by the people from these groups. No book can tell the complete story of any topic, and to claim as much is to assert only the author's hubris. My goal in writing this book is therefore to contribute to an ongoing conversation in which Native Southerners drive the story through their words and deeds. The book is also an invitation to readers to engage with the debates, disagreements, and warfare between and among Native Southerners and European colonizers. It's my hope that such engagement will inspire empathy and raise new questions that deepen our collective understanding of the histories featured throughout this book.

Native Southerners is divided into six chapters. Chapter 1 takes a broad approach to the controversial question of origins and how these questions relate to issues of storytelling and identity among Native Southerners.

Indigenous origin narratives are therefore juxtaposed against Western theories of Native American migrations. In keeping with a broad approach to questions of origins, the chapter also considers the impact of technological and horticultural change in helping Native Southerners build and renew communal identities. Set against a backdrop of fluctuations in climate and local ecosystems, this often-neglected aspect of the origin question helps us focus on how Native Southerners incorporated technologies such as the bow and arrow into material culture and highlights the importance of agricultural innovation to the development of cooperative group identities.

An appreciation of the importance of technological and agricultural innovations provides the ideal starting point for analysis of Mississippian chiefdoms. Chapter 2 introduces readers to chiefdom societies. This chapter explores the rise and fall of chiefdoms, details the social and political structures that buttressed chiefdom societies, and considers the impact that early European contact with chiefdoms in North America's Southeast had on preexisting trade, diplomatic, and social networks.[20]

Chapters 3 and 4 focus on the seventeenth and eighteenth centuries. These chapters introduce readers to a transformative phase in the Native South and the communal identities nurtured by its Indigenous people. Indeed, this epoch witnessed the decline and splintering of chiefdoms and the emergence of what anthropologists call coalescent societies. As the chapters reveal, both large coalescent societies and *petite nations* emerged in the Native South during these centuries. The communal identities that coalesced, or came together, in larger societies like the Creeks and Cherokees were built on a foundation of multiethnic and multilingual societies emerging at a time of slave raiding, unprecedented disease outbreaks, and an increase in Indian-European engagement, which all had the potential to exacerbate preexisting tensions among Native polities.

Chapter 5 covers a period roughly from the mid-eighteenth century to the emergence of a nascent United States republic. Native Southerners witnessed some dramatic changes in their communities and in the world outside their towns and villages during this time. Violence and warfare between Native polities combined with the involvement of Native Southerners in imperial wars involving the French, Spanish, British, and American colonists—most notably the Seven Years' War (sometimes referred to as the French and Indian War to denote the American theater of a global war between 1754 and 1763) and the American Revolutionary War—precipitated small-scale migrations within the Southeast, most notably among the Cherokees, as displaced Native Southerners worked to breathe new life into their communal identities after the wars. Moreover, this was an era in which the ethnogenesis of Native polities such as the Seminoles comes fully into focus and in which Native war chiefs and prophets from the Native South and beyond tried to forge pan-Indian alliances to deal with ongoing threats to their territorial sovereignty and cultural traditions.[21]

Chapter 6 surveys the era of removal, an era commonly associated with the 1820s and 1830s. These decades did indeed see a concerted effort to remove not only Native Southerners but all remaining Native people in the eastern half of the United States and its territories, culminating with the removal of the Miami people in the mid-1840s. As the slave frontier expanded westward in the Southeast and settler populations swelled in the Ohio and Illinois River valleys, pressure for Indian removal grew. Eventually, the federal government oversaw the removal of 70,000 to 100,000 Native Americans from the eastern United States to reservations west of the Mississippi River. While the 1820s and 1830s bore witness to the hardships and tragedies of coerced removals, the drive of Euroamericans to remove, or eliminate, Native people from the eastern half of the United States did not suddenly emerge in the 1820s; the intent to remove Native people (whether in the form of assimilationist policies or the physical relocation of Native Southerners) was present at the founding of the republic. Set against such immense pressures, how could Native Southerners maintain any sense of social cohesion and continue to nurture their communal identities? Indeed, how would the stories of who they were, and who they were becoming, change?

That tens of thousands of Native Southerners held onto their social and cultural traditions, maintained Native languages, and worked to nurture bonds of kinship and community is borne out in this book's epilogue. The coerced removals of the 1820s and 1830s and racial stereotypes about what constitutes an "authentic" Indian continue to haunt the stories that Native Southerners tell about themselves. But since the 1830s and 1840s, these stories have also remained connected to long-held tales of migration, place, and collective identities forged in both diaspora and in the Native South. Thus, today, Native Southerners maintain family connections, nurture communities, and share stories of a common and ongoing encounter with settler colonialism from their homes in the southeastern United States, the American West, and beyond.

Finally, a few words about terminology. Throughout the book I refer interchangeably to the Native South and the Native Southeast to designate the Southeastern culture zone defined above. In terms of communities of people, where possible I use specific chiefdom affiliations—such as Cahokia, Etowah, or Moundville—or the identifications that have come to be associated with the coalescent societies of the Native South—such as the Cherokees, Creeks, Choctaws, Chickasaws, Seminoles, Lumbees, Catawbas, and many others. When not using these specific designations, I use phrases such as "American Indian," "Native American," "Indigenous," or "Native Southerners," recognizing that each of these terms is the product of settler colonial histories, and as such, culturally freighted in different ways for Native American peoples.[22] In other words, while the terms commonly used to refer to "American Indians" or "Native Americans" tend to reduce people with very specific tribal identities that efface the complex history of identity formation among Native Southerners, it is not my intention to disrespect the members of different tribal nations when using these terms.

This book is ultimately an attempt to introduce readers to the stories of who the Native Southerners were and who they became following the invasion of North America by Europeans in the sixteenth and seventeenth centuries. At the same time this is a book that is mindful of the fact that the histories recounted in the following pages inform the identities of Native Southerners—in both the Southeast and in diaspora—to this day.

CHAPTER ONE

ORIGINS

In the beginning there was the water and the air. Water beings and air beings punctuated the vast expanses of water and air. Some of these beings were humanlike, others resembled animals. In time, these beings began having families. Some hunted for food, others traveled, and still others led efforts to develop cultural and ceremonial traditions that bound communities together in a common sense of belonging that was rooted in geography, or a sense of place.[1]

The Yuchis and Tuskegees, Native Southerners who became part of the Creek Indian Confederacy during the seventeenth and eighteenth centuries, told and retold versions of this story to their children and grandchildren. It's a story of beginnings, of origins. Elders committed these stories to memory, eventually entrusting future generations with the retelling of such narratives—a responsibility that continues into the present.

Like the Yuchis and Tuskegees, Native communities throughout the Southeast nurtured origin stories.[2] Native polities such as the Natchez, Hitchitis, Alabamas, Koasatis, Catawbas, Nottoways, Waccamaws, and larger societies like the Choctaws, Chickasaws, and Cherokees, all developed oral traditions that helped to explain the origins of the universe and the place of kinship groups in the world, and gave meaning to life on earth.[3]

The origin narratives nurtured by Native Southerners (and recorded, albeit imperfectly, by Europeans and Euroamericans) between the seventeenth and nineteenth centuries were thousands of years in the making. Stories about how a people came into existence connected spiritual beliefs and ceremonial systems, gave meaning to social, cultural, and political structures, and provided clues to Indigenous belief systems in pre-Columbian

15

North America.[4] Origin narratives also overlapped with stories about binary opposites, such as concepts like good and evil, light and darkness.[5] In other words, origin narratives did more than simply tell a story about the beginnings of the universe and human existence; they gave meaning and purpose to cultural life, helped to structure social and political conventions, and connected people to a place and a community.[6]

The dynamism of the cultures that Native Southerners developed throughout the Southeast prior to European colonialism gave them the ability to use stories to explain historical developments, such as the refinement of spear point technologies and the introduction of the bow and arrow, or changes in agricultural practices that revolved around the three sisters of corn, beans, and maize. Native storytelling therefore informed political and cultural identities, in addition to transmitting scientific and medicinal knowledge from one generation to the next.

This chapter takes an intentionally broad approach to the notion of "origins." While the following analysis reflects on the well-worn question of "where the Indians came from," it also presages the analysis in subsequent chapters by reflecting on social, political, and technological changes in the Native South. Borrowing from the insights of archaeologists and anthropologists, it's possible to extrapolate meaning from human behavior and to try to understand how Native Southerners articulated new beginnings in their political and ceremonial traditions. Finally, the chapter concludes with a brief summation of Western scientific arguments about Native American origins. These theories cannot be ignored because they constitute a part of the enduring legacy of settler colonial logic and the drive to empirically know, categorize, and confine Native people. As this portion of the chapter reveals, Indigenous leaders, elders, and intellectuals continue to meet such efforts with critiques of their own.

◇◇◇◇◇◇◇◇◇◇◇◇◇◇◇◇◇◇◇◇◇◇◇◇◇

The oral traditions that Native Southerners developed over many centuries helped to give meaning to a collective sense of beginning and an understanding of place in the world. Stories focusing specifically on the creation of the universe and human societies fall under one or a combination of the following genres: earth emergence stories, earth-diver creation stories, deluge stories, migration narratives, human creation associated with the Sun or Moon, and corn mother narratives.

Earth emergence tales (stories about the emergence of a people from an opening in the ground) and earth-diver narratives (involving animals diving into primordial waters) were the two most common types of origin narratives associated with the societies of the Native South by the seventeenth century. As in other parts of Native North America, variations on these narrative genres emerged over time, with different types of stories overlapping and complementing one another.[7] For example, if we return to the Yuchi it's possible to identify oral traditions that emphasize earth-diver tales. Similarly, members of other groups, like the neighboring Cherokees, nurtured earth-diver narratives but also incorporated other oral traditions, such as deluge stories and migration narratives, perhaps reflecting how Cherokees incorporated the origin legends of Europeans into their own narratives of beginnings.[8]

Increasingly after the seventeenth century, both small and large polities in the Native South had their origin stories and beliefs filtered through the ethnographic writings of colonial military officers and officials, ethnologists and missionaries, and more recently, professional anthropologists, archaeologists, and historians. This has proven to be the case with, for example, the Natchez. Seventeenth-century French observers interpreted Natchez origin stories through the lens of Catholicism. French missionaries and colonists sometimes recorded Natchez origin narratives in language that reinforced their own Christian beliefs about the origins of the world. For instance, one historian has noted that French colonists observed that "the Natchez followed a moral code of divine origin that was not unlike those found in the Old Testament."[9]

Disentangling the threads of Native American and Christian culture remains one of the major challenges confronting students of the Native South. The Natchez, for example, didn't passively allow the French to interpret their oral traditions; instead, they actively sought ways to incorporate outside belief systems into existing traditions to empower elders and medicine men and women to better address new social problems, such as the spread of diseases like smallpox.[10]

Other challenges also exist for students of the Native South. From the sixteenth century, the loss of knowledge that occurred in Indigenous communities across the Southeast following the invasion of European colonizers and the forced relocation of slaves from Africa to the Americas meant that origin narratives became fragmented at times. The anthropologist Charles Hudson made such observations during his fieldwork among the Catawbas.

Hudson claimed that many people didn't seem particularly interested in their origin stories.[11] Hudson was not the first (and by no means last) anthropologist to make such observations. In the early twentieth century, University of Pennsylvania anthropologist Frank Speck lamented what he believed was the distinct lack of insight among the Catawbas about their origins, something he attributed (in an overly racialized and condescending way) to the Catawbas being "lax and shiftless in vital concerns."[12]

Catawba people did in fact have narratives about their origins. Some of these stories reveal the influence of Christianity in the Native South. For instance, twentieth-century Catawbas recounted how their ancestors were connected to the "Lamanites"—a group of apostate Hebrews who migrated to the New World—a belief that can also be found in Mormon theology and which is a reflection of the porous and adaptable nature of oral storytelling.[13]

If Catawba origin narratives highlight the significance of cultural syncretism in the Native South, the oral traditions of other Native Southerners display similar complexity and a range of possible cultural influences. The multiethnic Creek Indians—a group that included people who spoke the Muscogee (Muskogee or Maskókî), Hitchiti, Euchee (Yuchi), Natchez, and Alabama languages—developed a number of narratives to help explain the origins of their ancestors. These cosmogonies, or creation stories, have long been nurtured by Creek people in oral storytelling and scattered through written ethnographies dating back to the sixteenth and seventeenth centuries.[14]

Creek creation narratives focus on two major traditions. In the Eastern Creek tradition, narratives emphasizing earth-diver creation stories predominate. The Yuchis, the Hitchitis, and the Tuskegees, for example, developed earth-diver creation stories to account for their origins. Among Creek people, earth-diver creation stories posit a beginning point in which only the sky, water, and the beings inhabiting each space exist. Many Creek origin narratives focus on a crawfish diving into the water several times and ultimately succeeding in pulling a piece of the earth to the surface of the water.[15] Shortly after the earth is created, the Yuchi origin narrative instructs that the first humans came into being.[16]

The Alabamas, Koasatis, and Muscogees also developed creation stories that emphasize their emergence from the earth. Earth emergence narratives share many similar plotlines. Muscogee narratives usually don't speak of the earth's creation before human beings. In fact, both Alabama and Muscogee narratives highlight the emergence of humans from underground. These original people are said to be made from the earth's clay and to emerge from a cave. Such traditions hold clues to the importance of the land in providing a sense of geographical rootedness and go part of the way to understanding the importance of communal agricultural activity in Creek communities. Slight variations in earth emergence stories exist; the Alabamas, for instance, developed stories about "the Great Spirit" who made the universe and its human inhabitants, while the Muscogees emphasize the Rocky Mountains as the backbone and foundation of the earth.[17]

In the Western Creek tradition, groups such as the Kashitas emphasized migration in their origin narratives. Such narratives presented a story of the first humans emerging in the West shortly after the formation of dry land. One of these narratives recounted the emergence of the Kashitas and their eastward migrations.[18] In other instances, non-Creek people recorded stories of east-west migrations as part of Creek origin legends. During his travels through Georgia and Florida in 1773 and 1774, the naturalist William Bartram speculated that "the Creeks or Muscogulges, arose from, and established itself upon, the ruins of the Natches." Bartram contended that Creek informants told him that after some people established settlements, others continued migrating in a northeasterly direction.[19]

The people of the Creek Confederacy were not alone in sharing migration narratives about their origins with Europeans during the seventeenth and eighteenth centuries. The neighboring Cherokees (Tsalagi, or Ani-Tsalagi, the plural of "Cherokee") also developed a variety of origin narratives that including stories about travel, migration, and resettlement. The Cherokees, an Iroquoian-speaking people, had called the southern Appalachians home since at least the year 1000. The Cherokees developed a matrilineal clan system. Cherokees belonged to one of seven clans—Aniwahya (Wolf), Ani Tsiskwa (Small Bird), Anikawi (Deer), Anigilohi (Twister or Long Hair), Anisahoni (Blue), Anigatogewi (Wild Potato), Aniwodi (Red Paint)—and lived in "demographically amorphous" towns nestled along riverbanks.[20]

One narrative recited to explain the origins of the Cherokee people is the story of a mythical ancient priesthood, the Ani-Kutani. Eighteenth-century ethnographers claimed that Cherokees recounted stories of this ancient priesthood migrating from a mythical island and settling in the southeast. However, the Ani-Kutani became excessive in their exercise of power, prompting a bloody uprising that led to their overthrow and gave rise to the communal, consensus-seeking form of politics that emerged in Cherokee towns by the seventeenth and eighteenth centuries.[21]

The most popular Cherokee creation stories focus on earth-diver narratives. Some of these stories emphasize the motif of the sun-catcher. Historically, Cherokee creation stories are recounted at night and during the winter to ensure listeners had the fire of life rekindled inside of them. Of all the Cherokee origin narratives, the most famous is that which tells the tale of a time when everything was covered by water. This narrative is similar to that recounted by the Yuchis and involves the belief that all living things lived in Galunlati, the sky vault. The narrative recounted how Galunlati became overcrowded, prompting a quest for more space. At first the animals populating Galunlati sent a Water Beetle to dive into the waters to search for more space. When the Water Beetle returned he spread a small amount of mud over the surface of the water. Over time, this mud became the muddy beginnings of the earth. In fact, the earth was so muddy and soft that it could not support any animals and so was affixed to the sky vault by four cords—areas of the earth in which mountains emerged. Once the muddy earth was secured, Grandfather Buzzard was sent to investigate a patch of earth that would eventually become the Cherokees' southeastern homeland, a homeland illuminated by Sister Sun who was pulled out from behind a rainbow.[22]

What of the first Cherokee people? Cherokees developed narratives that told of the Great Spirit who made all the plants and animals and who also made the first man and woman. As is the case for other Native Southerners, a number of these Cherokee narratives survive today and highlight both the durability of Indigenous belief systems and the religious syncretism, or the blending of Indigenous and Christian beliefs, in the oral traditions of Native Southerners after the sixteenth century.

Missionaries, botanists, and ethnologists diligently recorded oral traditions about horned serpents and the Great Spirit.[23] Such narratives emphasized how the "red man" constituted the first human.[24] These types of narratives also provided a platform to explain the origins of corn, squash, and beans in the Native South. Indeed, stories about corn reinforce the importance of agriculture and buttress a sense of place among Native Southerners. Choctaws, for example, told of a crow bringing the first corn seeds after a "great flood," or of Choctaw ancestors finding corn at the sacred mound site of Nanih Waiya.[25] While these stories differed, they both refocused the listener's attention on an important agricultural staple after a journey that ultimately connected people to a specific place.

The Cherokee narrative of Kana'ti, the "lucky hunter," and his wife, Selu (or Corn), remains one of the most famous in American folklore.[26] Like the Choctaw stories above, the tale of Selu and Kana'ti explained how the Cherokees acquired game and corn. It also outlined a rationale for the gendered division of labor in Cherokee society—men hunt, women tend to the crops. But the story of Kana'ti and Selu offered more than this.[27] It constituted a story of transformation that pivots dramatically when Kana'ti and Selu's only son discovered the Wild Boy by a riverbank. The Wild Boy sprang from the blood of game that Kana'ti killed and which Selu cleaned by the river. Kana'ti and Selu believed they'd tamed the Wild Boy, but the Wild Boy had not been tamed. He was not only wild, but cunning, and possessed magical powers. Kana'ti and Selu thus gave the Wild Boy a name appropriate to the traits he displayed: Inage-utasunhi, "He-Who-Grew-Up-Wild."

Inage-utasunhi led his brother into mischief as they followed their parents, discovering how Kana'ti procured game and how Selu collected corn by rubbing her stomach and acquired beans after rubbing her armpits. On seeing this, the boys decided to kill Selu because they became convinced she must be a witch. On discovering the boy's intent to kill her, Selu instructed them that once she was dead they should clear a piece of land in front of their home and drag her body in a circle seven times. She instructed the boys that after completing this task they should stay up all night and in the morning there would be ample corn. But the boys ignored Selu's instructions, instead dragging her body in a circle twice, and clearing seven small spots. This story explained to Cherokees why corn grew only twice a year and in limited places.[28]

The story of Kana'ti and Selu also provided Cherokees with an outline for the administration of justice, while the adventures of Kana'ti and Selu's sons appeared in other narratives, such as the story of Anisgaya Tsunsdi (Little Men), or Thunder Boys. At the heart of Cherokee oral tradition was an effort to explain creation, account for the origins of the Cherokee people, and to underscore the importance of balance and harmony in the Cherokees' relationship with local ecologies. Cherokees who adopted identities as men and women played different, albeit complementary, roles, in Cherokee society. Thus, Cherokee oral tradition taught people the importance of communal responsibilities and reciprocity. To maintain harmony in Cherokee society, opposites required constant balancing.

Like the Cherokees, the Choctaws developed creation narratives that, as noted above, explained the origins of corn. They also developed stories that recounted earth-emergence and migration tales of Choctaw beginnings. Choctaw society was matrilineal in nature. Choctaw matrilineal clans included the Wind, Bear, Deer, Wolf, Panther, Holly Leaf, Bird, Raccoon, and Crawfish. Geographical divisions were also important to the Choctaws. By the eighteenth century, Choctaw geopolitics was structured around the Okla Hannalli (people of six towns), Okla Tannap (people from the other side), and the Okla Fayala (people who are widely dispersed).[29]

The Choctaw earth-emergence story focused on the legend of Nanih Waiyah. There emerged different versions of the Nanih Waiyah story, but most followed roughly the same narrative trajectory. The story recalled a time when the earth was a flat plane, its surface a quagmire not dissimilar to the muddy clay described in Cherokee oral traditions. Some versions of the story speak of "the Great Spirit," others of "a superior being" (a "red man" in appearance) descending to earth and creating a large mound. This mound, or hill, is called Nanih Waiyah, the stooping or sloping hill. From this mound, the Choctaw people emerged and were granted eternal life. Some versions of the narrative indicate that the people did not understand what the Great Spirit told them as they rose out of the mud and began to form life. Angered, the Great Spirit took eternal life from the Choctaws.[30]

Choctaw oral tradition includes tales of ancestral migrations that are similar to those in Creek and Cherokee oral narratives. These stories focus on an ancestral population migrating from west to east. Such tales connect the Choctaws and their northern neighbors: the Chickasaws. The earliest published version of the Choctaw migration narrative appeared in the 1820s. It told the story of Chahta and Chikasa, two brothers, who had the responsibility of ruling populations that had grown too large for the land to support. In response, the brothers led their people from west to east. Each day the brothers and their fellow travelers took a sacred pole with them. They planted this pole in the ground at the end of each day's journey. When they arose the following morning, the direction in which the pole leaned told them the path they should travel that day.[31]

This went on for months. Then, one day, after crossing the Mississippi River, and with rain teeming down upon them, they stopped. The people under Chahta had found their new homeland; with their oracle pole standing erect, they knew they were home and settled on lowlands near Nanih

Waiya Creek and the tributaries of the Pearl River. However, the migrants under Chikasa pressed on, not settling until they reached lands around the Tombigbee. Despite requests from Chahta's people to join them, they refused; they became the Chickasaws.[32]

The Chickasaws' connection to the Choctaws extends beyond creation narratives; they were also close linguistic relatives. Like the Choctaws, the Chickasaws developed a matrilineal totemic society. Two major moieties structured Chickasaw social life—the Imosaktca ("their hickory chopping") and Intcukwalipa ("their worn-out place").[33] Chickasaw moieties have received other names from ethnologists and anthropologists since the eighteenth century—such as Panther and Spanish; Tcukilissa and Tcukafalaha. What is important to note about Chickasaw moieties is that they were binary in nature, the balancing of moieties being vital to the harmony of society. At the same time, moieties helped to give order to matrilineal house groups, which provided the basis for membership in an *iksa* (clan).[34]

Chickasaw creation narratives, migration stories, and eschatology provided the Chickasaw people with the cultural threads necessary to stitch together a coherent sense of who they were as a people. Chickasaws believed that a supreme being, Ababinili, was a composite force that combined "the Sun, Clouds, Clear Sky, and He that Lives in the Clear Sky." The Chickasaws referred to these as the "Four Beloved Things Above." Like other large societies in the Native South, Chickasaws narrated stories about how certain creatures created specific physical markers on the earth. The crawfish, for example, reached down into the water to bring up the earth from the "universal watery waste." In similar ways, the Chickasaws nurtured oral traditions that helped them to explain light and darkness, the mountains and the forests. Of particular importance to the Chickasaw creation narratives was the sun, or the "great holy fire above." To signify the life-giving importance of the sun, each Chickasaw town charged guardian priests to ensure the sacred fire remained alight at all times.[35]

<hr />

While Native Southerners have nurtured traditions about their respective origins for several millennia, Europeans sought their own explanations of where Indigenous Americans came from. Where Native Southerners set out traditions that explained their respective connection to the landscape and local ecologies, and provided the basis for social structures and institutions,

Europeans sought to circumscribe Native identities by presenting origin stories as "myth." An analysis of non-Indigenous theories of Native origins constitutes the starting point for understanding European and Euroamerican perceptions of Native Americans after 1492.[36] The following section reveals some of these Western cultural constructions, noting that migration theories—the Beringian standstill theory, the Solutrean hypothesis, the Bering Strait theory, and the coastal migration theory—continue to dominate Western academic and popular discourses about Native American origins.

From the fifteenth and sixteenth centuries, European explorers, soldiers, colonial officials, missionaries, and settlers postulated theories about Native origins. These theories varied from religious hypothesizing to the reduction of Native Southerners to "objective" and racialized categories of human existence. The "scientific" theories developed by Europeans and Euroamericans about Native American origins went hand in hand with settler colonial attempts to dispossess Indigenous people of their lands and waters, elements critical to the collective identities of Native Southerners.

Some of the European and Euroamerican theories about Native American origins have veered toward the intellectually absurd.[37] Take for instance Benjamin Smith Barton's theory. Barton, a noted American botanist, speculated in a 1792 letter to his friend and prominent Welsh naturalist Thomas Pennant that the Indigenous people of North America were "Welsh-Indians."[38] Pennant had long maintained that Native Americans were the living descendants of ancient Welsh migrants, and now, after lengthy study, Barton agreed with his friend. Like the popular theory that Native Americans descended from the "Lost Tribe of Israel," Barton and Pennant's speculations about American Indian origins were as far-fetched as they were Eurocentric.[39]

In addition to fanciful speculation about American Indians descending from ancient Welsh migrants or being "remnants" of the Lost Tribe of Israel, Europeans (and ultimately Euroamericans) have posited a variety of theories about American Indians possessing Celto-Iberian, Norse, Greek, Egyptian, Libyan, Phoenician, or Viking ancestry.[40]

These wild claims say more about European settler colonial knowledge and their desire to know, categorize, and control Indigenous Americans. Indeed, fanciful claims about the origins of America's First Nations have long had both political and cultural agendas associated with them because they bring into question the indigeneity (and claims to land and territorial sovereignty) of Native American peoples. In other words, the pursuit of "origins" can have the political effect of presenting Native Americans as simply another migrant group who settled in what became part of a multicultural republic.

Additionally, European and Euroamerican speculation about Native origins implied (and continues to imply) a belief that pre-Columbian Indigenous people could never have formed complex social and political structures worthy of sovereignty. In what became the United States, theories about Native American origins have supported the idea that North America constituted *res nullius* (ownerless property) prior to the arrival of European settler colonists. The result has been endless cycles of speculation about American Indian origins and the erasure of Indigenous histories and cultures. Such puzzlement manifested itself during the nineteenth and into the twentieth century when white Americans speculated about the origins and purpose of the mound complexes that dotted the Arkansas, Mississippi, and Ohio River valley landscapes. Such grand and elaborate structures, amateur archaeologists insisted, must surely have been the work of ancient European-descended peoples.[41]

For the past century, archaeologists and anthropologists developed migration theories about Native American origins. For example, the anthropologist Charles Hudson argued that the "first men in the New World came out of Siberia and across the Bering Strait land bridge into Alaska during the Pleistocene geological period—the Ice Age." Hudson thus adopted the twentieth century's dominant academic position on the origins of Native American people. As Hudson explained it, over a period spanning two million years the ice that comprised the Bering Strait land bridge expanded and contracted at least four times. Between 70,000 and 10,000 years ago, the last time the ice advanced and moved southward toward North America, archaeological evidence suggests that human beings began arriving in North America.[42]

Twentieth-century archaeologists refined their theories and acquired increasingly sophisticated scientific equipment to help them test their hypothesis that Native North Americans descended from peoples who migrated across the Bering Strait land bridge many thousands of years ago. But this theory, represented in the map on the next page, is by no means new. In 1590, the Jesuit missionary José de Acosta became the first to publicly speculate that the ancestors of modern American Indians migrated across the Bering Strait land bridge and colonized the Americas.[43]

Like other Spaniards arriving in the Americas during the sixteenth and

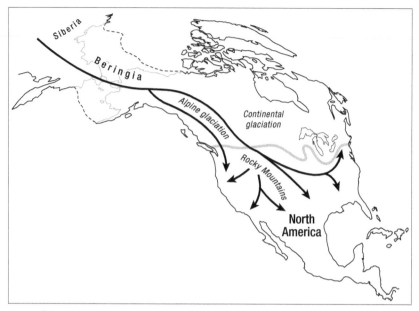

Map of the Bering Strait migration theory. *Erin Greb Cartography.*

early seventeenth century, Acosta puzzled over who the Native peoples were. The Bible, the historical compass for the vast majority of Europeans at the time, proved virtually useless as it offered only silence about the origins of American Indians. Perhaps Acosta could elaborate on the Bible's teachings to gain greater insight into the origins of Native Americans. Having spent time among Indigenous peoples in modern-day Peru and Mexico, Acosta did just that. He read the biblical story of Adam and Eve as literal truth and therefore refused to countenance the idea that American Indians came from the "mud" of the Americas. Such a theory, Acosta believed, implied a separate origin for Indigenous Americans and Christian Europeans. Monotheism represented a core belief among sixteenth-century Christians, and so Acosta insisted that American Indians must be descended from a single original pair of human beings—Adam and Eve—just as Europeans has descended from this single human creation. As such, there was but one explanation for the existence of American Indians: they must have migrated.[44]

From the earliest encounters between Europeans and American Indians, Europe's intelligentsia posited migration as the most logical explanation for the presence of Indigenous people throughout Turtle Island, or what became known as the Americas. From Acosta's biblically inspired speculations at the end of the sixteenth century, to archaeological investigations in the twentieth and twenty-first centuries, the question of Native American origins has remained a constant source of debate and speculation.

Questions about Native American origins certainly continue to stir controversy in our own time. Scientists now contend that during a sixty-thousand-year period of fluctuating temperatures, the Bering Strait land bridge was twice exposed—between fifty and forty thousand years ago, and between twenty-eight and ten thousand years ago. Archaeologists have long maintained that evidence for human migration across the land bridge is strongest for this second period, a period of much cooler temperatures and a wider land bridge that enabled large numbers of people to migrate. This theory is sometimes referred to as the "Clovis-first scenario," so named after the spear points that archaeologists have excavated and analyzed from a site near Clovis, New Mexico.[45] Archaeologists contend that by chipping or flaking new materials like flint, chert, jasper, or chalcedony into a spear point, "Clovis Man" crafted weapons used for hunting game.[46] In the late 1960s, paleoecologist Paul Martin led the championing of the Clovis-first scenario, arguing that big-game hunters migrated across the Bering Strait land bridge and arrived at the southern end of the ice-free corridor about 11,500 BCE.[47]

However, the discovery of archaeological sites containing artifacts that predate Clovis has undermined the Clovis-first scenario.[48] This newer archaeology suggests that human life in the Americas predates the Paleo-Indians who purportedly used Clovis technology. Archaeologists refer to these human inhabitants as pre-Clovis. The most famous pre-Clovis archaeological site in the Americas is at Monte Verde in Chile.[49] The discoveries at Monte Verde include flakes and pebble-choppers that some archaeologists insist are suggestive of human occupation in the Americas many thousands of years prior to Clovis culture. These pre-Clovis tools were likely used to forage for food. Archaeologists have therefore begun to differentiate pre-Clovis tools according to chronology, with pre-projectile points (200,000 to 60,000 BCE) and pre-Clovis tools (60,000 to 12,000 BCE) framing revised time frames.[50]

During the first decade and a half of the twenty-first century, speculation about the origins and migratory paths of ancient American Indians has been reinvigorated not only by new archaeological discoveries but also by a growing interest in family genealogy. As genetic science continues to improve, increasing numbers of Americans have invested in DNA testing and made some surprising discoveries about their racial and/or ethnic heritage. Professional geneticists have seized upon these technologies to also make some startling, and controversial, claims of their own about the genealogy of North America's Indigenous peoples.

Among the more notable discoveries are those by Harvard University geneticist David Reich. Reich assembled a team of sixty experts to analyze genetic data from more than five hundred individuals from fifty-two Native American and seventeen Siberian groups. Reich's research aimed to analyze the genetic similarities and differences in their trial samples. Reich's team discovered that "the great majority of Native American populations—from Canada to the southern tip of Chile—derive their ancestry from a homogeneous 'First American' ancestral population, presumably the one that crossed the Bering Strait more than 15,000 years ago."[51]

This was not a particularly startling discovery; it supported the archaeological consensus about Native American migrations across the Bering Strait land bridge and fell within the chronological range typically reported by archaeologists. But Reich's team went further. Their research indicated that the genetic makeup of Indigenous Americans included DNA that could be traced back to Han China. Reich's team reported that there exists "three deep lineages in Native Americans: the Asian lineage leading to First Americans is the most deeply diverged, whereas the Asian lineages leading to Eskimo–Aleut speakers and the Na-Dene-speaking Chipewyan are more closely related and descend from a putative Siberian ancestral population more closely related to Han [Chinese]."[52]

Reich's research garnered widespread media attention, particularly in the Native American press, and has spurred renewed debate about Native American origins.[53] Significantly, his findings reveal how important DNA testing of human remains has become in the study of Native American ancestry. The analysis of mitochondrial DNA, for example, has led some scientists to postulate the so-called Beringian standstill theory as an explanation of how and when the ancestors of modern American Indians arrived in North America. According to proponents of the Beringian standstill theory, analysis of mitochondrial DNA reveals that the descendants of modern American Indians entered the Americas about fifteen thousand years ago, after being stationary on Beringia for approximately ten thousand years.[54]

While the Beringian standstill theory tends to support archaeological and scientific arguments about the Asian origins of modern American Indians, proponents of the Beringian standstill theory go further. They assert that "before spreading across the Americas, the ancestral population paused in Beringia long enough for specific [genetic] mutations to accumulate." This argument contends that a Beringian pit stop of sufficient duration occurred to "separate the New World founder lineages from their Asian sister-clades." In other words, a distinct genetic population adapted to the climate of Beringia developed over thousands of years and subsequently contributed to the peopling of the Americas. As proponents of this theory argue, "after the Beringian standstill, the initial North to South migration was likely a swift pioneering process, not a gradual diffusion."[55]

A small but vocal group of scholars dispute the Beringian standstill theory and offer a radical alternative. Dennis Stanford and Bruce Bradley are two of the most prominent proponents of the controversial Solutrean hypothesis. The Solutrean hypothesis contends that Ice Age Europeans were the first human beings to migrate to, and settle in, the Americas. Proponents of this theory speculate that similarities between European Solutrean and early Clovis technologies in the Americas (ca. 13,200–12,900 years ago) hint at a shared ancestry.[56]

What exactly is the Solutrean hypothesis? It is the theory that Solutreans from Europe traversed ice sheets and traveled by boat across the Atlantic Ocean to colonize North America. According to Stanford and Bradley, "during the Last Glacial Maximum, sometime between 25,000 and 13,000 years ago, members of the Solutrean culture in the southwest coastal regions of Europe were led by subsistence behavior appropriate to their time and place to exploit the ice-edge environment of the polar front across the North Atlantic and colonize North America." Stanford and Bradley argue that these European migrants contributed to the formation of the Clovis peoples of the Americas and constituted the forebears of modern American Indians.[57]

The Solutrean hypothesis is without question the most contentious theory of American Indian origins.[58] It should be noted, however, that Stanford and Bradley do not reject the idea that Paleolithic migrants from northeast Asia to the Americas traversed the Bering Strait land bridge, but their theory does suggest to proponents of the Solutrean hypothesis that the genetic makeup of ancient American Indians is far more diverse than scholars previously imagined.[59]

The most recent, and now widely embraced, theory of origins is the coastal migration theory. This theory has gathered momentum since it was first proposed in the 1960s. Its leading proponent, archaeologist Knut Fladmark, advanced the coastal migration theory by focusing some of his research on the Pacific Northwest. Fladmark's research postulated oceanic migrations across the Pacific. He proposed that these migrations were characterized by "sea-level refugia," or island-hopping.[60]

In the decades since the 1970s, archaeological research along the Pacific coastline of North America has tested Fladmark's research findings. Proponents of his coastal migration theory—such as Ruth Gruhn and Richard A. Rogers—have contended that Asian groups island-hopped as they traveled by boats across the Pacific.[61] Advocates for the coastal migration theory believe that these Ice Age migrants arrived on the west coast of North America about sixteen thousand years ago (with some scholars extending this time frame to between fifty and twenty-five thousand years ago).[62]

Of all of the migration theories posited by scholars, the Bering Strait theory remains a lightning rod for Native American criticism. American Indian people express a variety of perspectives on scholarly theories about their origins. For example, Ruth Hopkins (Spirit Lake Tribe of North Dakota), echoes the sentiments of many American Indian people when she writes that "as an American Indian scientist, I find that both the Bering Strait Land Bridge theory and the Solutrean hypothesis smack of arrogance and ethnocentrism."[63] Alexander Ewen, a member of the Purépecha Nation, expresses similar sentiments, characterizing the Bering Strait migration theory as a product of Western racism.[64]

Hopkins and Ewen's pointed critiques of the Bering Strait land bridge theory reiterates the criticisms of a long list of Native American scholars and social commentators. Arguably the most prominent post–World War II American Indian activist and scholar, Vine Deloria Jr., set the tone for such critiques. In Deloria's 1995 book, *Red Earth, White Lies,* he wrote eloquently about how "most scholars today simply begin with the *assumption* that the Bering Strait migration doctrine was proved a long time ago."[65] Deloria wanted to complicate such theories by reminding readers that scholars have now demonstrated that the descendants of modern-day American Indians were indeed capable of building boats to travel to the Americas by ocean; they did not simply walk into North America. Far from Indigenous Americans being a technologically backward people, Deloria laid out an argument for the innovativeness of Native American cultures.[66] Jack Forbes (Powhatan) shared Deloria's skepticism about migration theories. Writing of the coastal migration theory, Forbes noted the merits of the argument about ancient mariners traversing the Pacific aboard "floating devices," but expressed concern about the tendency of coastal migration theorists to blanket these ancient Pacific seafarers with the term "south Asian."[67]

◇◇◇◇◇◇◇◇◇◇◇◇◇◇◇◇◇◇◇◇◇◇◇◇

The origin traditions of Native Southerners and the theorizing of academics reveal only part of the "origins" story. Native Southerners developed social systems centered on hunting and gathering, and ultimately embraced communal agriculture, technological advances, and diplomacy and warfare among Native polities long before the arrival of European colonists.

We can only guess, however, at how Native people understood their place in the small hunter-gatherer communities that populated North America during the Pleistocene Ice Age (ca. 2.5 million to 11,700+ years ago). The seasonal campsites and tools left behind by these small bands and studied by archaeologists suggests they valued some degree of communalism.[68] But why? Was the pursuit of sustenance the primary driver in the formation of small communities? It's possible. Then again, developments in material culture suggest creative forces also drove Native people to define distinctive identities adapted to local ecologies and specific to certain groups of people.

Such developments came into focus during the Archaic period (ca. 11,500 to 2,000–1,000 BCE). Archaeologists observe a stabilization in regional cultures during the Early and Middle Archaic periods (ca. 11,500 to 6,000 BCE), something that's observed through analysis of tools, dwelling sites, and changes in consumption habits. As Native people altered hunting practices, shifting away from hunting megafauna, it's possible they began experimenting with cultigens and attempted to domesticate dogs and turkeys.[69] By the Middle Archaic period, Native Southerners appeared to make a concerted effort to establish clear territorial boundaries—most notably to accommodate social adaptations to riverine economies of fishing and hunting and gathering—and to use rising temperatures to continue agricultural experiments, all of which suggests growing communal population bases and a conscious association of group identity with a defined sense of place.[70]

Reinforcing communal identities at specific geographical locations gathered momentum during the Late Archaic period (ca. 3,000 to 1,000 CE) and continued into the Early Woodland period (ca. 1,000 BCE).[71] At a site that archaeologists call Poverty Point, located in the Lower Mississippi Valley in modern-day Louisiana, the efforts of Native Southerners to reshape their social and geographical environment are clear. Poverty Point (ca. 1700 to 800 BCE) supported a relatively large population that required Native people to systematically plan agricultural cycles, engage in fishing, hunting, and gathering, and organize themselves in the defense of local resources and to engage in long-distance trade with peoples as far away as present-day Indiana and Georgia.[72] At the same time, the construction of mounds to bury the dead highlights how Native people combined their scientific knowledge and engineering skills to embed an attachment to place. Moreover, the layers of sand used in the construction of mounds at Poverty Point hints at a desire for permanence, and thus, behaviors that reflect a conscious sense of the sacred and the ceremonial.[73]

The systematic planning of towns and mound complexes continued to develop during the Woodland period as climate stabilized and populations increased. During this era, Native Southerners remained engaged in technological experiments. Pleistocene-era stone tools had long given way to manufactured items made with copper. Native Southerners imported copper from the Midwest, providing one example of how Indigenous people established extensive riverine and overland trade networks prior to the arrival of European colonizers.[74]

Innovations in ceramics, agriculture, funerary traditions, and town planning also characterize the Woodland period, reflecting the establishment of trade networks at the same time that material and cultural exchange informed the development of distinctive communal identities. From the Gulf Coast to what we know today as the state of Kentucky, regionally distinguishable polities emerged throughout the Native South.[75]

The developments described above continued to shape and reshape the identities of Native Southerners throughout, and beyond, the Woodland period. One technological adoption that would have profound implications for the social and military history of the Native South was the bow and arrow. Native warriors in the Southeast incorporated the bow and arrow into warrior culture between the years 600 and 800 CE—a relatively late technological advance given Native people in the Arctic regions of North America appear to have been using the bow and arrow as early as 9000 to 6000 BCE.[76] As an indispensable article of military technology, the bow and arrow was used throughout the world and could be found from ancient Egypt to the Polynesian islands. In the Native South, warriors understood

Four Native American Indians of New France (Canada): two men at top in war attire, with shield, bow, and arrows; mother holding paddle and nursing infant; and men clothed for winter, wearing snowshoes. *Library of Congress, Prints and Photographs Division, Washington, D.C.*

the importance of the bow and arrow as it became an integral piece of material culture in defining the identities of young warriors.[77]

The story of Native American origins is complex. While archaeologists and geneticists continue to debate migration theories and analyze DNA data, Native peoples turn to their time-honored traditions and oral narratives to articulate who they've been, who they are, and who they imagine they'll become. In other words, where empirical studies often raise as many questions as they answer (and serve the eliminationist drive of settler colonial regimes of power), Indigenous origin narratives provide people with an important cultural compass with which to tell stories that define their identities.

The origin narratives of the coalescent societies that emerged in the sixteenth and seventeenth centuries have a number of key elements in common (or at least interconnected) with the technological and cultural innovations cited above; however, communal identities predated the coalescent societies. The origin narratives of Native Southerners therefore reflect long histories of accumulated knowledge and a conscious effort to foster a collective sense of place, communal belonging, and responsibility for local ecologies.

Origin narratives are a small part of the stories that Native Southerners told about themselves. The following chapters consider how Native Southerners structured their social and cultural lives in the centuries immediately before European colonization. How did Native Southerners form allegiances and identities that bound people together in communities, diplomatic alliances, and trade networks? These are questions that we now turn to.

CHAPTER TWO

THE CHIEFDOM ERA

The cultural traditions, religious ceremonies, networks of trade, and social organizations that Native Southerners developed from the Pleistocene to the Archaic and into the Woodland period contributed to an accumulation of knowledge, refinement of belief systems, and the development of political institutions. Native Southerners experienced major changes in climate during this vast swath of time, but they were not simply acted upon by climatic and ecological changes; they were active agents in trying to shape their environment and to define relationships with kin and non-kin peoples.

Archaeological work at the Poverty Point site suggests that Native Southerners organized themselves into highly complex societies by ca. 1700 BCE. Over the ensuing millennia, changes in climate altered hunting and gathering practices and inspired innovations in horticulture and technology throughout the Americas. From South to North America, Native people adopted the bow and arrow and refined agricultural tools made from materials such as wood, bones, stone, slate, and copper.[1]

Similar developments occurred in other parts of the Americas. The Poverty Point site, the best example of the first mound-building epoch and central to understanding social and cultural changes in the Native South, is not the only example of how Native Americans reorganized their communities. In the Middle Ohio Valley during the early and middle Woodland period, mound-building societies developed sites known to archaeologists as Adena and Hopewell.[2] As at Poverty Point, the Adena and Hopewell burial mounds reflect a self-conscious understanding of community and an apparent appreciation for the respective customs and beliefs of the recently deceased.[3]

Archaeologists begin the third mound-building epoch, the focus of this chapter, with the Cahokia mound complex, located just outside of modern-day St. Louis. Cahokia was by no means the first mound-building society to emerge after 700 CE, but as an example of a chiefdom, or ranked society, it has become something of an archaeological starting point for understanding the relative complexity of other mound-building chiefdoms in eastern North America. And as the following analysis reveals, not all chiefdoms were the same. Archaeologists classify the polities of the Native South between 700 and 1600 CE as simple, complex, or paramount chiefdoms.[4] These categories denote the relative level of social and political organization in chiefdom societies, complexity that was dynamic and changed over time.

◇◇◇◇◇◇◇◇◇◇◇◇◇◇◇◇◇◇◇◇◇◇◇◇◇◇

Cahokia remains the most famous example of a paramount chiefdom between 700 and 1600. It emerged, flourished, and eventually declined in political significance and economic prosperity fairly rapidly. During an eight-hundred-year period that coincided with the Late Woodland period (ca. 500 to 1200), Cahokians produced and ultimately left behind artifacts that continue to help archaeologists understand Native life prior to European invasion and colonization.[5]

The Late Woodland period in which Cahokia rose is significant because it bore witness to dramatic population growth and dispersal throughout the Native South, especially along the river valley corridors of the interior Southeast. It is in these places that Native people renewed communal relationships, adapted the technologies noted in the previous chapter, and developed distinctive material cultures.[6]

The history of the chiefdoms is also important because it provides us with insights into how Native Southerners dealt with the impact of rapid changes in climate. Between 950 and 1250 CE, a major climactic event occurred that altered the communal life of tens of thousands of Native people. Archaeologists and climate scientists refer to this event as the "medieval warm period." A particularly intense period of global warming triggered a series of "megadroughts" across North America between 900 and 1400. Life became increasingly unstable for Native societies as people tried to sustain themselves by living mobile, foraging lifestyles. Further changes in climate ultimately led Native people in the Southwest and Southeast of North America to become, in the words of one scholar, "predominantly agrarian."[7] As agriculture became an increasingly important part of Native economies

Map of the major Mississippian chiefdom regions. *Erin Greb Cartography.*

and a growing source of caloric intake, mound-building societies in Louisiana and Mississippi began prospering.[8] From the social stresses produced by climate change Native Southerners gave birth to the chiefdom era.

As a central organizing feature of communal identities in the Native South, chiefdoms emerged as a means of uniting people in a sense of communalism (albeit in a ranked politico-economic structure) and for group protection. Native Southerners lived in chiefdoms that varied in size and political complexity. Larger chiefdoms, or complex chiefdoms, were characterized by a hierarchical sense of communalism with clearly defined political structures buttressed by elaborate cultural ceremonies. The monumental architecture of mound complexes helped to both order space and create a sense of place that reinforced social distinctions.[9]

Within the chiefdoms of the Native South, kinship both defined social relations and gave meaning to identity. While political leadership was often determined by birth and legitimated through religious ideology, chiefs did not exercise unlimited control over all functions of government, such as the use of military force. Typically, a number of individuals from different parts of society had a voice in deciding how to use military power.[10]

Cahokia is the most famous example of how Native people organized societies, cultures, and identities of chiefdom-era peoples after 700 CE. The Cahokia chiefdom became the largest of the mound-building societies during the Mississippian period—a historical fact that makes it exceptional in North America. During its spectacular history, Cahokia's population ranged from a few thousand to as many as fifty thousand.[11] Archaeological evidence suggests Cahokians built their domiciles—segregated by size and form—for the long term. In all likelihood, the average Cahokian lived in the same home for as many as three decades.[12]

Cahokia emerged relatively quickly around 1050 CE, taking as little as one generation to form into a distinct polity. Cahokia constituted what archaeologists call a "paramount chiefdom." Other Native polities in what we know today as the Midwest and Southeast varied in size and complexity, from small, or simple, chiefdoms to complex chiefdoms and paramount chiefdoms like Cahokia.

What did these different types of chiefdoms look like? Simple chiefdoms were, as the name suggests, small. They constituted clusters of people from as few as four towns, built a single mound, and had a population that rarely exceeded 5,400 people. Complex chiefdoms were much larger in terms of number of towns, mounds, and population size. Typically a complex chiefdom was ruled centrally by a single chiefdom and could, as occurred during the Late Mississippian period, consist of a number of simple and complex chiefdoms existing alongside one another that were overseen by a paramount chief.[13]

A paramount chiefdom was an even more highly developed social and political structure. Complex chiefdoms could include within their orbit of power numerous other polities and comprise a population of as many as thirty thousand to fifty thousand people. Given the geographical and demographic size of paramount chiefdoms like Cahokia, some archaeologists liken them to a collection of smaller chiefdoms that were bound together by nonaggression pacts. Additionally the size of paramount chiefdoms suggests that political power was dispersed more widely than it was in a complex chiefdom.[14]

While archaeologists continue to debate the nature of chiefdom societies, one thing seems clear: irrespective of their size and political structure they all at some point bore witness to a process that involved the breakup—or "fissioning"—of communities within their social and political orbits. In such instances, Native people had a decision to make; they could form a new polity and attempt to establish new bonds of kinship or they might attempt to reestablish older political and kinship ties.[15]

Cahokia displayed all the hallmarks of a paramount chiefdom. It became the largest settlement north of modern-day Mexico before contact with Europeans in the sixteenth century. In fact, Cahokia became so large that by 1250 its population was larger than that of London. The complexity of Cahokian society and the ordering of social spaces were stunning. Cahokia included over one hundred earthen mounds, the largest extending thirty meters into the air.[16] Structures of such size and scale were made possible by large and well-planned labor projects. These construction projects included not only mounds but also the construction of rectangular plazas, palisades, and housing projects.[17]

Cahokia's rapid emergence and growth owed much to the rich soils of the floodplain on which it evolved. Agriculture, which was highly organized, combined with hunting and fishing (which supplemented the diet with protein in the form of red meat, waterfowl, and fish), sustained its people in sedentary communities.[18] But the development of agriculture—which included the cultivation of maize, cucurbits (gourds), and starchy seeds—does not fully explain Cahokia's stunning rise.[19] Social and cultural developments—and the sense of community and order that these developments gave meaning to—provide a deeper understanding of how Cahokians mediated ecological knowledge, scientific inquiry, and agricultural advances, and developed diplomatic networks and trade relations with other chiefdoms. Using overland and riverine trade routes, the Cahokians imported copper from the Great Lakes, chert (used in the making of stone tools) from what is today Oklahoma and Arkansas, stone from Wyoming, salt and lead from Illinois, mica (often used for painting) from North Carolina, and shells from the Gulf of Mexico.[20]

Still, agriculture proved critical to the rise of Cahokian society. With the climate shifting from warm and dry to warmer and wetter weather, the right combination of soil and atmospheric conditions emerged to make maize agriculture possible and the development of large sedentary communities sustainable after 1050. Considerable planning and scientific experimentation went into not only growing maize (and shaping and reshaping the environment) but also to storing it. Cahokians constructed belowground pits in which they stored surpluses of maize for up to two years. While the growing and storing of food did not end hunting and gathering practices, it did provide people with much more time to devote to the production of crafts, practice religious ceremonies, hone specialized skills, and engage in leisure activities. In other words, Cahokian culture continued to develop and evolve, adding new intellectual layers that helped to inform communal identities.[21]

The archaeological study of Cahokian society and culture has proven influential in the way Mississippian cultures throughout the American Bottom are perceived by scholars. One area in which we see this influence is in the social structures that archaeologists point to as a characteristic of Mississippian cultures after 1050.[22] These sociopolitical hierarchies were the products of adaptive cultures that tied social and religious organizations, ritual practices, and agricultural fertility to the patterns of social and political life.[23]

However, while social, political, and even architectural structures gave daily life the appearance of stability, the social and cultural world of Mississippian peoples was anything but static. To the contrary, Mississippian cultures were dynamic and adaptive; they were also relatively competitive, with rivalries punctuating the life of Mississippian chiefs. That said, the exogamous nature of marriage—that is, marriage outside of one's kin group—among Mississippians meant that marriage to a rival chief's kin could take the edge off economic and political rivalries; it could even result in long-lasting alliances and the creation of an extended kin network.[24]

◇◇◇◇◇◇◇◇◇◇◇◇◇◇◇◇◇◇◇◇◇◇◇◇

Cahokia was not the only large chiefdom to emerge between 700 and 1600. Across the interior South and along the Gulf region, chiefdom societies rose, fell, and were reconstituted around new political structures. One of those societies, Etowah, rose to regional prominence between 1000 and 1100. In what is today the Etowah River valley of northern Georgia, individuals formed bonds of kinship and divided themselves—sometimes violently—into ranked political and social identities. An elaborate complex of earthen mounds—structures used as burial chambers or ceremonial platforms made from gravel, sand, rocks, and debris—provided a sense of architectural order to the social landscape not unlike the order provided by Cahokian architecture. And within this complex society, ritual and ceremonial practices helped Native people to narrate communal identities and give meaning to political and social rankings, while trade with outsiders brought exotic goods into local villages.[25]

Etowah became one of the most powerful and prosperous chiefdoms in the interior Southeast between 1000 and 1600. Etowah's social and political structures, and the rich cultural and ceremonial life that its members enacted, highlighted the sophistication and diversity of Mississippian societies. We've learned much more about these societies since the 1950s, with archaeological evidence complementing oral traditions and providing important insights into the material culture of Mississippian polities. It was at the midpoint of the twentieth century that archaeologists truly began to grasp the richness of Mississippian cultures and societies like Etowah.[26]

The people of Etowah lived in a paramount chiefdom. Like Cahokia, Etowah's people undergirded their social and political structures with an ethos of communal redistribution. Specifically, the redistribution of economic resources helped to integrate settlements from diverse ecological regions. In turn, the people from these different regions provided labor, their surplus crops being placed into a central pool and redistributed among members of the chiefdom or used to fund public construction projects, feasts, or support military activity.[27]

Irrespective of their complexity, the people who formed chiefdoms often brought with them memories of experiences in other social and political communities.[28] For example, in what we know today as north-central Florida and southeastern Georgia, the Timucuan chiefdoms brought people together to form a "multicommunity political unit" that included a central bureaucracy and regional population nodes ranging in size from a few thousand to tens of thousands.[29]

In the Timucuan chiefdom, which formed around 700, kinship was critical to a collective identity. Kinship reminded Timucuans of their responsibilities to each other, gave meaning to everyday life, and invested purpose in sacred ceremonies.[30]

The Timucua people were not alone in nurturing kinship bonds. To their west, along the Florida panhandle and the borderland region between

A Timucuan chief of Florida, ca. 1585–1593, by
John White. © *The Trustees of the British Museum.*

present-day Georgia and Alabama, the Chattahoochee chiefdoms also
developed kin-based societies. Like other chiefdom polities to emerge in
the Southeast, the Chattahoochee nurtured a sociopolitical system defined
by kin and non-kin people. Non-kin, such as captives, did not receive the
same protections or access to resources that kin members enjoyed. Through
participation in group rituals and ceremonies non-kin could become part
of kinship networks and the collective social identities associated with kin
membership. Such traditions served the chiefdoms well, and would later

prove invaluable to Native Southerners when they reorganized their polities during the seventeenth and eighteenth centuries.[31]

The kin-based societies of the Mississippian period varied in size and complexity. Polities such as Etowah and Coosa were examples of paramount chiefdoms.[32] Smaller polities also existed in the Native South. The Timucuas, for example, displayed the features of small-scale chiefdoms for parts of their history.[33]

Importantly, Native chiefdoms did not constitute static social and political entities. In some cases, complex chiefdoms grew even larger, forming a paramount chiefdom. The Coosa chiefdom, located in modern-day northwestern Georgia, developed out of smaller polities and grew to become a paramount chiefdom. The Coosa chiefdom extended over a vast distance, incorporating between seven to ten simple and complex chiefdoms and encompassing an area of approximately five hundred kilometers in length.[34]

Alternatively, throughout the Tombigbee and Black Warrior River region in Alabama and Mississippi, the Tombigbee chiefdoms displayed the social and political qualities of simple chiefdoms. These communities comprised small villages of uncertain political allegiance, some with palisaded mound centers. Community members sustained themselves by farming on a small, localized scale.[35] Decision-making in simple chiefdoms like Tombigbee was likely left in the hands of the household or local community. Unlike complex chiefdoms, then, simple chiefdoms lacked the large centralized bureaucratic structures that assumed responsibility for decision-making and military defense.[36]

Archaeological evidence suggests that simple chiefdoms could, and did, change over time. This process, which archaeologists label "cycling," involved the breakup (or "fissioning") of chiefdoms. When people from these splintered communities formed new kin-based polities, they engaged in a process archaeologists and anthropologists refer to as "fusion."[37]

Such was the case for the Moundville chiefdom. Moundville refers to an archaeological site in what is today central Alabama.[38] Moundville's center, located near present-day Tuscaloosa, eventually gave rise to a large paramount chiefdom that extended over approximately three hundred acres of fertile floodplain.[39]

Moundville's archaeology suggests that its Native inhabitants designed mound centers with a high degree of formality. In the layout and the symmetry of Moundville architecture, we glimpse clues about how the architects of those structures imagined the ordering of human space. Moundville's architecture could, for instance, operate as a mnemonic device, providing its residents with structural and symbolic reminders of the importance of ceremonial centers, social distinctions, and spiritual beliefs within the larger kin-based society.[40]

How did the people of Moundville sustain themselves and their kin? Moundville's economy involved the movement of subsistence goods, such as corn, beans, and pumpkins, from the site of their production at local centers and smaller, domestic localities to the paramount center. In turn, these goods were exchanged for locally and nonlocally produced prestige items. People who resided at a single-mound site might, for example, have access to craft items to which they attached ceremonial and symbolic importance. At smaller domestic sites, far from the center of the paramountcy, people had access only to goods that had utilitarian value.[41]

Moundville's exchange economy therefore reinforced social ranks while also operating to connect the larger polity to Indian chiefdoms beyond its boundaries. The paramount center, for example, seems to have engaged in economic exchanges to its north, south, and west. While the people of the Moundville chiefdom appear to have manufactured most of their ceramic items locally, archaeological evidence indicates that materials such as copper, mica, and conch shells were imported from outside the chiefdom.[42]

Moundville's highly developed political ranks, its ceremonial traditions, and its economic structures all combined to give meaning to a communal identity. But nothing lasts forever, and this proved true for chiefdoms like Moundville. Approximately a century before Hernando de Soto's entrada through the Southeast between 1539 and 1542, Moundville collapsed.[43] Between 1300 and 1450 Moundville's people began migrating and forming new chiefdoms—the Taliepacana, Moculiza, and Apafalaya, for example— along the Black Warrior River. Others migrated down the Tombigbee River, some journeying into the Tallapoosa, Alabama, and Chattahoochee River valleys. There they formed new chiefdoms and began telling new stories about the cultural parameters of their collective identities—the largest and most famous being the Tascalusa chiefdom on the upper Alabama River.[44]

◇◇◇◇◇◇◇◇◇◇◇◇◇◇◇◇◇◇◇◇◇◇◇◇◇◇◇◇

In the centuries after 1000, large and small chiefdom societies flourished throughout the American Bottom, or the Mississippi floodplain, and through

Water spider shell gorget. An example of a mnemonic symbol to structure a larger oral narrative and worldview. *Frank McClung Museum, University of Tennessee, Knoxville.*

the interior Southeast and Gulf region. It was during this period that the South emerged as a distinctive geocultural place. Kin-based societies dotted the southeastern landscape, with chiefdoms like Coosa and Etowah developing into particularly complex and powerful societies.[45]

In addition to developing well-organized political and economic structures, Native Southerners crafted rich cultural lives expressed in pictoglyphs, ceramics, and a variety of other material culture forms. The Cox Mound style, centered on the Tennessee Valley and including major sites such as Etowah and Moundville, provides clear archaeological examples of cosmic narratives translated to material culture forms. The archaeologist George Lankford observes that during the thirteenth and fourteenth centuries the people who lived in the Tennessee Valley made shell gorgets, carved pendants worn around the neck, in one of five motifs: the cross, the rayed circle, the looped square, crested birds, and the circular shell.[46]

Lankford explains how these different motifs reflected how Native Southerners worked to adapt their cosmic stories to the changing cultural, political, and ecological circumstances in which they found themselves. Mnemonic devices, for example, were used to represent humans in a complex relationship with the larger cosmos—the sky, land, and water. Often humans were depicted occupying the middle strata of the cosmos, with travel underwater presenting great risks due to the presence of beings such as the Underwater Panther. While certain types of travel were presented as risky, the layers of the world were usually portrayed as interconnected, often a cosmic tree uniting the various layers.[47]

Other motifs help to explain how Native people acquired land. From Cahokia to Etowah, water spiders appear on shell gorgets to help tell a story of how the land and the sun helped make Native life in the various regions of the Southeast possible. Such representations constituted important components of origin stories, but they did so in ways that left scope for oral storytellers to tailor narratives to the natural and social environments in which people lived. In these ways, material culture and oral histories constituted dynamic elements of ancient storytelling cultures that grounded communal identities in time and place.[48]

Color and symbolism in material objects such as gorgets and distinctively stamped ceramics, in addition to tattooing, jewelry, clothing, petroglyphs and pictographs, and burial mounds and mortuary traditions, also contributed to external displays of Indigenous worldviews. Indeed, material culture had the potential to convey social rank and kinship ties. Material objects also helped Native Southerners keep a tangible record of their respective group's cultural heritage and identity.[49] In other words, the material culture that Native Southerners created had the potential to sustain a cohesive sense of group identity in a world shaped by regular engagement with outsiders. Long-distance trade, carried out by overland trading paths and large flotillas of traders in canoes, connected Native Southerners to the people, beliefs, and customs of other polities. While these encounters had the potential for cultural exchange, they also reminded people of the importance of nurturing their own distinctive sense of social belonging and identity as traded items and new ideas became woven into the fabric of their respective societies.

Reinforcing dynamic group identities occurred through the maintenance of kinship ties and the establishment of social ranks. Physical appearance proved critically important to Mississippians who wanted to project their social status to others. For example, cranial modifications (specifically the flattening of one's head) and body adornment proved particularly important in communicating social or political status. Additionally, archaeologists have uncovered a range of artifacts that provide clues about the material culture of Mississippian societies. Body art and jewelry, as noted above, in addition to cultural practices like the smoking pipes, all had the potential to remind Native Southerners of their sense of place in the cosmos and in the social structures that governed daily life.[50]

A person's occupation also informed one's status, defined gender roles, and bound people together in a society in which one's labor served to ensure the general peace and harmony of the polity. Men, for instance, often filled the roles of warriors, traders, and diplomats. These occupations provided men with opportunities to travel beyond the loosely defined geographical limits of the chiefdom—opportunities generally not available to people assigned female roles, with the exception of women who accompanied men into war.[51]

When Mississippians traveled outside of the chiefdom by overland route or along rivers in canoes, their identities were projected to outsiders in a number of ways. Body adornments appeared to have been a common form of communication. So too were hairstyles important to the projection of identity; indeed, nothing highlighted the arrival of a defeated warrior in a community more quickly than a man with a shaved head.[52]

Women performed a number of jobs integral to the prosperity of Mississippian society. Historically, women collected nuts and fruits, but with the introduction of cleared-field agriculture around the year 800 women developed agricultural knowledge and gained responsibility for overseeing the growth and cultivation of corn, beans, and squash. In fact, evidence of tool differentiation suggests that men and women knew very little about each other's world of work other than grasping the concept of their roles being mutually reinforcing.[53]

Significantly, as Native women acquired important agricultural responsibilities their autonomy and sociopolitical influence increased. Horticultural knowledge and an understanding about agricultural cycles amounted to a form of scientific knowledge that gave women considerable influence over the distribution of resources, something that likely provided women with insight into the ability of the chiefdom to sustain its population. Thus, kinship identities based on matrilineal inheritance invested women with considerable political power. So great was this power that women possessed, they typically decided the fate of war captives.[54]

"A wife of a 'werowance' or chief of Pomeiooc [located in
present-day North Carolina] carrying a child," ca. 1585–93,
by John White. © *The Trustees of the British Museum*.

European documents from the mid-sixteenth century indicate that
Mississippian women also exercised control over how to receive and treat
outsiders. Early Spanish sources, for example, suggest that women exercised
diplomatic influence. Hernando de Soto reported that during his march
through the South, the Lady Cofitechequi enlisted him as an ally. Several
years later, Juan Pardo made similar claims about Mississippian women in
what is today North Carolina.[55]

While evidence does exist to suggest that Mississippian women engaged in diplomacy and went into battle, it's probable that most women never experienced combat. For the vast majority of Mississippian women, their social and political influence was greatest around the village and fields, in making pottery and caring for children, in working together to prepare the soups and stews that Mississippian people were so fond of, and in determining the fate of captives that their warriors brought back from wars or raids. These were not marginal roles; they constituted vital social and political responsibilities that helped bind communities together.[56]

If gender roles helped to structure Mississippian societies, so too did architecture. Mississippian societies built mounds for ceremonial purposes, to order space, to demarcate rank or social status, and to tell a story about a particular society's wealth and power.[57] Mounds thus served multiple functions, acting as sites of burial and places of worship in addition to being visible assertions of political power and economic prosperity. The planning and location of mounds asserted not only an ordering of space and a polity's collective identity but also a declaration of what we understand today as sovereignty.[58]

It's possible that the inspiration for mound building in the Native South came from Central America and the extensive networks of trade and travel developed over centuries.[59] Irrespective of its regional and political origins, Native Southerners used mounds for a variety of purposes. In some instances, earthen platform mounds, built in stages, became the site of a high-ranking chief's house. Social and political status certainly played a role in determining the location, dimensions, and purpose of a mound. Atop other mounds sat sweat lodges or the council house, while still other mounds were built specifically to bury the remains of high-ranking members of society.[60]

Some mounds held symbolic meaning for Native Southerners, and, for that matter, Native people throughout eastern North America. Effigy mounds built in the shape of eagles, lizards, turtles, bears, and panthers appear to have held sacred meaning. These mounds were constructed relatively low to the ground, typically did not contain the remains of the dead, and likely became places where community members came together in ceremony.[61] Mounds, like the other aspects of material culture discussed above, reflect a creative desire on the part of Native Southerners to enrich their lives and connect people through symbols, town planning, and storytelling.

Mississippian chiefdoms such as Cahokia, Etowah, and Moundville experienced stunning growth and material prosperity. However, the social structures that gave the appearance of rigid, hierarchal societies were in actuality quite unstable. By identifying the processes of cycling, fissioning, and fusion, archaeologists and anthropologists have shown how Mississippian societies were often changing; simple chiefdoms could cycle and fuse with other smaller chiefdoms to form a complex chiefdom, while paramountcies could fissure, the former members of its polity finding refuge in other chiefdoms.[62]

By the late sixteenth and early seventeenth century, a number of factors combined to further destabilize Mississippian societies, ultimately paving the way for the formation of the coalescent societies that became known as the Cherokee, Creek, Choctaw, or Chickasaw, for example. The so-called Little Ice Age—a period that extended over the sixteenth century and into the mid-nineteenth—contributed to changes in agricultural and settlement patterns throughout the Mississippian world. During the same period, the arrival of Europeans sparked violent conflicts with Indigenous people, spread previously unknown diseases through Native communities, and intensified preexisting rivalries among Native polities. The sixteenth century was therefore a period of population loss and migration, an epoch in the Native South's history in which large tracts of land emptied of human inhabitants as the previous occupants succumbed to disease, violence, or migrated to and resettled in a new land.[63] As one scholar observes, "The interior of the native Southeast between 1560 and 1650 must have been a cauldron of demographic instability, political volatility, and social fragmentation."[64]

The Mississippian world had become an incredibly dangerous place by the latter half of the sixteenth century.[65] If kinship ties became important to life in the eleventh and twelfth centuries, for many Native Southerners those protections likely seemed even more important by the sixteenth and seventeenth centuries. Indeed, while warfare was always a threat, the scale of violence increased following the arrival of European colonists. Moreover, the inability of medicine men and women to cure the sick brought the social and cultural knowledge of the chiefdom era under renewed scrutiny.

The technologies used to unleash violence on the Southeast had significant consequences for Native Southerners in the century after de Soto's entrada. For example, Indigenous people from Central and South America to southeastern North America confronted the brutalities of colonial violence when the Spanish unleashed their mastiffs on Native populations.[66] In other instances, the introduction of horses, particularly the Spanish mustang, aided Spanish violence against Native communities. These must have felt like sudden changes to Native Southerners; indeed, most were slow to incorporate the horse into the military cultures of the Native South, preferring instead to kill horses for their meat.[67]

By no means did all sixteenth-century technologies of warfare give Europeans an edge over Native warriors. The Spanish, for instance, may have introduced the mustang and firearms to North America, but Native Southerners had the bow and arrow, often a more efficient weapon in sixteenth-century warfare. As chapter 1 observed, the bow and arrow became ubiquitous throughout the Native South between 600 and 800. The adoption of the bow and arrow increased the impact that the raids of Indian warriors had on non-kin communities. In response, Native Southerners began building wattle and daub dwellings to protect against fire arrows.[68] By the sixteenth century, though, Indian raiding became even more common. This raiding was not simply about conquest; rather, population losses caused by European diseases and growing European–Indian violence encouraged Native warriors to engage more frequently in captive raiding and trading.[69]

The arrival of the Spanish, and later the French and English, in the Native South, added a new dimension to trade and warfare for Native Southerners. It's important not to lose sight of the fact that the history of European–Native encounters did not unfold in a linear invasion–violence–conquest model. Violence was unquestionably part of Indigenous relations with Europeans during the sixteenth century, but Native people often held strategic advantages over Europeans.

The Natchez, for example, continued to dominate substantial swaths of the Mississippi into the sixteenth century due to their skill as mariners and their adroit diplomacy. French reports noted the skilled manner in which the Natchez navigated the Mississippi River, skills and knowledge that empowered them to play a leading role in trade and captive networks. Nonetheless, the consequences of disease and persistent warfare (with both Europeans and Native enemies) resulted in a contraction of Natchez landholdings during the final quarter of the seventeenth century. The loss of territory, and sustained pressure from the Spanish and French (to say nothing of the social instability caused by the Indian slave trade) saw the Natchez reorganize into more confined areas along the Mississippi. Additionally, smaller tribes to the North, such as the Tioux and Grigra, joined the Natchez. This type of coalescence occurred throughout the Southeast during the sixteenth and seventeenth centuries, resulting in a reformulation of communal identities and enabling groups like the Natchez to better confront the challenges being posed by the French and Spanish.[70]

The types of geopolitical changes that polities like the Natchez experienced during the sixteenth and seventeenth centuries occurred during a time of increased violence and warfare that the Indian slave trade exacerbated. Raiding parties in search of captives became so common in the southeastern section of North America that Native communities began constructing and/or reinforcing defensive palisades. For example, the Spanish observed that the sixteenth-century Timucua Indians built defensive walls around their villages. Guards armed with spears and bows and arrows manned these walls. The Timucuans were not alone. Up and down the eastern seaboard and across the interior of the Southeast, American Indians built ditches, embankments, moats, and palisades to protect villages from attacks by Native captive raiders.[71] In the first century after contact with Europeans, the anthropologist Harold Driver speculates that as many Native people were killed fighting each other as were killed in wars against Europeans.[72]

Native violence was therefore motivated by a number of overlapping factors during the late chiefdom era. For example, warriors might use deadly force to exact revenge on a non-kin group for the murder of one of their kin. Alternatively, and increasingly after the fourteenth century, Native warriors engaged in combat and raiding to protect landholdings, to secure supplies, or to augment populations through captive raids. One of the unintended outcomes of horticultural development in the Native South was that it placed pressure on resources, pressures that sometimes spilled over into warfare and which the arrival of European invaders exacerbated.

The ubiquity of violence in eastern North America was such that it stretched from what we know today as the Great Lakes, the Mid-Atlantic, and into the interior Southeast by the sixteenth century. Around the Great Lakes region and what became known as upstate New York, pressure on resources sparked violence among the Iroquoian-, Siouan-, and Algonquian-speaking peoples. As the following chapter reveals, this violence resulted in Siouan-speaking Indians being driven out of their territory, while the Iroquois formed a confederacy designed to protect the interests of its people.[73]

The raiding of villages and the taking of captives increased in both frequency and intensity after the sixteenth century. In a tradition that continued after the chiefdoms began to fissure during the fifteenth and sixteenth centuries, captives faced one of three fates: death, captivity (which meant having none of the kinship rights and protections of one's captors), or being traded away. Significantly, captivity in Mississippian societies did not necessarily equate to a life of enslavement. Captives could, and were, incorporated into kinship groups. The adoption of captives was a slow process that involved confinement, involuntary labor, and torture. For captives to be adopted into a kin group they had to undergo a complete social and cultural transformation, or rebirth. In some cases, the leaders of chiefdoms might use the adoption of captives for diplomatic purposes (for instance, to seal an alliance with a rival chiefdom), or to reward supporters.[74] In other words, captivity was both an assertion of power and the potential beginnings of a transformation process involving rebirth and adoption.[75]

◇◇◇◇◇◇◇◇◇◇◇◇◇◇◇◇◇◇◇◇◇◇◇◇◇

The European invasion of the Americas at the end of the fifteenth century and into the sixteenth accelerated changes in the lives of Native Southerners. But if the chiefdom era proved anything it was that Native Southerners possessed both the ability and the willingness to adapt to change and reinvent their social, political, and cultural identities.

The chiefdoms of the Mississippian period played a profoundly important role in the history of the Native South. Out of the simple, complex, and paramount chiefdoms—polities that rose and fell for well over half a millennium—societies that archaeologists and anthropologists refer to as "coalescent societies" began emerging during the sixteenth and seventeenth centuries. For example, from the Tombigbee chiefdom arose the proto-Choctaws; the Chicazas became the Chickasaws; and where the Etowa chiefdom once thrived, towns such as Apalachicola in what is today Florida developed and helped the Creek Confederacy's emergence.[76] That these coalescent societies developed in the varied ways in which they did reflects how sixteenth-century Native Southerners engaged in a profound period of political change and ethnogenesis. As the following chapter reveals, Native Southerners formed multiethnic polities during the post-Columbian centuries.

While Native Southerners adapted chiefdom-era cultures to this new era, economically a shift away from the production of maize surpluses toward a growing trade in captives and deerskins sped the transformation of south-eastern societies during the seventeenth century. And as the relationship between labor and power changed, so too did the distribution of social and political power take on new forms. Historian Theda Perdue observes one such example, arguing that the seventeenth- and early-eighteenth-century tendency toward the commodification of captives reduced the role of Native women in warfare.[77]

Such commodification of human beings was not inevitable in 1500. However, in the post-Columbian Native South—whether along the Atlantic or Gulf Coasts, or through the interior of the Southeast—life was changing. By the seventeenth century, both Natives and the invading peoples from across the Atlantic truly were building "new worlds for all."[78]

CHAPTER THREE

CAPTIVITY, COLONIALISM, AND COALESCENCE

The invaders appeared suddenly. As they approached the town these foreign men encircled its residents and brandished weapons that emitted a foul odor when discharged. The war party had traveled from the north, entering the Native South by traveling, in part, the Occaneechi Path. This unwelcome band of northern warriors eventually reached a point some 240 miles north of the Apalachee Indians. The invaders came not to exchange goods or to renew diplomatic bonds; they came to plunder and take captives.[1]

In 1659, these invaders from the North were not Europeans; they were one of a growing number of Native American tribes that recognized the utility of firearms and understood that European colonists had a seemingly insatiable demand for Indian slaves. This most unwelcome band of invaders, the Erie-Westos, whom the Virginia English referred to as the Richahecrian, sought out trade alliances with Europeans in hopes of acquiring the firearms that made their trade in captives so efficient. To date, their strategy had proven successful. As they moved rapidly over the landscape, the Westos enjoyed success in Virginia. They established a short-lived town, Rickahockan Town, and as their warriors moved farther South the Westos continued to find Europeans willing to trade firearms in exchange for Indian slaves.[2] When the Westos eventually appeared on the frontier of the Apalachee chiefdom in 1659 their arrival added to the stresses being placed on Apalachee social structures by a different group of invaders: the Spanish.

The Spanish, like the French and the English, arrived on the coast of Florida and the Gulf region in large vessels and equipped with firearms. No one could be sure where these particular strangers came from. They spoke a foreign language, wore strange garments, and were pale-skinned and hairy. The vessels that transported these strangers were much larger than the canoes made of birchbark and poplar that Native Southerners used to shuttle goods and people throughout North America's Southeast and beyond. We can only imagine the questions that must have run through the minds of Native Southerners. Did these vessels have any relation to the horned serpents that Native people spoke about in their stories and represented in material culture? Would the Europeans want to form alliances with Native Southerners? Sixteenth-century accounts from the North Carolina coastline, for example, suggest that any trepidation that Indigenous people held for these newcomers soon gave way to curiosity and an effort to engage the Europeans aboard their ships.[3]

Native Southerners like the Apalachees made efforts to discover whom these pale-skinned invaders were and what their intentions may have been. Uncertainty, curiosity, suspicion, and possibility intermingled in these encounters. Native Southerners quickly discovered that the Spanish, like the Westos, had a capacity for extreme violence and cruelty. European and Indigenous outsiders displayed a tendency to contribute to the violence and social dislocation that characterized vast swaths of the Native South during the seventeenth century. For the Apalachees, violence and captivity fractured group identities. By 1704, a year in which English colonists massacred hundreds of Apalachee people, the Apalachees were struggling like so many other Native Southerners to retain their cohesiveness as a community.[4]

The violence of the Indian slave trade and European colonialism led to the fissuring of chiefdoms like the Apalachee, prompting Native migrations and resettlements that resulted in self-conscious attempts to redefine communal identities.[5] The Westos and other aggressive captive-raiding parties, such as those from Occaneechi communities, played a significant role in magnifying the social and cultural pressures that Indigenous people struggled with during the sixteenth and seventeenth centuries. The Westos' reputation as slave raiders and "man eaters" and the Occaneechis' reputation for terrifying levels of violence struck fear into the hearts of Native Southerners.[6] Compounding such anxiety, French, Spanish, British, and other European settler colonialists fanned out across the Native South and in so doing helped to magnify long-held disputes over land and resources among Native Southerners.

No one knew with certainty what the future held. What thousands of Native Southerners understood during this transitional epoch—punctuated by outbreaks of disease, violence, and the threat of slave raids—was the need to reconstitute social, cultural, and political systems if they hoped to successfully navigate the new threats to lands, waterways, and population.

◇◇◇◇◇◇◇◇◇◇◇◇◇◇◇◇◇◇◇◇◇

Students of North American history know, at least in broad and generalized outlines, who the Spanish colonists were and the wealth they hoped to extract in the Americas during the sixteenth and seventeenth centuries. Their invasion of Central and South America and the Gulf region (including Florida) of North America is well chronicled by historians.[7] But who were slave-raiding and trading groups like the Westo Indians?

Until recently we knew very little about the slave-raiding and trading polities like the Westos.[8] A generation of ethnohistorical research has provided students of seventeenth-century North America with some answers. The Westo Indians had their origins far to the north of the Native South. Violence, struggles over resources (such as access to beaver pelts) and political fractures among Iroquois peoples who ultimately formed the Six Nations, or Haudenosaunee, Confederacy, led to the large-scale displacement of Native people.[9] The Westos became one of those displaced groups, forcing members into migrations from Lake Erie to the Mid-Atlantic region and ultimately into the Native South.

The Westos' migrations coincided with the nascent decades of European colonialism in North America, a coincidence of chronology that the Westos and other slave-trading Indians tried to exploit by providing Indigenous captives to Europeans in exchange for firearms and other material items.[10] In the Native South, the Westos targeted and took captive people belonging to the Cherokees, Chickasaws, Timucuas, Guales, Mocamas, Calusas, Cuseetas, and members of scores of other Native polities.[11]

The Westos won few friends in the Native South. In fact, their lightning raids and violent abductions of Native Southerners invited retribution. The Occaneechis, an agricultural community whose warriors also engaged in captive raids and whom the late-seventeenth-century English referred to as the "Akenatzy," exacted a degree of vengeance on a small party of Westos in 1670. According to John Lederer, a German surgeon and explorer of the Appalachian region, the Occaneechis invited a "Rickohockan Ambassadour, attended by five Indians" to "a Ball of their fashion." At "the height of their mirth and dancing," Lederer reported that the Occaneechis "barbarously murthered" the Westos. According to Lederer, the Occaneechis' violence constituted "a bloody example of their treachery"; in truth it was an act of resistance against a violent slave-raiding competitor.[12]

The Westos certainly earned enemies throughout the Native South. While they were an example of ethnogenesis, the Westos were not a typical example of how Native people from fractured chiefdoms tried to reconstitute their collective identities.[13] Having said that, the Westos certainly weren't alone in participating in an expanding slave trade and endeavoring to redefine whom they were as a people. A confluence of factors—the collapse of chiefdom political structures, Native political reorganization, competition for natural resources, and the arrival of European traders and settlers—precipitated the emergence of reimagined Native polities and warrior tribes like the Westos. Europeans tried to leverage these changes to their advantage. The English, for example, built an empire in North America on the backs of Indian slaves, while the Spanish and French—who fretted as much as the English about the violence associated with the Indian slave trade—also availed themselves of the trade networks made possible by Indian slavery and groups such as the Westos in North America.[14]

By 1680, the Westos were gone as an identifiable group, defeated militarily by the Carolina colony and their Indian allies. But for Native Southerners, slave raiding and trading did not end with the demise of the Westo Indians. The Indian slave trade continued to have a profound impact on the Native South, as did other factors such as disease, violence, and the encroachment of European colonialism. All of these historical forces contributed to the demographic collapse of scores of chiefdoms and the emergence of new communal societies and group identities. Socio-political fissures hastened the establishment of what archaeologists and anthropologists call "coalescent societies," or Native polities comprised of members from former chiefdoms (and different, but related, language groups, cultures, and social conventions). In a rapidly changing world, the members of former chiefdoms began reorganizing their communal identities by adapting older notions of kinship into clan systems of identity.[15] As we'll see, some migrated and resettled their communities in the Native South. The Occaneechis, for example, migrated from their island homeland at the confluence of the Dan and Roanoke Rivers in Virginia to the North

Carolina Piedmont and the Eno River where they established connections with other Siouan-speaking people like the Saponis, Enos, and Tutelos.[16] In other instances, new polities emerged and coalesced during the sixteenth and seventeenth centuries to become known as the Cherokees, Creeks, Chickasaws, Choctaws, Catawbas, and many others.[17]

◇◇◇◇◇◇◇◇◇◇◇◇◇◇◇◇◇◇◇◇◇◇◇◇

The century between the 1550s and 1650s proved a transformative time for Native Southerners. The Little Ice Age (ca. 1300–1870), the invasion of European colonists, large-scale disease outbreaks, violence, slavery, and changing patterns of trade—specifically the integration of the Native South's deerskin trade into transatlantic commercial trade networks—all impacted Native Southerners. Once powerful chiefdoms fell, leaving thousands of Indigenous Southerners bereft of meaningful kinship ties. In the Lower Mississippi Valley, for example, Native communities along the Red River and Gulf Coast regions collapsed during this period. These people, and scores of now kinless Native people across the Southeast, became prime targets for the Indian slave-raiding parties that swept through the region. Some Native Southerners found themselves confined to refugee communities, such as the Native people of Savano Town on the Savannah River, while still others migrated in search of a new home and hopes of reforging kinship bonds.[18]

The anthropologist Robbie Ethridge describes the Native South during the sixteenth and seventeenth centuries as a "shatter zone."[19] Ethridge explains that European colonialism and military might were not the only factors that helped transform the chiefdoms of the Native South. As the above example of the Westos highlights, Native people also played active roles in that process.[20] Ethridge's conceptualization of the Mississippi shatter zone—chiefdom societies shattered and transformed by a multitude of forces—was also a world that Native people actively strove to remake. This transitional period for Native Southerners ultimately gave rise to new Native polities.[21]

New Native polities emerged against a historical backdrop characterized by different forms of violence. Much of the Native South became a military zone for significant periods of the sixteenth and seventeenth centuries.[22] In the Lower Mississippi Valley, for example, smaller nations—such as the Tunica and Houma—provided military scouts for warrior parties from larger polities, such as the Chickasaws. The members of smaller nations—or *petite nations,* as the French called them—looked, often in vain, for allies among the French and Native Americans to protect them against the violence and social dislocation caused by disease or Indian slave-raiding parties.[23]

As the sixteenth century unfolded, warfare became a routine part of life in the Native South. In fact, this proved true in other parts of eastern North America too. Virginia, for example, was the site of three Anglo-Powhatan Wars (between 1610–1614, 1622–1632, and 1644–1646) and Bacon's Rebellion during 1676 and 1677. In the Great Lakes region, the Beaver Wars between 1641 and 1701 punctuated life and disrupted social and political networks for both Native and settler communities.[24]

In addition to conflicts over resources, warfare and violence occurred for at least three main reasons. For Native Southerners, military activity was often woven into the ceremonial dispensation of justice or to establish the reputation of a young warrior. Secondly, the violence associated with captive raids could result in those captives not sold into the slave trade potentially being adopted into kinship systems. Finally, violence could help Native leaders project regional power.[25]

While warfare had both ceremonial and political implications, the cycles of violence that swept across eastern North America between 1400 and 1700 became so common that Native communities built defenses around their villages.[26] As the previous chapter noted, the Spanish observed that the sixteenth-century Timucua Indians of Florida built defensive walls to protect community members from possible violence. Walls were made from wood, were twelve feet high, and circled a town. Defensive walls were manned by guards and in some instances encircled by a moat. Up and down the eastern seaboard, along the Gulf Coast, and into the interior Southeast, American Indians also built ditches, embankments, moats, and erected palisades to protect villages from attack.[27]

During the sixteenth and seventeenth centuries, the weapon of choice among most warriors in the Native South was the bow and arrow. While Native warriors grew to appreciate the military utility of European firearms (and later, the mobility provided by horses) during the sixteenth and seventeenth centuries, the bow and arrow remained the weapon of choice for most warriors because of its speed and accuracy. Whereas the matchlock arquebus and flintlock musket preferred by Europeans tended to misfire when powder became wet, and took much longer to reload, a skilled archer could fire off dozens of arrows in a relatively short time and strike a target—typically an opponent's face and legs—with extreme accuracy.[28]

Native Southerners also developed body armor. Cherokee warriors used buffalo-hide breastplates, roughly eight to ten inches across. Algonquian-speaking warriors in the Carolinas fashioned wooden breastplates.[29] The materials used to make this equipment reflected that Native Southerners were all too aware of the dangers of combat; it also revealed the close relationship that they had with local ecologies. For example, strips of rawhide, hemp, or agave were used to manufacture bowstrings. The use of an animal's intestines was also common among some Native Southerners. Cherokees, for instance, used twisted bear's guts to fashion the bow, a practice repeated among other tribes throughout the Southeast.[30]

The use of local raw materials to manufacture weapons and palisade towns does not, however, explain why warfare and slave raiding became endemic across the Southeast—and eastern North America more generally—after 1300.[31] In general terms, warfare and captive raiding grew in volume and intensity as the people of Native polities strove to both protect and consolidate their communal landholdings and property. Cycles of violence were in turn perpetuated by the general increase in Native and settler populations—facilitated by the rise of horticultural economies, networks of exchange, and migrations—and the ongoing conflict over resources. From the Great Lakes to the Mid-Atlantic, Iroquoian-, Siouan-, and Algonquian-speaking people became ensnared in a cycle of warfare that gave rise to new confederacies—such as the Iroquois, or Haudenosaunee, League—and migratory slave-raiding polities like the Westos. The Westos were not the only slave-raiding polities to contribute to the reshaping of the Native South. Other polities, such as the Occaneechis and Yamasees, engaged in violent slave raids that contributed to the reworking of Native polities, while the Choctaws found themselves in the crosshairs of Chickasaw, Creek, and Alabaman slave-raiding parties.[32] The expansion of Indian slave-raiding and -trading activities occurred at a time when Europeans began establishing settler colonies that had the potential to add further strain to Indigenous communities and radically reshape the Native South.[33]

Given the centrality of slave raiding to the "shatter zone" South it's worth pausing to consider what slavery looked like in the Native South in the centuries after 1300. The first point to note is that it did not look like the racial slavery that characterized slave labor during the nineteenth

century. The captives of Native Southerners did not remain slaves for life.
Still, the raiding of Native communities and capture of slaves was violent,
but slaves who were put to work in a community (and not, for instance, sold
away) could experience a series of ritual and ceremonial traditions. Some of
these traditions had the potential to result in adoption into a kinship group.
A captive, for example, might be exposed to subordination rituals, such as
confinement, involuntary labor, and sometimes violence. These practices
served a longer-term purpose: the resocialization of captives that culminated
in their rebirth and adoption into kinship systems.[34]

Native Southerners used captivity as an "assertion of power over a person."[35] Among the people who formed the Creek Confederacy, captives
were known as "owned people," or *este vpuekv*. Siouan-speaking people in
the Carolinas referred to enslaved people and animals by the same term:
"slave."[36] The Iroquois-speaking Cherokees referred to captives as *atsi
nahshi'i* ("one who is owned," or "dependent"). As was the case throughout
the Native South, the *atsi nahshi'i* in Cherokee society had liminal identities
and remained outside the kinship system until they were "reborn" and
adopted into a Cherokee clan.[37]

The arrival of Europeans and their insatiable demand for land and slave
labor added a new dimension to these assertions of power. Throughout the
western regions of the Native South, for example, Natchez and Choctaw
peoples experienced the violent effects of slave raids and losses of population
as Native slaving parties fueled the Spanish, French, and English demand
for tractable labor.[38] Among the *petite nations* of this region, such as the
Acolapissas, Biloxis, and Capinas, population losses were also experienced.
In all cases, women and children seemed most vulnerable to the violence
of the Indian slave trade.[39] In the 1680s, an English observer noted that
the "Sevanas" (Shawnees) engaged in the Indian slave trade in the interior
Southeast. The Shawnees became a major slave-raiding and -trading power as
they sought trade networks to supply them with firearms and, as our English
observer noted, to "make war upon their neighbours, ravish the wife from
the husband, and kill the father, take the child, and burn and destroy the
dwellings of the poor people who cheerfully received us into their country."[40]

The cycle of slave raiding, captivity, and adoption that increased in the
Native South during the sixteenth and seventeenth centuries involved both
overland expeditions and river raids. Such was the demand for slaves that
some raids took as many as 1,200 captives.[41] Most captives found themselves

sold away to other parts of the Native South and as far away as New England and the Caribbean.[42]

The captive raids that supplied the Native and European markets for slaves involved well-coordinated attacks overseen by war chiefs.[43] Slave raids followed a familiar set of practices. First, the war chiefs gathered warriors together and observed purification rituals. With these rituals complete, the chief provided his warriors with tactical instructions. Typically, slave-raiding parties surrounded a targeted village in a half-moon shape, just as they would surround game. When the chief gave the whistle to advance, the warriors launched their surprise attack by letting out a loud war whoop while also closing the half-moon formation to completely encircle the town.[44] Such raids supplied captives to the Indian slave trade and made it possible for invading warriors to keep some slaves. Between 1670 and 1715, some twenty-four thousand to fifty-one thousand captives were traded in the Southeast and to points beyond.[45]

The expansion of both captive-raiding and slave-trading networks were not the only factors to cause widespread social dislocation and the fragmentation of communal identities in the Native South during the sixteenth and seventeenth centuries. Indeed, the Indigenous and European exchange networks that crisscrossed the Native South brought not only slaves and new trade goods into Indigenous towns, but microbes. No one was immune. In fact, the French worried so much about disease that they carefully examined African slaves for smallpox before they disembarked at port, fearful that such diseases would spread quickly through North America's Southeast and disrupt exchange networks with Native traders.[46]

The unwanted exchange of microbes throughout the Atlantic world constituted a potentially deadly dimension of the Columbian Exchange.[47] As the name suggests, the Columbian Exchange refers to the impact that Christopher Columbus's so-called voyages of discovery had in spreading vectors of disease and initiating a trans-Atlantic exchange of food items, animals, and myriad plant species.

For Native Southerners, disease became yet another dramatic reminder of the growing pressures on their communities as a consequence of European colonialism.[48] Typhoid, smallpox, measles, diphtheria, yellow fever, yaws, sleeping sickness, filariasis, and malaria all impacted tens of thousands of Native Southerners between the sixteenth and eighteenth centuries. Diseases previously unknown left Native communities reeling and thousands dead along the Atlantic and Gulf Coasts, in the mountain South, and throughout the American Bottom.

Smallpox became by far the most feared disease in the Native South. One of the deadliest outbreaks occurred between 1696 and 1700. The Great Southeastern Smallpox Epidemic cut a swath of death and destruction from the Gulf Coast to the mountain South. Smallpox—with its symptoms of chills, fever, and delirium—proved a sinister disease, traveling over vast distances with Europeans and Africans acting as unwitting carriers. As occurred with other smallpox outbreaks, the Great Southeastern Smallpox Epidemic afflicted thinly populated regions as seriously as it impacted densely populated towns. As many as 152,000 Native Southerners died from smallpox between 1696 and 1700.[49]

Smallpox continued to devastate parts of the Native South during the eighteenth century. Outbreaks in 1718–1722, 1728–1733, 1738–1742, 1747–1750, 1759–1760, 1763–1765, and 1779–1783 highlighted the frequency with which smallpox afflicted Native communities. These outbreaks caused a crisis of confidence in, and among, Native healers and priests. When Cherokee medicine men saw the effects of one of these outbreaks their response proved tragic. According to one eyewitness, "some shot themselves, others cut their throats, some stabbed themselves with knives and others with sharp-pointed canes; many threw themselves with sullen madness into the fire and there slowly expired, as if they had been utterly divested of the native power of feeling."[50]

Colonial newspapers also reported the dread experienced by Native Southerners when disease outbreaks began. On August 13, 1760, the *Pennsylvania Gazette* observed that "we learn from Cherokee country, that the People of the Lower Towns have carried smallpox into the Middle Settlements and Valley, where the disease rages with great violence, and that the people of the Upper towns are in such a Dread of the Infection, that they will not allow a single Person from the above named places to come amongst them."[51]

Disease epidemics had the potential to temporarily change how kin members interacted with one another while at the same time compounding the demographic stresses that Native communities experienced in the Southeast during the seventeenth and eighteenth centuries. Death and captivity defined both the literal and metaphorical reality of Native Southerners, periodically giving rise to fears that the South had become a haunted place where the specter of social dislocation and death hung over its inhabitants.

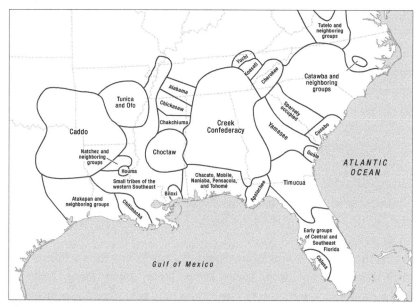

The major coalescent societies of the Native South. *Erin Greb Cartography.*

◇◇◇◇◇◇◇◇◇◇◇◇◇◇◇◇◇◇◇◇◇◇◇◇◇◇

Slavery, disease, and violence all hastened social and political changes in the Native South during the seventeenth and eighteenth centuries. It's true that the pressures from European colonialism magnified the impact of these factors and gave rise to some dark moments in the Native South. However, in this climate of uncertainty and change, Native Southerners took action and began forming new societies.

Coalescent societies, such as the Cherokees, Catawbas, Chickasaws Choctaws, and Creeks, brought people from different (though related) linguistic and cultural backgrounds together under a single polity. Coalescent societies were far less hierarchal than their chiefdom predecessors, although elements of older military and cult institutions remained. In the Southeast, most Native societies observed a matrilineal division of labor and clan identification, one of the few exceptions being the Shawnees, some of whom migrated south from the Ohio River valley and settled along the Savannah River.[52]

Coalescence was not the only strategy use by Native Southerners to renew kinship bonds and maintain a sense of community identity in the face of slavery, disease, and settler colonial expansion. The Apalachees, located near present-day north Florida, the Caddos of western Louisiana and eastern Texas, and the Natchez on the Mississippi all strove to maintain social, political, and cultural structures akin to those that existed during the chiefdom era. By the 1730s, these societies had become severely weakened by disease, colonial warfare, slave raids, and/or migration and dispersal as coalescent polities took shape.

The Native Southerners who embraced the process of coalescence, or the formation of multilingual and multiethnic polities as a means of reforging kinship and clan-based identities, included the Chickasaws and Choctaws, the latter bringing together people from smaller chiefdoms and focusing their settlements along the great bend of the upper Pearl River in what is today Mississippi.

To the east of the Chickasaws and Choctaws, lived the Cherokees and the Creeks—the latter forming core and periphery towns among the Upper and Lower Creek settlements—and the Catawbas, whose clan members coalesced from the ruins of the old Cofitachequi chiefdom. The people who shaped these and other Native polities typically adopted a matrilineal form of coalescence. Chapter 4 of this book explains in greater detail the cultural traditions and social structures that gave these coalescent societies their meaning during the eighteenth century while also exploring the colonial pressures that faced Native Southerners like the Natchez.

For now it's important to remember that coalescence did not unfold in an unproblematic, linear fashion. Disease and warfare, captivity and colonialism, all impacted Native Southerners and the innovations they strove to bring to their political and kinship systems. As coalescent societies of the interior Southeast slowly solidified their communal institutions, colonial trade and diplomatic networks with the British, French, and Spanish added layers of social and economic complexity to life in the Native South.

Most significantly, the deerskin trade became both economically lucrative and an important commodity that connected the economies of the Cherokees, Creeks, and other Native Southerners to colonial and trans-Atlantic economies. From the 1670s, the combination of Native demand for European goods and European demand for deerskins led to the overhunting of the white-tail deer. By the middle decades of the eighteenth century, the commodification of deerskins had supplanted the Indian trade and captives and altered both the social and economic fabric of the Native South. Horses, for example, become critical to facilitating the trade. While Native Southerners became expert horse breeders and "skillful jockies," the use of horses to expedite the delivery of skins to market led to overhunting. In the fierce competition to supply the market, Native warriors moved beyond their traditional hunting grounds, prompting violence with neighboring tribes as competition for new hunting lands intensified.[53]

The drive to maintain the supply of deerskins ultimately hurt the terms of trade in the Native South. By flooding eighteenth-century markets with skins, Native traders unwittingly contributed to some sharp reductions in commodity prices—a phenomenon exacerbated by downturns in demand. Closer to home, Native traders came into conflict with Indian elders. Elders

TABLE

Major eighteenth-century battles and resistance involving Native Southerners, in alphabetical order.

BATTLE OR CONFLICT	YEAR
Anglo-American campaigns against the Cherokees	1760–1761, 1773–1774, 1776–1777, 1779–1780, 1782
Anglo-Cherokee War	1758–1761
Chickamauga Wars/Resistance	1776–1794
Chickasaw Wars	1721–1763
Choctaw-Chickasaw War	1752
Choctaw Civil War	1746–1750
Creek-Cherokee Wars	ca. 1716–1754
Creek-Choctaw Wars	1702–1776
Natchez Revolt/Natchez Massacre	November 29, 1729
Natchez Wars	1716–1733
Queen Anne's War*	1702–1713
Tuscarora War	1711–1713
War of Jenkins Ear†	1739–1748
Yamasee War	1715–1717

* Queen Anne's War led to major attacks on peoples of the Tampa Bay region and major loses among the Tocobaga chiefdom.

† The War of Jenkins Ear was a major imperial conflagration between the British and Spanish that engulfed Native polities in Florida and Georgia.

became increasingly concerned about the cultural and spiritual consequences of overhunting for pecuniary purposes. They worried that the rush of some Native Southerners to increase their wealth through participation in the deerskin trade was destabilizing the delicate gender balance in labor and political life while also undermining the important principle of balance and harmony.[54]

Still, Spanish, French, and British agents worked with chiefs and headmen to "brighten the chain of friendship" and keep diplomatic and economic networks open. However, as French and Spanish agents worked to forge alliances with polities such as the Choctaws, Chickasaws, Upper Creeks, and Overhill Cherokees, growing competition among British traders from Virginia and the Carolinas, and the eventual separation of North Carolina from South Carolina in 1712, created fluid colonial boundaries and trade networks that prompted Native chiefs and traders to begin questioning the mixed messages they received from the British.[55] War always seemed a possibility.

But violence, warfare, and mixed diplomatic and trade messages did not always involve Europeans. Native Southerners had a long economic and diplomatic history and as a result old enmities had the potential to spill over into violence in this new colonial context. In the Gulf Coast region, along the Mississippi, and into the interior South, tensions between Native polities became heightened as alliances and trade agreements were renegotiated. In the early eighteenth century, the people who formed the Creek Confederacy—most prominently Ocheses warriors—and those known as the Choctaws engaged in a series of battles and warfare over slaves, access to hunting lands, and the breakdown of diplomatic friendships. While tensions between Creeks and Choctaws predated the arrival of Europeans, Creek–Choctaw violence often became ensnared in European imperial rivalries.[56]

This proved the case during the first quarter of the eighteenth century (and in subsequent decades, as the following chapter demonstrates in relation to French–Indian violence). Queen Anne's War (1702–1713), for example, embroiled Creeks and Choctaws in a war between the French and English.[57] The Creeks had forged an alliance with the English, and after the Act of Union in 1707, the British, to supply slaves to the Anglo colonists. In contrast, the Choctaws formed an alliance with the French. With new alliances in place, in 1711 about 1,000 Creek warriors took the weapons supplied them by the British and launched an attack on their Choctaw enemies.[58] In the ensuing decades, Creeks and Choctaws initiated both small- and large-scale assaults on each other, using the weaponry supplied by their European allies to exact maximum losses on their Native opponents.[59]

The ongoing danger of violence between Creek and Choctaw warriors was overlaid with Native Southerners jockeying for European alliances that might benefit their communities. Red Shoe, a powerful Western chief from the Choctaw town of Cushtusha, massaged French and British alliances for a variety of reasons during the 1730s and 1740s. In the process he upset not only the balance of power with the Creeks but also with the Chickasaws and Choctaw chiefs (especially those from the eastern division). In one instance, Red Shoe turned against the French and cultivated an alliance with the British after he caught a French soldier engaging in a sexual relationship with his wife. Diplomatic and trade alliances in the Native South required constant attention; however, a slight of the magnitude experienced by Red Shoe not only ended alliances but had the potential to spark violence.[60]

The Creek–Choctaw Wars were not the only examples of large-scale warfare between Native polities in the early eighteenth century. The Creek–Cherokee Wars, the first of which occurred between 1716 and 1727, provided another example of such violence to sweep across the Native South. The Creek–Cherokee Wars engulfed Creek and Cherokee relations after disputes over claims to hunting lands on the Creek–Cherokee borderlands erupted in violence. As the Creeks and the Cherokees formed two of the largest coalescent societies in the Native South (in terms of geography and population size), diplomatic and trade entanglements with Europeans and access to hunting lands vital to the supply of the deerskin trade and the identity of their young warriors enhanced tensions and magnified the significance of violence.[61]

Violence between Creek and Cherokee warriors continued into the mid-1720s. European colonists, especially British officials in Charles Town, South Carolina, worried that Native warfare might endanger the future expansion and prosperity of frontier settlements. As a result, the British sent Tobias Fitch, who'd served as an agent to the Creeks, to negotiate peace between the Creeks and Cherokees. However, in March 1726, Cherokee and Chickasaw warriors joined forces to attack and destroy the Lower Creek town of Cussita. A Creek counteroffensive fueled British concerns that their frontier settlers might once again be exposed to Native warfare. Renewed efforts to end hostilities between the Creeks and Cherokees resulted in peace in 1727, a peace agreement that proved temporary as violence between Creek and Cherokee warriors broke out once more in 1740.[62]

◇◇◇◇◇◇◇◇◇◇◇◇◇◇◇◇◇◇◇◇◇◇◇◇

Violence between Native polities continued into the middle and latter decades of the eighteenth century as Native Southerners fought with each other over control of hunting grounds and a larger slice of the lucrative deerskin trade, while Native chiefs strategically shifted alliances among European allies. Additionally, a number of wars involving Europeans and Native warriors had profound implications for the shape of the Native South's geopolitical map. These included the Natchez War (discussed in chapter 4), and the Tuscarora and Yamasee Wars.

The Tuscarora and Yamasee Wars revealed how quickly Anglo–Indian relations could sour during the early eighteenth century. In the eastern half of North Carolina during the first two decades of the eighteenth century, Native Southerners were losing patience with European colonists. This proved the case in eastern North Carolina, home to Chowans, Pasquatanks, Hatteras, Poteskeets, and Yeopims. These Algonquian-speaking peoples called the lands settler colonists labeled "Albemarle County" home. North Carolina officials tried to manage Indian–settler relations by designating tributary status to Indigenous peoples, a governing strategy similar to that employed in seventeenth-century Virginia among polities like the Nottoways and which involved the establishment of Indian reservations.[63]

As North Carolina officials tried to envision effective ways of governing Native communities, their efforts became complicated by colonial factionalism. In the early eighteenth century, North Carolina was home to a motley assortment of pirates, debtors, common criminals, Quakers, and a diverse cross-section of religious dissenters, aspiring planters, and Britons who considered themselves part of the proprietary elites. These non-Indigenous outsiders not only squabbled among themselves but they competed with Native peoples for land and resources and began altering local ecologies as their settlements, farms, plantations, and foreign species of flora and fauna penetrated into Native territory.[64]

Herein lay the problem for these settlers; Iroquoian-speaking people also called the eastern half of North Carolina home.[65] Mehrerrins, Cores, Nueses, Pamlicos, Weetocks, and Bear River Indians all forged communal identities for themselves in eastern North Carolina. The Tuscaroras, however, constituted by far the largest and most power Native polity in the region. With a population exceeding five thousand, the Iroquoian-speaking Tuscaroras had the potential to put large numbers of warriors into the field of battle, something that worried North Carolina's settlers.

This proved no small concern for North Carolina officials. As the settler population grew from about 1,400 in 1679 to 15,120 in 1710, encroachments onto Native land holdings increased.[66] Pressure from Albemarle County settlers had long ago placed territorial strain on the Pasquatanks, Hatteras, Poteskeets, Yeopins, and Chowans throughout the Outer Banks.[67] When a new county, Bath County, was added to the burgeoning colony and new settler societies sprang up along the Pamlico, Neuse, and Trent Rivers, tensions between settler populations and Bay River Indians, Core Indians (or Corees), and Machapungas increased. And the Tuscaroras, the largest Native polity in eastern North Carolina, posed a very real impediment to the internal expansion of settler communities.[68]

Tuscaroras, of course, saw things differently. The Tuscaroras began having regular contact with European traders in the mid-seventeenth century. However, the steady encroachment of colonial settlements on their hunting lands had grown increasingly irritating to the Tuscaroras.[69] Additionally, late seventeenth- and early eighteenth-century colonial traders routinely exploited Tuscaroras and kidnapped Tuscarora women and children to supply the burgeoning slave trade, something that caused deep unease in Tuscarora towns. This train of ills prompted Tuscarora attacks on settler farms, cattle, and boats. These attacks were matched by the inflammatory rhetoric that began to characterize Indian–settler relations throughout much of eastern North Carolina. When one colonial official threatened a Native leader in 1704, the Indian leader responded by telling the settler to "kiss his arse." And in the vicinity of Tuscarora Country, one settler observed that "ye neighbouring towns of ye Tuscororah Indians are of late dissatisfied with ye Inhabitants of this place."[70]

This was an understatement. The Tuscaroras had grown weary of traders exploiting them and angry about settlers encroaching on their lands.[71] Tensions had reached a tipping point when, in September 1711, Christopher de Graffenried, a prominent leader of a colony of Swiss and German Palatine settlers, and John Lawson, the surveyor general of North Carolina, set out on a surveying trip along the Neuse River.[72] Tuscarora warriors detained Lawson and de Graffenried—neither having permission from the Tuscaroras

to survey Native lands—as they journeyed along the Neuse. As captives, de
Graffenried and Lawson were fed while awaiting trial. Both men might have
survived their captivity had Lawson not impudently insulted his captors.
Where de Graffenried expressed contrition to the Tuscarora chief, Tom
Blount, Lawson displayed arrogance. Lawson's lack of contrition and threats
of military retribution sealed his fate. One account of his death suggested
that Lawson's captors removed a knife from the haughty settler's pocket
and slit his throat. Whatever the actual cause of his death, Lawson's demise
at the hands of the Tuscaroras sparked a war.[73]

Historian James Taylor Carson has argued that what scholars have long
called the Tuscarora War should actually be thought of as a series of overlapping conflicts. At the heart of these conflicts was settler colonialism, a
violent system of invasion and conquest that sought to dispossess Native
Southerners of their lands and control to their waterways.[74] These issues
prompted the detainment of de Graffenried and Lawson and ultimately
led to Tuscarora warriors launching a series of lightning attacks on settlers
at New Bern. These attacks resulted in the destruction of crops, homes,
and the mutilation of several settlers.[75] The Tuscaroras' defense of their
homeland had begun.

Tuscarora attacks on settlers outraged colonial opinion. In Virginia,
calls to kill every Indian rang out as Governor Spotswood moved swiftly
to muster Virginia's militia. In North Carolina, however, the pacifist beliefs
of the Bath County Quakers posed a serious military problem for North
Carolina officials. If the Bath County settlers did not take the fight to the
Tuscaroras, who would? The answer came in the form of support from
Virginia, and the South Carolina legislature's appropriation of £4,000. North
Carolinians used these funds to support a force of white and allied Indians
(which included Esaw, or Catawba, warriors), and approximately 250 North
Carolina militiamen. Under the leadership of Colonel John Barnwell, the
colonists and their Indian allies brought total war to Tuscarora Country.
They attacked not only Tuscarora warriors but their towns and villages too.
Tuscarora warriors under the leadership of King Hancock fought valiantly,
only to fail in halting destruction to their towns and farms and preventing
the devastating loss of life in one Tuscarora community after another.[76]

From a settler colonial perspective, the battles that historians later labeled
the Tuscarora War constituted an attempt to extirpate the Tuscaroras, Cores,
Neuses, and other Native Southerners in eastern North Carolina, Native

people whom colonists deemed an obstacle to the growth of the colony. From a Native perspective, these battles tell us an important story about how the Tuscaroras worked to remain united in a larger effort to preserve their territorial and cultural sovereignty. Once the war ended in 1713, Tuscaroras continued to cling to family and community identities that their warriors fought to preserve. But the strain caused by the previous years' violence proved hard to ignore. As the Tuscarora population declined, whole communities became refugees and potential victims of the Indian slave trade. In response, scores of Tuscaroras made the decision to migrate north and resettle among the Haudenosaunees (with whom they had long maintained good relations), eventually becoming the sixth member of this powerful Iroquoian Confederacy. The Tuscarora War therefore had implications that reverberated well beyond Anglo–Indian relations in the Native South.[77]

Indian–settler relations in the Carolinas remained on edge in 1713 and 1714. This proved the case with Anglo–Yamasee relations. The relationship between the Yamasees and British had simmered for the best part of a decade. In 1714 and 1715 these tensions boiled over, engulfing the region in violence in what became known as the Yamasee War.

Understanding what caused the Yamasee War requires us to go back in time and to the English founding of the Carolina colony in the 1670s. For Native Southerners along the Atlantic and Gulf Coast, the founding of the Carolina colony added to the uncertain future many of them faced following the collapse of chiefdom societies. The kinship identities and polities that emerged, such as those among the Lower Creeks, built on the multiethnic and multilingual heritage of their members. Their regional neighbors, such as the Apalachees and the Yamasees, held on to as much of the older chiefdom political and social structures as was practically possible while their chiefs attempted to negotiate new exchange networks with Native and non-Native communities.[78]

The Yamasees were themselves no strangers to the impact of European colonialism and the ravages of both disease and slave raids. As early as the 1680s, some Yamasee communities tried to migrate away from the Carolina coastline in an effort to find refuge from the violence associated with the Indian slave trade.[79] As the Yamasees worked to reestablish their towns they also became entangled in European trade networks. Thus, when Yamasee traders continued purchasing English firearms and other manufactured items, Yamasees racked up large debts.[80]

At the same time, Yamasees became important suppliers of Indian slaves to the English in South Carolina and the Caribbean. Many of these slaves were acquired from the western regions of the Native South—to which the French laid claim—with Upper Creek traders selling captives to slave traders farther south. In 1700, approximately 200 Indian slaves toiled in the Carolina colony, a number that increased to 1,500 by 1710. The Yamasees also supplied slaves to the Carolina English by launching raids into Spanish Florida and targeting the Apalachee and Timucua peoples.[81]

Despite the Yamasees regularly selling Indian slaves to the British, their debts continued to grow. Debts owed to British creditors proved instrumental in ratcheting up tensions between the Yamasees and the Carolina colony. A series of other issues and slights also magnified tensions. For example, the Yamasees felt that they had not received adequate compensation for supporting the British in the latter's war against the Tuscaroras in 1713. Yamasee warriors had played a major role in helping the British subdue the Tuscaroras, enslaving over 1,000 of them and killing a further 1,400. Other factors also raised tensions, such as the expansion of rice plantations and British cattle ranches, both of which encroached onto Yamasee lands and began altering local ecosystems.[82]

All of these factors played a role in souring relations between the Yamasees and Carolina settlers and traders. What truly undermined the Yamasees' trust of the British, however, were the mixed messages they received from British traders and colonial Indian agents. Of the former, traders worked to enlarge their profits among local Native communities. Such profit-seeking pursuits ensnared Yamasees in transnational networks of trade and led to ballooning debt among the Yamasees, all of which hastened the decline of the exchange economy.[83]

The growing indebtedness of the Yamasees made clear the economic pressures that tribal leaders came under during the early eighteenth century.[84] But what truly undermined Anglo–Yamasee relations were those mixed diplomatic messages that Yamasees heard from Indian agents Thomas Nairne and John Wright, two men who harbored a deep dislike for one another.[85] The result of their personal animosity ultimately proved disastrous. Where Nairne strove for a diplomatic friendship between the Yamasees and South Carolina, Wright actively undermined his efforts. Consequently, the Yamasees became increasingly suspicious of the British.[86]

The frustrations of Yamasee chiefs boiled over in April 1715. On April

14, Nairne feasted with the Yamasees at the town of Pocotaligo. Nairne was in Pocotaligo to bring the Yamasees talks that emphasized the importance of peace and friendship. He probably went to bed that April evening satisfied with his diplomatic overtures, not knowing that Wright had arrived in town to undermine his words of friendship, or that his life was about end violently. In the dead of night, Yamasee warriors burst into Nairne's lodgings, dragged him from his bed and tied him to a post in Pocotaligo's town square. While Nairne's British companions, including Wright, reportedly died quickly that night, Nairne was not so fortunate. According to British reports, Nairne "suffered horrible torture" for several days, his body punctured with "a great number of pieces of wood, to which they set fire." Nairne's death was slow and agonizing, the nature of his death reflecting how deeply the Yamasees now distrusted the British and their Indian agents.[87]

Nairne's and Wright's deaths brought to life settler fears of Native Southerners rising in open rebellion against the colony. Colonial leaders in Charles Town complained that despite the Yamasees showing outward signs of "friendship" toward the British, their "bodies were painted with red and black streaks," a statement that told the British that the Yamasees were now at war and prepared to kill. These "devils come out of Hell" had suddenly placed the British colony in South Carolina in a "deplorable state."[88] Fearing a broader regional war against Native warriors, the British saw in the Yamasee uprising a grave threat to British colonialism. These fears became a reality when the Yamasees gained military support from smaller polities such as the Waccamaws and the neighboring Lower Creeks, prompting colonist George Ross to warn in May 1714 that if "this Province were lost the whole continent would suffer."[89]

The Yamasee War did indeed reverberate into other parts of Native America. In the interior Southeast, the Upper Creeks, Cherokees, Catawbas, Chickasaws, among others, killed rogue traders and drove a hard bargain with French, Spanish, and British agents over access to Native towns, the locations of trading forts, and the parameters of the lucrative deerskin trade.[90] To the British, these developments proved troubling, a threat to their colonial ambitions in the interior South. Everywhere the British looked they imagined they saw French and Spanish agents working to turn the Indians against them, and Native warriors "burning and destroying the plantations" and "very cruelly" killing British traders and livestock throughout the Southeast.[91] The Yamasee War thus brought Native

Southerners together in a military alliance against European colonists and sparked European agents into action as they sought out Indigenous allies and trading partners.

Was all of this a sign that Native Southerners were willing to form new military and diplomatic identities? Perhaps. While British colonial officials worried about pan-Indian alliances, none of any enduring military consequence emerged during the early eighteenth century.[92] Nonetheless, in the wake of the Yamasee War, the Lower Creeks and Yamasees did form the core of an anti-British coalition.[93] The Huspaw (or Huspah) king, chief of the Yamasee town of Huspaw, informed the Carolina British that the Indian agent John Wright had been killed because of rumors that "the white men would come and Ketch all the Yamasees in one night, and that they would hang four of their head men, an take all the rest of them for Slaves, and that they would send them all off the country."[94] The Huspaw king and his people relocated, ultimately finding refuge in Spanish Florida, prompting the Carolina colony to issue a reward for his capture and return.[95]

Yamasees were not willing to relinquish their sovereignty as a people or to succumb to the clutches of slavery. While Native Southerners like the Yamasees had a complex relationship with the Indian slave trade, they, along with Native peoples throughout eastern North America, knew that they must remain proactive in maintaining their communal identities. The British understood this, one official observing that Native Americans considered "ye lands are theirs and they can make warr and peace when they please."[96]

The Yamasee War reminded European colonial officials of the importance of Indian allies and the need to nurture those alliances. Among the British, however, the war also sparked efforts to forge closer ties between the Carolina colonies and Virginia.[97] What the Yamasee War didn't do was avert European attention away from the interior South of North America. In fact, the British turned aggressively to the interior regions of the Southeast and worked to cultivate diplomatic and trade relations with the Upper Creeks, Catawbas, and Cherokees, while the Spanish and French vied for alliances with Choctaws, Chickasaws, and smaller nations, alliances the British worked to undermine as the eighteenth century unfolded.[98]

Rumors of French desires to use their Indian allies to cut off the Cherokees led to some dire predictions from British officials. One warned that the British should increase efforts to court the Cherokees, stating that "the

Cherikees being a numerous Nation consisting of upwards of 4000 fighting men, and seated in the fastness of the great mountains are not so easily to be destroyed."[99] Thus, to stymie French ambitions in the interior South, the British needed to make overtures to the Cherokees and the neighboring Catawbas and establish articles of friendship with them.[100]

But before the British could turn their diplomatic and trade attentions to the interior South, they had to survive the Yamasee War. The war was brutal; Yamasee warriors and their Lower Creek allies used surprise and stealth tactics against the British. Smaller polities such as the Waccamaws, whose towns and villages dotted the landscape along the Pee Dee River, joined the hostilities and attacked English settlements during the war.[101] The war, however, ended badly for the Yamasees. Scores of Yamasees were captured and transported to the Caribbean as slaves. Once the violence finally ceased colonial diplomats did indeed focus on cultivating a new ally: the Cherokees.

◇◇◇◇◇◇◇◇◇◇◇◇◇◇◇◇◇◇◇◇◇◇◇◇

Warfare, slavery, and disease all impacted the efforts of Native Southerners to reconstitute and stabilize their communal identities during the early eighteenth century. However, the nature of slavery was changing as the Europeans who invaded the Native South increasingly turned to African slaves by the 1720s. As growing numbers of enslaved Africans entered the region they were also bought and sold by Native slave traders and slave owners. Indeed, violence and slavery, trade and diplomacy, and cultural exchange did not end with the Tuscarora or Yamasee Wars.

As the following chapter reveals, how Native Southerners structured daily life, understood ritual and ceremony, and defined a communal sense of belonging bore at times a faint resemblance to, and at other moments a clear outline of, the region's chiefdom antecedents. In the eighteenth-century Native South, tradition remained alive and meaningful because Indigenous people fought for it and were willing to breathe new meaning into the stories they both enacted and told about their communal identities.

CHAPTER FOUR

PETITE NATIONS, TOWNS, AND CLANS

Tomochichi saw a lot of change in his lifetime. Born in the 1640s, he grew to manhood among the Lower Creeks. Like other young Creek men, Tomochichi experienced all of the rites of passage necessary to ensure he became a skilled warrior and proficient hunter. Such was the esteem in which contemporary Yamacraws held him that they entrusted him with the responsibility of traveling to England in 1734 to represent the interests of his people. Although an old man by the early eighteenth century, Tomochichi had earned the respect of the British, the neighboring Yamasees, and the members of his town, Yamacraw.[1]

But in 1715, Tomochichi's future as a trusted elder was by no means guaranteed. Nor for that matter was the future of the Yamacraw people a sure thing. The outbreak of the Yamasee War saw the splintering of the Yamasee people and their Lower Creek allies. These events altered the course of Tomochichi's life. As the war raged on, however, communities among the Lower Creeks regrouped. Many Lower Creeks coalesced around the Creek chief Brims of Coweta.[2] Under Brims, the Coweta Creeks broke with the Yamasees and pursued a policy of neutrality—a label that doesn't fully do justice to Brims's diplomatic goals—with the British and other European colonial powers in the Southeast.[3]

Tomochichi had a choice to make: follow Brims or go in a different direction. How would Tomochichi and the people close to him define themselves at this moment of change? He reflected on the immediate future and rejected Brims's strategy. Tomochichi and some two hundred Yamasees

Portrait of Tomochichi. *Hargrett Rare Book and Manuscript Library, University of Georgia, Athens.*

and Lower Creeks broke with the Coweta Creeks and formed the town of Yamacraw. Under Tomochichi's leadership, the Yamacraws actively pursued diplomatic and trade relations with outsiders, including neighboring Europeans. Tomochichi, whose father was Yamasee and mother Creek, sought out the white path of peace, a path that eventually reopened trade and diplomatic friendships with the Yamacraws' various neighbors.[4] Tomochichi thus eschewed the idea of neutrality in preference for well-established practices of diplomacy and trade designed to nurture bonds of reciprocity between the Yamacraws and their neighbors.

Tomochichi's decision to lead approximately two hundred people to form the town of Yamacraw and pursue economic and diplomatic policies seemingly at odds with the Coweta position of neutrality reveals the importance of local identities in the Native South. Against a backdrop of slave raids, warfare, disease outbreaks, and economic and diplomatic challenges magnified by European colonialism, Native Southerners like Tomochichi and his followers found comfort and meaning in town life. This chapter reveals the importance of town and regional identities among Native Southerners between the 1720s and 1760s. During these decades, Native communities worked to nurture meaningful relationships with townspeople and members of their kin groups. Native Southerners also worked to maintain trade and diplomatic friendships with Native and European outsiders. Native Southerners did not adopt a single formula for carving out a meaningful sense of belonging. Some followed the path taken by Tomochichi and decided to start over, others chose the hatchet and warfare, and still others looked to time-honored traditions to retell the stories of their kin and communities.

◇◇◇◇◇◇◇◇◇◇◇◇◇◇◇◇◇◇◇◇◇◇

At the opening of the eighteenth century, Native Southerners continued to innovate and adapt tried-and-tested cultural traditions to renew communal identities. As the members of former chiefdoms reconstituted their communities, clan identities and local affiliations were rewoven together in an example of Indigenous political innovativeness.[5] For Native Southerners from the Gulf Coast—such as the Chitimachas, Biloxis, Apalachees, and Ocales—to the communities of the interior South—like the Koasatis, Alabamas, Cherokees and Hitichitis—traditions associated with matrilineal kinship and exogamous marriage practices made it possible for many to migrate, resettle, renew, and nurture clan identities over geographical distances much larger than they had been during the chiefdom era. Regional, and specifically, town, identities, structured daily routines and reminded people of communal responsibilities among Native Southerners while also making it possible for macroregional affiliations to develop within polities such as the Catawbas, Cherokees, Creeks, Chickasaws, and Choctaws.[6]

These coalescent societies helped to remake the Native South as an Indigenous *place* during the first half of the eighteenth century. Despite the best efforts of European colonial powers to control the Native South, large macroregional coalescent societies—in addition to smaller Native polities—continued to exercise sovereignty over the land and rivers of the region and shaped trade networks and diplomatic friendships with Europeans.

The European traders who ventured into the interior South understood these power dynamics better than most outsiders. They recognized the control that Native warriors maintained while also acknowledging the feelings of connection that Native Southerners felt for their towns, each with its respective local ecology. For example, the English trader James Adair noted as much when he traveled through Creek Country. Adair claimed that "it is called the Creek country, on account of the great number of Creeks, or small bays, rivulets and swamps, it abounds with."[7]

The land, the mountains, and the rivers and creeks etched into southeastern North America's landscapes permeated Native culture and gave meaning to a place. Despite the violence of the Indian slave trade, the ravages of disease, and growing diplomatic, economic, and military pressure from European imperial powers, Native Southerners lived in societies where the principles of balance and harmony between human society and local ecosystems and the ideal of reciprocity trumped any drive for profit and individual advancement.[8]

These principles inspired Tomochichi, just as they motivated scores of other chiefs, *micos* (town chiefs), and the townspeople whose respect these leaders constantly strove to win. It was the case for demographically and geographically smaller polities as much as for larger macroregional societies.

◇◇◇◇◇◇◇◇◇◇◇◇◇◇◇◇◇◇◇◇◇◇◇◇

The people of one of these smaller polities, the Caddos, worked together to maintain a coherent sense of communal identity.[9] Located in modern-day western Louisiana, eastern Texas, and portions of Arkansas and Oklahoma, the Caddo people belonged to kinship groups whom Europeans called the Hasinais, Kadohadachos, and Natchitoches. The Caddos, whose neighbors included the Wichitas, Tonkawas, Kitsais, and Natchez, were a horticultural people whose diet was based around corn, beans, and squash. As was the case throughout the Native South, the Caddos nurtured trade networks with Native and European traders while simultaneously using their horticultural base to reinforce a sense of place through the cycle of agricultural ceremonies.[10] The Caddos' sense of place and identity was further reinforced through mortuary rituals and a rich culture buttressed by ceremonial traditions that emphasized the importance of balancing dualistic forces—such as good and evil—that dated back to the chiefdom era.[11]

When the Caddos encountered the Spanish in the 1540s, their culture, social life, and economy were all vibrant. Kinship identities were maintained

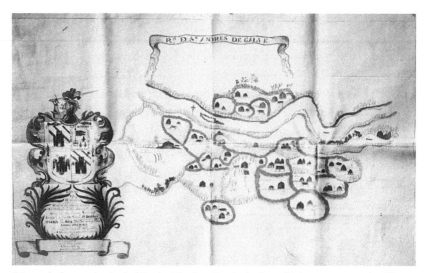

Mapa de la provincia habita la Nacion Casdudacho, which represents the Upper Nasoni community along the Great Bend of the Red River. Facsimile copy. *Eugene C. Barker Texas History Collection, Dolph Briscoe Center for American History, University of Texas, Austin.*

by a system of matrilineal inheritance, and both population and bonds of reciprocity were expanded through exogamous marriage practices.[12] These practices proved critical to the Caddos' understanding of reciprocity, with religious and political responsibilities being shared among the clans—an ideal that the Caddos expected the Spanish and the French to conform to after they began arriving in the region.[13]

Inheritance played a role in assigning some religious and political positions in Caddo society. For example, the *xinesi* (or Chenesi), meaning Mr. Moon, was an inherited position of spiritual leadership. The *caddi*, principal headman of a community, was a political position passed from father to son. The *caddi*, however, was not an autocrat as he received regular counsel from the *canahas*, or elders.[14]

The Spanish and French found the Caddos to be skilled traders and shrewd diplomats. Disease outbreaks and violence severely tested these skills as the Caddos sought ways to bring Europeans into their networks of exchange and social and cultural reciprocity during the seventeenth century. The Indian slave trade, particularly raids on Caddo towns by Chickasaw and Osage warriors, further strained Caddoan society. Between 1691 and

1816, as many as 75–95 percent of the Caddo population succumbed to disease, slavery, or a combination of both.[15]

The Caddo people responded to these historical forces by relocating and reestablishing their lives. The Hasinai Caddos relocated to east Texas while the Natchitoches Caddos sought refuge from epidemic outbreaks in northwest Louisiana. In the 1780s, the Kadohadacho people coalesced in communities along the Red River near Caddo Lake, located along what is today the Louisiana–Texas border. The Kadohadachos found respite at Caddo Lake from Osage attacks, ultimately remaining in the region until 1842.

The eighteenth century proved a challenging period in Caddo history. Caddoan people worked to renew a sense of connection to place, nurture kinship ties, and foster a sense of communalism. The Caddos persisted through the late eighteenth century, drawing strength from stories and cultural traditions that dated back to the chiefdom era and innovating them to meet the challenges posed by settler colonialism. Indeed, those traditions continue to give Caddos strength today.

If the Caddos renewed their collective identity by migrating and relocating their communities, innovating and adapting their social, cultural, and economic structures, the Natchez strove similarly to hold onto the traditional cultural practices and social structures that informed the identities of their chiefdom era forebears.

The Natchez, located to the south of the Caddos along the lower Mississippi River, were known as "the people of the Sun." Natchez people lived in towns and villages, their social and political structures surviving into the colonial period. Like other polities in the Native South, the Natchez engaged in exogamous marriage practices and organized their system of kinship along matrilineal lines. This system of matrilineality proved foundational to Natchez kinship identity; so too, according to Jean-Baptiste Le Moyne de Bienville, the governor of French Louisiana, was the organization of chiefs that included the "Great Suns," "Tattooed Serpent," "Little Sun," "The Bearded," "Old Flour Chief," "Old Hair," "Yakstalchil," and "Alahoflechia." Contrary to the French belief that Natchez chiefs oversaw a rigid political hierarchy, the Natchez structured their society around local chiefs in a loose confederation.[16]

The Natchez system of power, ritual, and identity was nonetheless "sedimented" in the landscape.[17] The reshaping of the landscape to reflect the ethnic diversity and social, cultural, and political identities within the Natchez chiefdom resulted in the construction of mounds and plazas that

"Dance générale," in volume 2 of Le Page du Pratz's *Histoire de la Louisiana* (1758). *Library of Congress, Prints and Photographs Division, Washington, D.C*

provided people with a sense of place, and a spatial compass with which to navigate the social world. Architecture, in other words, told a story about how the Natchez ordered the social landscape in ways that emphasized ranks and underscored the importance of reciprocity among Natchez people.[18]

When Europeans observed the Natchez social and political structures, they identified what they thought were systems analogous to their own. French and Spanish observers perceived in the hereditary leader, the Great

Sun, a figure of leadership similar to a hereditary European king or queen. If Europeans imagined that they saw in the Natchez "suns," "nobles," and "honored men" a system that approximated their own, did this mean that the Natchez and Europeans could coexist?

In the seventeenth century, the Natchez had an answer for this question: they worked to bring Spanish and French traders into their exchange economy. By the 1680s, the French actively sought new markets and colonies south of the Great Lakes. This brought them into the Louisiana Territory and regular contact with Native polities like the Natchez. The frontier exchange economy of which the French became a part connected villages across the Lower Mississippi and fit neatly into an established Native system that sought to absorb outsiders into reciprocal relationships.[19] However, the Indian slave trade discussed in the previous chapter had a terribly destabilizing effect on exchange networks and undermined the social stability of Natchez towns. By the 1720s, as the French looked increasingly to Africa for enslaved labor, new social tensions among the Natchez, Africans, and Europeans developed in the Lower Mississippi.

Natchez leaders continued working to smooth over tensions and bring outsiders into line with the traditions of reciprocity built into the exchange economy. However, French encroachments on Natchez lands and ongoing abuses by French traders and soldiers angered Natchez people. By the late 1720s, instability in Natchez and French relations looked set to boil over. And then, in 1729, Natchez leaders acted on repeated French abuses.[20]

At a meeting of *viellards* (elders), six days of discussions resulted in an agreed course of action. The Natchez must resist enslavement; they should also oppose the economic dependence that the French tried to impose over them. "The wares of the French," one Natchez Sun warned, "debauch the young women, and taint the blood of the nation." It was therefore decided that to prevent the French from whipping "us as they whip their slaves," military action was necessary.[21]

Natchez elders believed they were taking a stand against the abuses of French colonialism. Their course of action meant taking the path of resistance against colonial impudence and invasion. The French expressed different opinions. They viewed Natchez resistance as something more sinister: a plot so dangerous that it might also inspire African slaves to join a resistance movement that French officials began referring to as the "Natchez plot."[22]

The battle that ensued saw the French and their Indian allies—which included most Native polities in the vicinity of Natchez Country—embroiled in a bloody battle against Natchez warriors. The violence resulted in extensive damage to French properties and the loss of life on all sides. Natchez warriors destroyed French plantations and killed settlers and slaves.[23] The Natchez resistance, however, proved short-lived. When the violence ended, the French demanded that the People of the Sun leave the Apple Village, a particularly fertile region of the Natchez chiefdom that the Natchez people considered sacred. Despite French efforts to displace the Natchez, the communal identity of the Natchez burned strongly. The language used to express Natchez identity appeared to be changing, but the message seemed clear enough. As one holy man stated in the lead-up to the violence of 1729: the Natchez were "people who named themselves Red Men."[24]

In 1730, Natchez Country was again drenched in blood. A series of wars between Natchez warriors and the French ended badly for the Natchez. When the fighting ended, Natchez towns lay in ruins and kinship ties were fractured. Scores of Natchez people became refugees and began dispersing throughout the Native South. Some migrated to Chickasaw and Creek towns in search of refuge and the possibility of forging new kinship ties, while others traveled as far away as Cherokee Country. Not all Natchez refugees found new homes and kinship ties, however. An unknown number were sold into slavery and shipped to the Caribbean. Yet others avoided the slave catchers and despite taking refuge among the Upper Creeks strove to retain a sense of their Natchez identity. By the second half of the eighteenth century, approximately five hundred Natchez remained among the Upper Creeks. The U.S. government ultimately removed their descendants from the Southeast and relocated them to Indian Territory (modern day eastern Oklahoma) in the early nineteenth century.[25]

⬦⬦⬦⬦⬦⬦⬦⬦⬦⬦⬦⬦⬦⬦⬦⬦⬦⬦⬦⬦

The Caddos and Natchez are two examples of smaller polities along the western borderlands of the Native South who struggled to maintain a clear sense of community, tradition, and identity amid the violence, disease, and changing socioeconomic order unleashed by the growth in the Indian slave trade and European colonialism. For tens of thousands of Native Southerners, remaining members of small chiefdoms, or *petite nations,* to borrow the French term for them, proved an unsustainable option in an often volatile world. The members of some smaller polities—such as the

Houmas, Biloxis, and others—migrated, resettled, and lived quiet, dignified lives. For other Native Southerners, the future lay with the nurturing of macroregional coalescent societies.

One of those larger societies was that of the Choctaws. At the end of the seventeenth century, the Choctaws formed a loosely structured confederacy that worked to defend against all-too-regular slave raids and to protect the Choctaw homeland. The Choctaw homeland bordered Natchez and Tunica lands to the west, Chickasaw and Chakchiuma homelands to the north, the Alabamas and Mobilians to the east, and a number of small tribes like the Pascagoulas and Biloxis to the south.[26]

The first contact that the people who formed the Choctaw confederacy had with Europeans occurred when de Soto's entrada traveled through the Southeast in the 1540s. De Soto, like subsequent European invaders to the Lower Mississippi, noted that the Choctaws were a prosperous farming people. However, Europeans did not have regular contact with the Native peoples who became known as the Choctaws, and once they did, during the latter half of the seventeenth century, the Choctaws had formed a loose confederacy that provided them with the political structures and ceremonies to effectively trade and engage in diplomatic talks with outsiders.[27]

By the eighteenth century, the Choctaws, who called themselves "Chathas," divided themselves into three politically and geographically distinct categories. These included the western towns (or *Okla falaya*, "the people who were widely dispersed"), the eastern towns (*Coonsha*), and the southern towns (*Okla hannali*, "people of the six towns"). The eastern and western divisions comprised the two main geopolitical divisions in Choctaw society.[28]

These geopolitical distinctions provide clues about the ethnic and linguistic origins of the Choctaws. Eighteenth-century Choctaws descended from simple chiefdoms and spoke different, albeit similar, languages. The different interpretations of the Choctaw origin narrative about Nanih Waiya (Leaning Hill) mound builders suggests that while narrative differences developed, there existed a number of shared cultural concerns about the importance of place to communal identities.

Stories about origins may receive local interpretative applications, but ultimately the Choctaws developed a coalescent society in which kinship provided the cultural and political glue to bind people together in towns scattered over different regions in a common polity during the seventeenth and eighteenth centuries. Town and village clusters were usually autonomous among the Choctaws. Each Choctaw town included members from different kinship groups. These kinship groups comprised clans that were grouped into exogamous moieties, or social groups. This meant that when men and women married they had to be from different moieties.[29]

Choctaw social and political identities were informed by moieties, clans, and geographical distinctions (the latter consisting of membership in one of the over ninety towns situated throughout Choctaw Country). Choctaws belonged to one of two moieties—red (*iksa*) and white (civil chiefs). These moieties were divided into as many as eight clans. Clans in turn divided into local groups and included a series of villages and towns. As was the case in other larger polities throughout the Native South, and as we saw with the Yamacraw–Creek chief Tomochichi, there existed considerable fluidity in the geopolitical and social nature of collective identities. For instance, Choctaws had the ability to change moieties based on accomplishments, age, and the esteem with which community members held an individual.

The red–white moiety was likely an example of cultural and political continuity from the chiefdom era. Such organizational traditions, adapted to meet the new challenges of European colonialism, helped Choctaw chiefs in their diplomatic and trade negotiations with non-kin people. And just as Tomochichi transitioned from a Creek war chief to a peace chief over the course of his long life, so too did Choctaws maintain a fluid understanding of their social and political roles in society. It's worth emphasizing that this fluidity was based on merit and experience, and was always focused on ensuring balance and harmony in Choctaw society.

No area of life required more attention to the principles associated with balance and harmony than the environment. As a successful horticultural people, the Choctaws paid particular attention to the rhythms of the seasons, the health of the soil, and the flow of the rivers. Their towns, for example, were located far enough away from the flood-prone rivers to mitigate against constant flooding. By the latter half of the eighteenth century, European observers expressed fulsome praise for the agricultural skills of the Choctaws.[30] The English botanist William Bartram wrote in 1777 that the Choctaws constituted "most ingenious and industrious husbandmen, having large plantations, or country farms, where they employ much of their time in agricultural improvements, . . . by which means their territories are most generally cultivated and better inhabited than any other Indian republic that we know of."[31]

As in other parts of the Native South, a Choctaw's identity was also tied to labor. Men and women performed different, albeit reciprocal, roles in supporting the well-being of their towns.[32] Choctaw women thus developed a store of knowledge about agricultural production and food preparation that combined beans, corn, squash, sunflowers, and pumpkins, all of which were supplemented by the gathering of wild fruits such as strawberries, huckleberries, crab apples, and mulberries. Surplus produce became part of an exchange economy—the Chickasaws being the main market for Choctaw produce—and the Choctaws supplemented their diet with meat products, such as deer, which male warriors contributed to the communal economy.[33]

Labor was therefore reinforced by gendered identities. Indeed, gender, which was far more flexible than the male–female binary that existed in European culture, was not only important to horticultural production and the exchange economy but played a central role in the Choctaw kinship system. As a matrilineal society, when a man married a women he relocated and took up residence with his wife.[34]

Once married, Choctaw men and women worked to nurture a loving family environment. The family reinforced the importance of responsibility and reciprocity in Choctaw life. As one European observer noted, "The Choctaw had a warm, caring family system whose members worked together as a unit. Both sexes participated in farming activities; females joined males and hunted and fished on various occasions."[35] The family, in other words, reinforced the communal ethos that was the bedrock of Choctaw identity. Without kinship connections to a larger sense of community, life for eighteenth-century Choctaws became meaningless.[36]

The Choctaws' northern neighbors, the Chickasaws, also gave meaning to life by regularly renewing communal identities. The Chickasaws' Chiefdom-era forebears, the Chicazas, established their towns and agricultural fields in a portion of the Tombigbee River watershed—a region stretching from western Tennessee to northern Mississippi—around Tupelo, Mississippi. The Chicazas, who absorbed refugees from shattered Native polities, emerged in European colonial records as the Chickasaws. It was the Chickasaws, as we saw in the previous chapter, who became major players in the Indian slave trade—raiding Natchez, Chakiuma, Yazoo, Choctaw, and other Indian communities. Chickasaw slave traders and diplomats used the Lower Trade Path (the major north–east thoroughfare that connected the Atlantic to the Mississippi) and accessed Creek towns such as Okfuskee by the Upper

Trade Path. The Chickasaws also traveled along the North–South Trail, a path that connected Chickasaw towns with the French at Mobile Bay.[37]

The Chickasaws' kinship system revolved around as many as fifty "house names" (*intcuka hotcifo*).[38] House names, or house groups, included related females and their husbands, children, and unmarried brothers. They had names such as "little corn crib," "a lot of weeds in the crop," and "having a red house," all of which reflected local environments and the characteristics of houses in a Chickasaw town. These house groups defined the Chickasaws' social system, just as totemic clans such as Bear, Fish, Wildcat, and Raccoon reinforced a sense of kinship in other Native polities.[39] Like the neighboring Choctaws, the Chickasaws had a flexible clan system. Its exogamous nature enabled Chickasaw clan members to adopt outsiders, and, after European traders arrived during the seventeenth and eighteenth centuries, acquire limited privileges and responsibilities within the clan system if they married a Chickasaw woman.[40]

In addition to house names and clans, the Chickasaw system of kinship included endogamous moieties. Chickasaw moieties were known to Europeans and Euroamericans as Panther and Spanish, Imosaktca ("their hickory chopping") and Intcukwalipa ("their worn-out place"), and Tcukilissa and Tcukafalaha (sometimes designated as peace and war moieties, respectively). This dualistic system of moieties included clans that varied in number; the moieties also operated as part of a dual political organization designed to maintain balance, for example, between war (red) and peace (white) chiefs.[41]

Given that the Chickasaws became major players in the Indian slave trade, it should not come as a surprise that Europeans likened their military prowess to the ancient societies of Greek antiquity. Eighteenth-century Europeans referred to Chickasaw warriors as the "Spartans" of the southeastern tribes. Chickasaw warriors also earned the respect of fellow Chickasaws and became feared among the British and French. Chiefs such as Chincoboy, Micho, and Oboystabee earned the esteem of Chickasaws because of their skills as warriors. Such esteem no doubt proved critical to Chickasaw masculinity, but a chief's identity was not static. In the eighteenth century, Chickasaw masculinity demonstrated a degree of fluidity, something that Fattalamee highlighted when his status transitioned from war chief to peace chief. As a young warrior, Fattalamee earned the respect of his kin and through experience accumulated enough wisdom to warrant the transition to peace chief.[42]

Eighteenth-century Chickasaw identities did not simply revolve around the pursuits of warriors, and slave raiding. Chickasaws also nurtured religious and ceremonial traditions and worked to maintain reciprocal relationships. In religious life, the Chickasaws worshipped the deity Ababinili, the Supreme Being. Ababinili was a composite force consisting of Four Beloved Things Above—the Sun, Clouds, Clear Sky, and He that Lives in the Clear Sky.[43] Chickasaw belief informed ceremonial culture and a strong connection to nature. Just as reciprocity informed the kinship system, Chickasaws understood the importance of remaining observant of the lunar cycles, respectful of the local ecology, and acting responsibly toward all living things.[44]

These principles guided the formation of intimate relationships between a man and a woman. Family was an important part of a communal identity for eighteenth-century Chickasaws, so when a suitor from one clan proposed marriage to a woman from another clan the matter was taken very seriously. The marriage ceremony reflected how Chickasaws believed that such unions played a vital role in a communal society guided by the principle of reciprocity. James Adair described one Chickasaw marriage ceremony when he wrote of how

> the groom takes a choice ear of corn, and divides it in two before witnesses, gives her one half in her hand, and keeps the other half to himself; or otherwise he gives her a deer's foot, as an emblem of the readiness with which she ought to serve him; in return, she presents him with some cakes of bread, thereby declaring her domestic care and gratitude. . . . When this short ceremony is ended they may go to bed like an honest couple.[45]

Adair's description is framed by his patriarchal understanding of marriage and his misunderstanding of the ceremonial symbolism associated with Chickasaw marriage ceremonies. However, if we read between the lines of Adair's value judgments we glimpse the Chickasaw commitment to a bond defined by reciprocal responsibilities. A married couple's children further contributed to the health and vitality of Chickasaw kinship communities and perpetuated the principle of matrilineality. For example, children were brought up in the mother's clan, with girls reared entirely by their mother and her clan, while sons were assigned to a village or town elder between the ages of twelve and fifteen to complete their transition to adulthood.

Like the Chickasaws to their west, the multiethnic Creeks understood the importance of kinship, the principle of reciprocity, and living responsibly with the environment. The "Creek," a word used by English traders to designate those Indians residing along the Ochese Creek in Georgia, lived at "an elegant place of residence" near important rivers and their tributaries.[46] In fact, the name that the ethnically and linguistically diverse peoples—Cowetas, Kashitas, Coosas, and Abihkas—who became known as the Creeks adopted for themselves was an Algonquin word: "Muskogee," meaning "people of the swampy ground (or wet ground)."[47]

The Creek Confederacy included major geographical divisions, the Upper and Lower Creeks, and involved the coalescence of Hitchitis, Uchees (or Yuchees), Cowetas, Kashitas, Hilibis, Abihkas, Fishatchees, Atasis, Okchais, Natchez, Alabamas, and numerous other ethnically and linguistically diverse peoples.[48] The collapse of chiefdom societies, the demographic losses experienced due to disease epidemics, and the traumatic consequences of slave raids resulted in large populations of Native Southerners abandoning towns and farms and becoming refugees throughout North America's Southeast. Many of these refugees suddenly found themselves bereft of meaningful kinship ties. As a result, they migrated to, and coalesced with, the Muscogean core of the nascent Creek Confederacy during the seventeenth and early eighteenth centuries. Why seek protection in a Creek town? The answer seemed simple: safety and a renewed sense of kinship. Between the 1720s and the early 1760s, the Creeks emerged as a major diplomatic and economic power in the Native South, making Creek Country a magnet for Native refugees.[49]

The ethnopolitical confederacy that became known as the Creek Confederacy incorporated a region that included the Chattahoochee, Coosa, and Tallapoosa Rivers—spanning what is today Georgia and Alabama. The Creeks rose to political prominence and power in this region in the century after the 1670s, with groups such as the Ochese Creeks proving themselves skilled traders and diplomats.[50]

The eighteenth-century Creek Confederacy was comprised of politically decentralized towns. Identification with a town proved a centerpiece of communal identities for the people of the confederacy. Creek towns enjoyed autonomy in the day-to-day decision-making and nurtured matrilineal ties that deepened communal identities. A 1735 version of a Creek origin narrative, related to Europeans by Chigilli of Coweta, emphasized the importance of women to eighteenth-century Creek identity. Chigilli told his audience that his ancestors were daily being attacked and killed by a large bird. They responded by making an effigy in the shape of a woman, which they placed in the flight path of the bird. When the bird saw the effigy it carried it off, keeping the effigy for a long time before returning it to the Creeks. After some time, a red rat came forth from the effigy, believing the bird was its father. The Creeks then "took council with the rat [on] how to destroy its father. Now the bird had a bow and arrows; the rat gnawed the bowstring, so that the bird could not defend itself, and its people killed it."[51] This narrative underlined the importance of women in forming relationships with powerful or dangerous beings. In return for women mediating these powers, the Creek people were able to live in peace with all living beings and gained insights into how to interact with outsiders.[52]

A common core of origin stories bound Creeks together in a sense of historical connectedness. Stories and ceremonies that reinforced kinship ties played a similar role. These stories helped to explain the Creek kinship system's dynamism and the capability of Creek communities to adopt outsiders. Creek kinship consisted of two major moieties: the Hathagalgis ("people of the white") and the Tcilokogalgis ("foreigners," designated by the color red).[53] The exogamous clans that existed within this moiety system helped define matrilineal Creek identities.[54] Unlike the neighboring Cherokees, whose clans constituted structural units of identity, the Creek clans were segmentary units. This meant that where the Cherokees had a fixed number of clans, the number of Creek clans fluctuated and were smaller and more localized than Cherokee clans.[55]

For eighteenth-century Creeks, the clan system reinforced the importance of communal life and identities. Clan members therefore took on some important responsibilities, such as dividing communal land allotments among townspeople; establishing identity in accordance with Creek principles of matrilocal identity formation (which included, among other things, a husband joining his wife's household); and enacting Creek laws to ensure the maintenance of social harmony.[56]

As important as clan membership was to eighteenth-century Creek identity, town affiliation was also critical. According to historian Joshua Piker, "when we examine the logic and practice of Creek life, . . . the clan's importance diminishes, although it does not disappear, and towns return to center stage. Without the town, in fact, Creek society would not have existed."[57] In this respect, town and regional affiliation proved as important to the Creek people as it did throughout other regions of the Native South.

Creek towns were vibrant places in which individuals jockeyed and played out clan interests. The interplay of clan- and town-based networks, events, and rituals required that townspeople transcend—but not forget—personal and familial agendas. In Creek towns, then, relationships were negotiated, conflicts resolved, and communal responsibilities established.[58]

All of this suggests that communalism played a critical role in determining how Creek people defined land ownership and allocated agricultural duties. Among those responsible for overseeing Creek agriculture was the Master of the Ground, a position that derived from clan connections. The Master of the Ground worked the fields alongside other townspeople, reinforcing feelings of connection to family, community, and the local ecology.[59]

For the peoples who became part of the Creek Confederacy, fostering a communal sense of connectedness remained important, especially so after Spanish, French, and British colonialism began encroaching on the day-to-day activities of Creek people. In the region that Lower Creeks called home, the Spanish presence in "La Florida" impacted the lives of thousands. La Florida, part of New Spain at the end of the American Revolution, constituted a vast domain extending from modern-day Florida to California. Within these colonial boundaries Native Southerners initially engaged with Spanish soldiers and missionaries. Guale, Timucua, and Apalachee Indians, among many others, had regular encounters with Spanish soldiers and missionaries during the seventeenth century and experienced regular raids from Native Southerners (such as the Yamasees) not affiliated with a Spanish mission. But the eighteenth-century Lower Creek communities continued to trade with the Spanish, something that continued as the colonial map of North America changed through the American Revolution and beyond.[60]

Given that town and regional identities played a major role in diplomatic and political decision-making among the Creeks, both British and Spanish trading interests actively vied for Creek trading alliances after the 1680s.[61] Moreover, the Lower Creeks had regular contact with both French and Spanish traders via rivers such as the Chattahoochee and Alabama. The combination of riverine transportation and overland trading routes meant that Creek traders enjoyed relatively easy access to trading centers at Charles Town, Mobile, and Pensacola, among others.[62]

Eighteenth-century Creek people worked hard to foster diplomatic and trade relations with both Native Southerners and Europeans. Upper and Lower Creeks therefore approached diplomatic relations and economic exchange with Europeans from traditions of communalism that strove for the collective good of their respective towns. However, the chaos and bloodshed caused by the Indian slave trade, warfare, and the trauma of disease outbreaks, sparked moments of political instability. Indeed, different forms of physical trauma—whether caused by war, slave raiding, or disease—changed the social fabric of communities and often precipitated migrations and resettlements.[63] Recall, for example, Tomochichi's decision to lead a group of Yamacraws to split from the Lower Creeks. In that decision we glimpse how local autonomy and ethnic affiliations shaped collective identities and contributed to a reassessment of alliances and town location.

For Tomochichi, the breaking point was the leadership of Brims and his agreeing to the Coweta Resolution. On March 23, 1718, Creek chiefs— mainly Ochese and Tallapoosa chiefs—met with Seneca and Mohawk headmen in the Lower Creek town of Coweta. At issue was the future of economic and political relations with European colonists. At the same gathering of chiefs, Seneca and Mohawk representatives worked to convince the Creeks to join an anti-Cherokee alliance. Iroquois diplomats, drawing on the traumatic memory of King Philip's War (1675–1678), likely informed the Creeks about the dangers of siding with one European power. After extensive deliberations, the Creek chiefs agreed to a resolution to preserve "their political autonomy." That resolution, however, was more than a policy of neutrality; it aimed to turn European imperialism to the advantage of the Creek people, and to halt the western expansion of the Carolina colony. When in the presence of Europeans, Creek headmen began referring to this policy as an example of their desire to live in peace and friendship.[64]

The Coweta Resolution was certainly an important document in Creek history. Historian Steven Hahn credits it as being the document that gave birth to the Creek Nation, while fellow historian Denise Bossy notes that for British officials the resolution represented an example of Creeks turning away from alliances with them.[65] Indeed, not all Creeks saw the political and economic efficacy of the Coweta Resolution. Tomochichi was the most famous example of an elder from the Creek Confederacy breaking with fellow Lower Creeks. Pioneering historians of the Southeast such as David Corkran asserted long ago that Tomochichi and the mixed-race Creek woman Mary

Musgrove were far from neutral political operatives. Perhaps seeing the benefits in staying close to British allies, Tomochichi and Musgrove became instrumental in aiding the British soldier and politician James Oglethorpe, whom Tomochichi befriended in 1733, in founding the colony of Georgia.[66]

James Oglethorpe certainly hoped to co-opt Tomochichi into an alliance favorable to the British in Georgia. When Oglethorpe arranged for Tomochichi and his wife, nephew, and a number of Yamacraw headmen to travel to London in 1734, it was in the hope of advancing the cause of British settler colonialism in Georgia. It is true that Tomochichi relocated the Yamacraw settlement in 1736, but he did so to avoid the increasingly aggressive Savannah settlers. Tomochichi certainly had a political mind that wasn't easily co-opted. This was clear in his criticism of King George's palace (which he complained had too many rooms), and in his decision to break with the Lower Creeks. In the way Tomochichi held himself and came to decisions we see a Yamacraw *mico* determined to not simply become an intermediary between the British and Lower Creek peoples but a skillful leader willing to negotiate the best diplomatic and trade deals for the Yamacraws.[67]

Tomochichi's position highlights the continued importance of regional autonomy among the Lower Creeks. Examples of other Native Southerners acting in ways that highlight the importance of local allegiance punctuate the historical record from this era.[68] But Tomochichi's decisions were also important because they shine a light on how local chiefs and *micos* throughout the Native South wanted to draw Europeans into the reciprocal responsibilities of diplomacy and trade, thereby advancing local town and clan efforts to protect their scared lands, cultural traditions, and political structures.[69]

The local autonomy shown by Tomochichi and those who gathered around him continued to be a fact of life for the Creeks in the 1740s and 1750s. This proved especially true among the Lower Creeks, the region that gave rise to the Seminoles (see chapter 5). Local decision-making, not an overarching "national" policy, sparked periodic hostilities among the Creeks and between the Creeks and Choctaws, the Upper Creeks and Cherokees, and the Lower Creeks and the Cherokees.

Fighting between the Creeks and Choctaws, as the previous chapter revealed, punctuated Creek–Choctaw relations in the early eighteenth century. Indeed, violence and warfare continued between Creek and Choctaw warriors throughout the mid- and late eighteenth century. There existed many reasons for this violence, from disputes over hunting lands and territorial limits, alliances forged with competing European imperial powers, and the failure of treaties to secure peace.

Although violence and diplomatic disagreements among Creeks and Choctaws had the potential to spark violence, changes in European imperial fortunes also impacted the timing and scope of Creek–Choctaw violence during the latter half of the eighteenth century.[70] For example, in the wake of the Seven Years' War (1754–1763) and the eventual withdrawal of the French from southeastern North America, the British organized a regional congress of Native chiefs at Augusta, Georgia, in 1763. Acting on long-held animosity toward the Choctaws, a number of Creek warriors threatened to kill any Choctaws who traveled through Creek Country in hopes of attending the Augusta conference. Such threats kept many Choctaw chiefs away, but one chief who did attend was Red Shoe II.

Red Shoe II, who shouldn't be mistaken for the Red Shoe who angered the French for courting alliances with the British, was a minor Choctaw chief in the early 1760s when he set off for Augusta with fellow Choctaw warrior Shapohooma to join Creek, Chickasaw, Cherokee, and Catawba chiefs in conference with the British. Aware of the Creek threats of violence, yet determined to attend the Augusta conference, Red Shoe traveled through Chickasaw territory in the hope of avoiding a violent confrontation with Creek warriors. He succeeded, making his way to Augusta and engaging in talks with the British. Creek warriors expressed outrage. They wanted to prevent any alliance between the Creeks and British, prompting the reignition of the Creek–Choctaw Wars in 1763. Fighting raged on until 1776 and was brutal and bloody. In part, the British played a role in the carnage witnessed during these hostilities as they supplied weapons to both sides, a move that perpetuated the bloodshed.[71]

The formation of diplomatic and trade alliances, or "friendships," proved a fraught business during the eighteenth century. The stakes were high, so Creek *micos* weighed their options carefully when considering trade and diplomatic agreements with the French, Spanish, British, and other Native polities. Although Creeks drew closer to the British by the 1750s, in the two preceding decades the decentralized nature of Creek politics made a coherent set of alliances difficult, with some Creek *micos* forming alliances with the French, others with the British.[72] However, as the above passages suggest, the ground on which Creeks and other Native Southerners negotiated trade and diplomatic agreements routinely shifted during the middle decades of the eighteenth century.

That said, local identities remained important to the Creek people through the century. Despite regional differences, Creek communities generally thrived and populations grew. In 1714, the Creek population stood at approximately ten thousand; by the opening of the 1760s that figure had risen to about thirteen or fourteen thousand. More importantly, both the Upper and Lower Creeks controlled lands coveted by European settlers, so having upwards of 4,000 warriors ready and able to defend the vast domain that the Creeks called home proved important.[73] Creek territory, like that controlled by the neighboring Cherokees and Catawbas, was not only native ground, it was a spiritually and strategically important place for the people living there.

◇◇◇◇◇◇◇◇◇◇◇◇◇◇◇◇◇◇◇◇◇◇

The Catawbas are another example of a coalescent society whose members defined the parameters of communal identity from the fragments of older social and cultural traditions, such as those of the Esaws. The Catawbas began appearing in the written archive of British colonialism during the early eighteenth century.[74] The Catawbas are a Siouan-speaking people whose ancestors lived in what's today South Carolina, North Carolina, and Virginia.[75] The Catawbas, like the neighboring Cherokees, constituted a polity that ethnologists once referred to as the "hill tribes."[76]

The English explorer John Lawson encountered the hill tribes when he canoed and walked his way over five hundred miles in 1700 and 1701. During his journey Lawson saw a stunning diversity of cultures and polities. Among the people he observed were the Waxsaws (also spelled Washaws, and whom neighboring Indians called "Flatheads"), Keyauwees, and over a dozen other tribes. As Lawson traveled over lands owned by the Esaw and Sugaree Indians, he marveled at the richness of the soil and impressiveness of local rivers such as the Catawba and Wateree. In describing the lands and rivers of the Esaws, Lawson narrated the resources belonging to a people later known as the Catawbas.[77]

The origin of the word "Catawba" isn't clear. Sixteenth-century Spanish sources refer to the "Catapa," while a 1697 French map notes the existence of the "Katoba."[78] Whatever its origins, the term "Catawba" eventually designated a people descended from fragmented Indigenous polities. The

Catawbas lived in small towns. They built their houses on terraces near rivers and sustained life by farming, hunting, and fishing.[79] The exact size of the Catawba population during the eighteenth century isn't clear. Estimates range from 8,000 to 10,000 in 1700, to between 600 and 1,067 by the mid-1750s.[80]

The dramatic decline in Catawba population reflected their struggles with disease and warfare in the same way that the neighboring Tuscaroras suffered during the late seventeenth century and early eighteenth (see chapter 3).[81] Similarly, the ancestors of modern-day Lumbees (which included the Cheraw people and Tuscaroras) struggled to navigate the ravages of disease and colonial violence.[82] On the eve of the Seven Years' War, a British reporter suggested that a loose coalition of people, with no land rights, resided on their traditional homelands, located in modern-day Robeson County, North Carolina. The 1754 report declared that British surveyors were attacked at "Drowning Creek [Lumbee River] on the head of the Little Pedee, 50 families a mixt Crew, a lawless people filled the lands without patent or paying quit rents."[83]

Historian and Lumbee tribal member Malinda Maynor Lowery observes that the Lumbee people engaged in regular migrations and resettlements between the 1550s and 1750s. Far from a "lawless people," the ancestors of today's Lumbee communities fought to protect their lands, fend off the violence of Native and European slave raids, and worked together to recover from disease outbreaks.[84] Moreover, Lumbees kept their traditions alive. Herbal remedies and prayers used for healing survive into the twenty-first century and remind us that even through the violence and traumatic disease outbreaks of the eighteenth century, Lumbees kept faith in their traditions.[85]

The Catawbas, as noted above, also struggled through slave raids, war, and population loss due to disease. However, in the eighteenth century they constituted a sizable polity that Europeans and other Native Southerners could not afford to ignore. With regular contact with the Cherokees, routine visits from British traders from Virginia and the Carolinas, and contact with the French and Native peoples from the Ohio River Valley, the Catawbas became key players in both the Native South's engagement with European settler colonialism and the world of Native diplomacy during the eighteenth century.[86]

The Catawbas lived a communally focused life. Individual identities meant little to a people who shared meals in a single room and owned land collectively. At meals, large wooden and ceramic bowls and platters were brought to a table and food was eaten with hands or spoons.[87] In this seemingly mundane daily activity we glimpse the value placed on community cohesion.

The Catawbas also engaged in an exchange economy with other Native communities, and after English settler colonialism took root in Virginia and the Carolinas, a trading path—known to the English and Indians alike as the "Catawba Path"—connected Catawba communities with Virginia and Georgia.[88] Significantly, the Catawbas measured their world according to the relationships they nurtured. The famous Catawba deerskin map, for example, reveals the diplomatic and economic relationships coveted by Catawba people.

In the late seventeenth century, the Catawbas earned a reputation as fierce warriors and slave raiders, a reputation Catawba warriors kept alive into the eighteenth century.[89] For young Catawba warriors, warfare remained important to their masculine identities. Thus Catawba warfare with the Cherokees, tribes in Virginia, North and South Carolina settlers, and Indian warriors to the north reflected both the strategically important location of the Catawba homeland and also the importance of martial success in establishing a young Catawba warrior's reputation among his kin.[90]

Warfare also had broader strategic implications. During the Yamasee War, the Catawbas sided with the British in their fight against the Yamasees. In the decades following the war, Catawba warriors and chiefs, along with Cherokee and Creek chiefs, became increasingly important to British and French anxieties about settler expansion and the establishment of stable trade networks in the Native South. Of course, Native Southerners had their own diplomatic and trade agendas, but the perceptions that Europeans had of the region impacted Indigenous economic aspirations and diplomatic strategies. For example, in September 1722, William Burnet, the governor of New York and New Jersey, expressed the growing concern of British colonial officials about the perceived instability of the Native South and Mid-Atlantic regions. Burnet worried about a French conspiracy aimed at convincing Native peoples to form a pan-Indian alliance throughout eastern North America. Such anxiety prompted a conference with the Five Nations Iroquois.[91] At that conference a Five Nations chief admitted parties of warriors had been sent to war upon the Flatheads (Catawbas) and Natives reportedly allied to the French and residing among the Tuscaroras. In a bid to prevent warfare, an agreement was reached in which Iroquois warriors were not to pass south of the Potomac River.[92]

Such agreements occurred often and were contingent on the actions of Native and European parties. Still, the Catawbas routinely found themselves ensnared in such diplomatic dramas. The Catawbas' diplomatic allegiances, however, crystalized during the latter half of the eighteenth century. In 1757, for instance, Catawba chiefs informed Creek headmen of their determination to keep the path of friendship "clear and open" to the Creeks and the Chickasaws, the Catawbas' staunch Indigenous allies in the Native South. Of the French, the Catawba chiefs were clear: they were their enemies and the Catawbas would continue to take "up the Hatchet" against their common French foes.[93]

Diplomatic and trade alliances involved calculations, and in the above calculation the Catawba chiefs bet that their identities as thoughtful, trusted leaders would garner the support of fellow Catawbas in opposing the French and aligning with the Creeks, Chickasaws, and British. Ideally, such agreements, or friendships, would preserve peace and ensure the future cohesiveness of Choctaw communal identities.

◇◇◇◇◇◇◇◇◇◇◇◇◇◇◇◇◇◇◇◇◇◇◇

Chiefs among the Catawbas' neighbors, the Cherokees, made similar calculations about how best to preserve communal identities. The British in Virginia, North and South Carolina, and Georgia, in addition to French diplomats among the Cherokees in Tennessee—a region known as the Overhill Cherokee settlements—sent diplomatic overtures to the eighteenth-century Cherokees on a regular basis. For Cherokees, as for the neighboring Catawbas, Europeans opened the possibility of new trade and diplomatic networks as much as their presence brought disease and fueled slave trading in the region.[94]

The eighteenth-century Cherokees were descended from the Great Lakes Iroquoian family. At some unknown point in Iroquois history, discord led communities of Iroquoian people to migrate south through modern-day Ohio, Pennsylvania, and Virginia.[95] These Iroquoian migrants settled in, and claimed sovereignty over, a vast domain that included portions of what became Virginia, Tennessee, Kentucky, Georgia, North and South Carolina, and Alabama. The Cherokees nurtured a regionally diverse population, adopting outsiders into the responsibilities of kinship according to tribal custom and law, and becoming known to Europeans as mountain dwellers.[96]

Ascertaining just who the eighteenth-century Cherokee were, and who they thought themselves to be, is complicated by their relationship with other Native Southerners—particularly the Creeks—and the influence of European trade and culture in Cherokee life. Some sources suggest that the Creeks knew the Cherokees as the *celokokalke*, the "people of another language," or the *chilo-kee*, the "people of a different speech."[97] The eighteenth-century trader James Adair claimed that the Cherokees' name derived from *chee-ra*, which meant "fire," and when combined with *cheer-tahge* defined the Cherokees as a people "possessed of the divine fire."[98]

The Cherokees called themselves Tsalagi, the plural of which is Ani-Tsalagi, which roughly translates as "the people," "the real people," or "the principal people."[99] Although the Cherokees suffered losses from warfare, the Indian slave trade, and disease outbreaks during the seventeenth and eighteenth centuries, demographically they remained one of the larger coalescent societies in the Native South. In 1650, the Cherokees numbered as many as twenty-two thousand. Prior to the smallpox epidemics that cut through Cherokee communities during the first third of the eighteenth century, the Cherokee population ranged from seventeen thousand to twenty thousand. Those figures fell to as low as about ten thousand by the 1750s, slowly rebounding to approximately sixteen thousand by the opening of the nineteenth century.[100]

The eighteenth-century Cherokees lived in towns and developed a strong sense of allegiance to their respective regional homelands. By the mid-eighteenth century, European observers identified these regional identities as the Lower, Middle, Valley, and Overhill settlements. Cherokee towns became important places where people assembled for work, cultural ceremonies, and political deliberations. According to historian Tyler Boulware, the town was the most important locus of Cherokee identity during the eighteenth century, with the council house occupying a central place in the town—both geographically and culturally.[101]

As it was among other coalescent societies in the Native South, the Cherokees understood that not all towns were the same. For example, Mother Towns were thought of as the Cherokees' original towns and carried clan distinctions with them. Mother Towns, or Beloved Towns, became regional capitals that had important responsibilities to perform to ensure the well-being of nearby Brother Towns. There were seven Cherokee Mother Towns. These were the Overhill towns Tannassie and Chota; Tellico and Neyohee (also spelled Noyohee) among the Valley Town Cherokees; Keetoowah (or Kituwah) in the Middle and Out Towns; and Ustenary and Estootowie among the Lower Towns.[102]

While these town and regional designations reflected the importance of place to communal identities, the Cherokee people also defined identity on the basis of kinship. Clan membership constituted a tie to other Cherokees through blood, or matrilineal inheritance. In the eighteenth century, Cherokees belonged to one of seven matrilineal clans: Aniwahya (Wolf), Ani Tsiskwa (Small Bird), Anikawi (Deer), Anigilohi (Twister or Long Hair), Anisahoni (Blue), Anigatogewi (Wild Potato), and Aniwodi (Red Paint).[103]

Clan membership constituted one of the cornerstones of the Cherokee legal system—a system that strove to maintain balance and harmony in an interconnected world that included humans, flora and fauna, the animate and inanimate—and a world that connected individuals to a geographically larger understanding of Cherokee community. Towns, for instance, were the sites where Cherokees from different clans enacted laws and cultivated communal affiliations that anchored people to an embodied sense of place.

In Cherokee towns, the principle of balance and harmony guided human decision-making and daily routines. Men and women performed different but mutually beneficial labor to ensure the well-being of the community. Women were responsible for agriculture and cultivated corn, beans, squash, gourds, pumpkins, and sunflowers. Cherokee women and girls also collected wild blackberries, raspberries, mulberries, grapes, acorns, walnuts, hickory nuts, and chestnuts. Men joined women in the agricultural fields in addition to hunting and fishing, thereby supplementing their diet with meat from deer, buffalo, bears, opossum, raccoons, rabbits, wild turkeys, squirrels, pigeons, trout, catfish, bass, and shellfish.[104]

Seventeenth- and eighteenth-century Cherokees were part of an exchange economy that eventually gave way to networks of credit and transatlantic trade during the early eighteenth century. For the Cherokees, as for other Native Southerners, agricultural and hunting practices changed and became increasingly geared toward meeting market demands (especially in the lucrative deerskin trade), maximizing profits, and servicing debts.[105] In other words, the principles of balance and harmony were regularly tested during the seventeenth and eighteenth centuries.

In the early eighteenth-century, Cherokee chiefs recognized that they were being pulled into far-flung networks of trade and diplomacy. In 1725 a Tanasee headman gave voice to this recognition, exclaiming that the Cherokees could "not live without the English." But Cherokees did not see the changes in their economy as evidence of dependence on Europeans. Instead, they engaged in trade and diplomacy with the goal of bringing Europeans into their networks of reciprocity and responsibility. This was the goal of a Cherokee delegation that embarked for London in the 1730s. It was also the objective of Cherokee chiefs who traveled regularly to Williamsburg and Charles Town between the 1720s and 1750s. The alliances that Cherokee headmen such as Ouconastota, Attakullakulla (Little Carpenter), and Outacite (or Ostenaco), to name just three, worked to forge with the British during this period were sealed in the hope of protecting the regional interests of Cherokees within a trans-Atlantic economy.[106]

The regional objectives that Cherokee chiefs brought to diplomatic and trade negotiations became ensnared in a web of broader geopolitical tensions and cycles of violence.[107] Fluctuations in the deerskin trade, warfare with the Creeks (1715–1755), and the growing intrusiveness of the British—who coveted the Tennessee corridor (and control of the Tennessee and Little Tennessee Rivers) as an entryway to the Ohio and Illinois Valleys—meant that the efficacy of town and regional identities and the principle of balance and harmony faced growing pressures from multiple sources on the eve of the era of revolutions.[108]

The pressures on Cherokee communal bonds and collective identities were hardly unique. Throughout the Native South, the Seven Years' War (1754–1763) and the American Revolutionary War (1775–1783) overlapped with, and in some cases, intensified, wars involving the Creeks and Choctaws, and the Creeks and Cherokees. With the rise of the American republic at the end of the 1780s, Native Southerners faced renewed challenges to the social, cultural, and political structures that undergirded their communal identities.

Between the 1750s and 1830s, Native Southerners demonstrated a willingness to adapt their traditions to the changing world around them.

They'd need to be adaptive and innovative in the wake of the Revolutionary War in particular, a war that left much of the Native South a smoldering ruin. How would Native Southerners respond to the challenges of these decades? What stories would Native Southerners relate to outsiders about their cultural and political identities? And what type of future did communal identities have in the Native South as the American republic emerged on the world stage?

CHAPTER FIVE

WAR, REVOLUTION, AND PAN-INDIANISM

In the summer of 1759 the *South-Carolina Gazette* reported that Indian warriors had attacked British settlements.[1] In what European settlers called the "backcountry," tensions between settlers and Native Southerners had boiled over yet again.[2] The outbreak of the Seven Years' War in 1754 and the aligning of Native Southerners with either the French and British combatants meant the potential for settler–Indian violence to engulf the region seemed always imminent in the middle decades of the eighteenth century.[3] In the midst of the Seven Years' War (1754–1763), a war between Indians and settlers did indeed break out: the Anglo–Cherokee War.[4]

The spark that reignited settler–Cherokee warfare came in 1758. British-allied Cherokees, including the famed war chief Moytoy, became victims of an unprovoked attack by Virginia backcountry militiamen as they traveled back to their towns. That violent exchange led to Moytoy's death and a marked shift in Cherokee perceptions of British settlers.[5] The resulting Anglo–Cherokee War (1758–1761) undermined over half a century of diplomatic and trade friendships between the Cherokees and the British.

In the midst of the Anglo–Cherokee War, the *South-Carolina Gazette* seemed to describe something even more troubling than Indian–settler warfare. Its pages described Upper Creeks and Lower Cherokee warriors—"wolves in the shape of Indians"—attacking "our Back-Settlements." These daily "insults and barbarities" kept colonial officials up at night and prompted calls to "Keep the Indians in proper subjugation."[6] As the following chapter reveals, settlers, British colonial officials, and ultimately the elected leaders of the nascent American republic spent countless hours worrying about the possibility of Indian violence. Amid wars for imperial dominance in North America, a war that gave birth to the United States, and the first attempts at crafting the federal government's "Indian policy," the threat of pan-Indian, intra-Indian, and interracial violence seemed to stalk the settlers of British colonies and ultimately states and territories of the United States.

At least, Euroamericans thought so. For Native Southerners, the latter half of the eighteenth century and the opening of the nineteenth century constituted an era in which the territorial and cultural sovereignty of Native people needed to be fought for, rearticulated, and renewed. For some Native Southerners this meant taking up the hatchet and engaging in wars of resistance, perhaps even transcending tribal identities and forming pan-Indian alliances. For others it meant striving to redefine the parameters of Native politics, and for still more it meant reengaging with cultural traditions and ceremonies.[7]

◇◇◇◇◇◇◇◇◇◇◇◇◇◇◇◇◇◇◇◇◇◇◇

The alarm expressed in the *South-Carolina Gazette's* 1759 report might be explained by the previous two decades of violence among Native Southerners and between Native Southerners and settlers. British Colonial Office records from this period reveal a particular concern about the possibility of pan-Indian alliances. In truth, the middle decades of the eighteenth century were a period of shifting alliances and renegotiated diplomatic agreements in the Native South. For example, during the War of Jenkins' Ear (or the Anglo–Spanish War, 1739–1744) Cherokees aligned with the British while neighboring Creeks remained neutral. However, when Cherokee warriors entered Creek Country and were attacked by Creek warriors, renewed Creek–Cherokee warfare commenced. Hostilities continued into the 1740s when, in 1744 and 1745, the British worked to negotiate a truce between Creek and Cherokee combatants in a bid to win Indian allies for its war with France (King George's War, 1744–1748).

The British-mediated truce proved short-lived, however. In part this was due to the Cherokees having their own diplomatic and military objectives that didn't necessarily conform to British imperial ambitions. Cherokee chiefs thus agreed to allow Seneca warriors to use Cherokee Country as a staging ground for attacks against the Creeks. The result of this provocative decision

was renewed violence between Creeks and Cherokees. The reigniting of the
Creek–Cherokee War did not escape the attention of the French and the
British. For example, in 1748 South Carolina governor James Glen initiated
new peace talks, discussions that the French worked to undermine because
they feared such talks would benefit the British war effort against them.
The French therefore persuaded Acorn Whistler, a Creek headman, to lead
a band of Creek warriors in an attack on the Cherokees, thereby scuttling
peace talks. The plot failed and tentative treaty terms were reached.

As so often occurred during this period, the peace between the Creeks
and Cherokees did not hold. Again, long-standing disagreements rose to
the surface in diplomacy among Native Southerners and reignited violence.
In 1750, for example, Lower Creek warriors launched attacks on Cherokee
towns. The Lower Creeks were angered that Cherokees continued to aid
Indian warriors from the north in attacking Creek communities; they also
rejected the idea that Cherokees should have access to hunting grounds
(critical to the deerskin trade) that the Creek warriors claimed as their own.
Under the leadership of Brims's son, Malatchi of Coweta, the Creek cam-
paign to wrest hunting grounds away from Cherokees succeeded and resulted
in the destruction of the Lower Cherokee towns of Echoi and Estatoe and
the burning of Cherokee captives. Officials from South Carolina tried to
cool hostilities but their efforts failed. Indeed, in 1752 Acorn Whistler led
Creek warriors in assassinating Cherokee chiefs who were visiting Charles
Town. These were unsettled, and unsettling, times. No one was safe, least
of all Whistler, who was assassinated by a relative acting on the instructions
of Malatchi (and whom Malatchi subsequently killed). In the midst of intra-
Creek violence, Creek–Cherokee fighting continued until chiefs from the
respective tribes agreed to a peace deal at the town of Coweta in 1754.[8]

That same year, the outbreak of the Seven Years' War drew warriors from
the Native South back onto the battlefield. The Age of Revolutions—from
the Seven Years' War to the American Revolution and rise of the American
republic—would have profoundly transformative consequences for Native
Southerners and the communal identities they'd nurtured during the seventeenth and eighteenth centuries. Old alliances collapsed and new ones arose.
Some Native Southerners continued to emphasize the importance of town
and kinship identities, while others looked to form pan-Indian alliances with
Native people from as far away as the Ohio River valley and Great Lakes.

Through these tumultuous decades, Native Southerners worked to ensure that the Southeast remained Indian Country. It was during these decades that new communal identities emerged—most notably the Seminole—and signs that political power in the Native South was shifting away from town chiefs and elders and into the hands of a new class of Native leaders became clear. When the fog of war lifted, how would a redrawn map of colonial North America impact Native Southerners? In a rapidly changing world, what stories would bind Native communities together?

◇◇◇◇◇◇◇◇◇◇◇◇◇◇◇◇◇◇◇◇◇◇◇◇◇◇

Answering this question requires us to acknowledge the transformations ushered in by the Seven Years' War (1754–1763), the first truly global war. The North American theater of war—sometimes referred to as the French and Indian War—dislodged preexisting power dynamics among Native polities and European colonists. It also precipitated a redrawing of the colonial map in North America. The badly beaten French surrendered to the British lands east of the Mississippi River (with the exception of New Orleans, which came under Spanish rule). The British also acquired East Florida from Spain, although the Spanish gained control over West Florida, the western half of the Mississippi Valley, and the British returned Cuba to Spanish control.[9]

How would these changes impact Native Southerners? That's a question that requires historical contextualization to fully reveal some of the wrenching changes occurring across the Native South during the latter half of the eighteenth century.

As we've seen, during the first half of the century the Upper Creeks, Overhill Cherokees, Chickasaws, and Choctaws maneuvered and actively contested European imperial power. Native chiefs and headmen shaped trade and diplomatic relations with Europeans, and they did battle with Europeans (and other Native peoples) to maintain access to the lucrative deerskin trade, to attempt to influence the location of trading forts, and to maintain control over the land and rivers of the Native South.[10] But with the British emerging as the dominant colonial power in North America following the Seven Years' War, Native chiefs, *fannemicos* (local chiefs), *micos*, and headmen needed to rethink diplomatic and trade strategies.[11]

During the first half of the eighteenth century Native Southerners played off French, Spanish, and British traders and diplomats. This strategy served Native leaders well, giving chiefs and headmen considerable influence over the trade and foreign policy networks throughout the region. Moreover, the strategy forced Europeans to negotiate with Native polities (and conform to Native concepts of reciprocity) if they hoped to achieve their imperial objectives. For example, the French attempted to connect their territorial holdings in Canada with what became known as the Louisiana Territory, something that forced them into diplomatic and trade negotiations (and ultimately war) with groups such as the Natchez (see chapter 4).

French interest in Louisiana began increasing during the last third of the seventeenth century when Louis XIV received favorable reports about the wealth purportedly waiting for someone to extract from the Mississippi Valley. The French Crown's quest for wealth and a desire to ward off British interest in the region led to a policy not of Christian conversion among Native peoples, as had been the case in Canada, but of economic alliances.

In the Mississippi Valley, the French attempted to establish alliances with Choctaws and Chickasaws. These efforts unsettled the diplomatic balance of power in the region and contributed to an elevation in tensions between the Choctaws and Chickasaws and their relations with *petite nations* in the region. Still, the French hoped to cement alliances with the Choctaws and Chickasaws to help them extract the region's wealth and quash what colonial officials perceived as hostile Native groups (such as the Natchez) and the competing interests of the British.[12]

French ambition in Louisiana, however, did not automatically equate with an active role on the ground. The first French fort, located at Biloxi Bay, was not built until 1699, and the French population in the region remained small through the early eighteenth century. This meant that life for the local Biloxis, Pascagoulas, Moctobis, and other Native peoples of the region went on largely undisturbed by the French despite periodic tensions with larger polities like the Choctaws and Chickasaws.[13]

After the War of Spanish Succession (1702–1713), the French Crown left the governance of its Louisiana colony in the hands of a private corporation: the Company of the Indies. Between 1717 and 1731, the Company of the Indies shifted the focus of the colony inland to New Orleans and oversaw a population of roughly 5,400 colonists and 6,000 African slaves, the latter population representing the company's determination to shift from Indian to African slavery.[14] The Company of the Indies struggled to turn anything but a paper profit in Louisiana, resulting in the bursting of the so-called Mississippi Bubble in 1720.[15]

While French investors failed to profit from their speculative ventures in Louisiana, the French on both sides of the Mississippi River continued to seek out Native headmen in hopes of forging alliances.[16] These efforts continued into the mid-eighteenth century and constituted the delicate balancing between *petite nations* and larger coalescent societies. Indeed, the War of Spanish Succession provided an opening for British traders to capitalize on unmet demand for trade goods among polities such as the Natchez, Creeks, Choctaws, and Chickasaws.[17] Such trade posed a threat to both the French system of Native alliances and had the potential to reopen longstanding trade and diplomatic disputes among Native Southerners as chiefs and headmen jockeyed for favorable trade agreements.

In the decades leading up to the Seven Years' War, both French and British officials viewed trade links as an important diplomatic tool in the Native South. This competition for Indian allies resulted in growing tensions between European traders and diplomats and with Native chiefs and headmen. At issue was whether Europeans would have influence with, or control over, Native trade allies. Well into the latter half of the eighteenth century, Native Southerners guarded against the latter scenario. Chiefs worked hard to maintain control over their own diplomatic and trade affairs while also limiting the influence of Europeans in their communities. In this sense, the enduring importance of town and regional identities comes into focus as local chiefs pursued their towns' interests.[18]

As British trade among Native Southerners increased in volume, the British failed to enjoy the success that their French contemporaries experienced in forming alliances with, for example, the Iroquois in the northern colonies.[19] British colonial officials complained that they struggled to cement diplomatic friendships with Native Southerners because of French meddling.[20] At the same time, the British also worried about the seeming regularity with which outbreaks of violence between Native polities threatened the security of trade networks and settler communities, and how they may even portend pan-Indian conspiracies against the colonial "backcountry."[21]

As ill-founded as these conspiracy theories were, the governors of Maryland, Pennsylvania, and Virginia led calls to activate the militia at different points during the 1740s to combat perceived threats from pan-Indian armies in the mid-Atlantic region.[22] Farther south, Native Southerners exercised their considerable diplomatic skill to leave British officials perpetually frustrated about their inability to control diplomatic and trade relations in the Native South.

In the 1740s and early 1750s, that violence between Native Southerners undercut colonial efforts to solidify trade networks. Regional instability occurred as a result of the Choctaw–Chickasaw War and the Creek–Cherokee War, in addition to individual episodes of violence. Cultural slights, sexual impropriety on the parts of settlers toward Native women, and the theft of property—all had the potential to spark violence. For example, British settlers stole Cherokee deerskins on such a regular basis that bloodshed often accompanied the lucrative deerskin trade, forcing colonial officials to impose tighter regulations on trade relations—a trade that included the export of over eight hundred thousand pounds of deerskin from ports such as Charles Town and Savannah.[23]

In a bid to reduce trade-related violence, the number of British garrisons and taxes on trade with Native Southerners increased. However, none of these measures inspired confidence among Cherokee, Creek, Catawba, Choctaw, and Chickasaw traders.[24] Instead, Native traders perceived these measures as hostile attempts to undermine the ideal of reciprocity at the heart of the Native South's trade with the British.[25]

More than a few Native Southerners viewed British trade regulations with deep suspicion. For example, Cherokee chiefs such as Attakullakulla (Little Carpenter) expressed serious reservations about what they saw as British attempts to monopolize trade in Cherokee Country. In July 1753, Attakullakulla expressed his displeasure to the governor of South Carolina, James Glen. Attakullakulla argued that British policies undermined free trade in Cherokee Country. He complained that British taxes and a system of licenses effectively created trade monopolies in the region that increased prices for manufactured items in Cherokee communities. Attakullakulla insisted that he had not agreed to such a relationship in previous talks with the British, claiming that "when I was in England [in 1730] I was told that I might go any way for goods when I could get them the cheapest."[26]

◇◇◇◇◇◇◇◇◇◇◇◇◇◇◇◇◇◇◇◇◇◇◇◇◇◇◇◇

The aggressiveness of backcountry settlers compounded the suspicions of Native Southerners that the British were attempting to reduce their communities into submissive economic and diplomatic positions.[27] To an extent, they were right. This certainly proved the case with the aggressive and land-hungry Virginians, sparking both the Seven Years' War and the Anglo–Cherokee War.

In 1754, Virginia's governor Robert Dinwiddie dispatched forces toward the fork of the Ohio River valley. Dinwiddie placed a young George Washington in command of the mission to remove the French from the region. When they arrived, Washington's men attacked a small French patrol, prompting the French army and its Indian allies to mobilize against the Virginians. Under dark skies and heavy rain, Washington's Virginia forces were routed, prompting their surrender on July 4.

Washington's defeat was a setback for the territorially ambitious Virginians, but it wouldn't be the last battle in the long and costly Seven Years' War in North America. Native warriors in the Ohio River valley took the initiative in reigniting hostilities. Against the advice of the French, who wanted to avoid a protracted war, outraged Native warriors—Shawnees, Delawares, Mingoes, Caughnewagas, Ottawas, and Potowatomis—sought their retribution on British settlers by attacking their livestock in Virginia, Maryland, and Pennsylvania.[28]

In taking these actions, Native warriors played their role in bringing a global war to North America. The outbreak of the Seven Years' War between the British and French and their respective Indian allies became such a serious international concern that it prompted the British prime minister, William Pitt, to adopt an America-first policy. Pitt's focus remained in North America even after the Seven Years' War engulfed Europe in 1756. Pitt injected large sums of money and troops—some forty-five thousand British soldiers by 1758—into the war effort against the French.[29] Pitt's infusion of financial and military support for the North American theater of war ultimately proved decisive in defeating the French and their Indian allies. However, while French military defeat led to a redrawing of the imperial map in North America, British control over the Native South was no certainty.[30] For the time being, the Native South remained Indian Country.

The 1750s and 1760s were nonetheless a challenging period for many Native Southerners, a point that brings us back to the Anglo–Cherokee War. This war, which raged between 1758 and 1761, played a significant role in exposing cracks in the systems and structures that helped Native Southerners control their respective towns and hunting grounds. While the British characterized the Anglo–Cherokee War as a "Cherokee uprising," it was in reality the Cherokees' response to Moytoy's murder at the hands of Virginia backwoodsmen and part of a larger struggle to maintain their territorial sovereignty and control of trade networks. Thus, in 1758 Cherokee war chiefs Aganstata of Chota, Attakullakulla of Tanasi, Ostenaco of Tomotley, Round O from the Middle Towns, and Wauhatchie from the Lower Towns led Cherokee warriors into battle against the British.

Despite the early efforts of South Carolina governor William Lyttelton to mollify Cherokee war chiefs, the Anglo-Cherokee War had some bloody moments.[31] Through 1759 and 1760, Cherokee warriors took both prisoners and scalps. The blood spilled in the regions near the Lower Towns told a clear story about Cherokee discontent and disappointment over backcountry settler outrages and perceived British failures to fulfill their responsibilities in diplomatic and trade agreements. Through violence—the tomahawking, scalping, and decapitation—Cherokee warriors gave voice to a general sense of frustration with the British.

The legacy of the Anglo-Cherokee War, and the Seven Years' War more generally, exposed the economic and diplomatic instability in Anglo-Indian relations in the Native South. Such instabilities continued despite Cherokee emissaries traveling to London in hopes of restoring calm to trade and diplomatic relations with the British. The Cherokee emissaries Ostenaco, Mankiller, and Pouting Pigeon toured London and persuaded the British Parliament to pass the Act to Regulate the Trade with the Cherokee Indians (or Indian Trade Act) in 1762. The Indian Trade Act led to the establishment of a trading factory at Fort Prince George, banned private trade from South Carolina, and established a public monopoly over trade with the Cherokees. If the goal of the act was to bring fairness to trade with the Cherokees, it failed, with unscrupulous traders from Virginia, Georgia, and North Carolina carrying on an illicit trade with the Cherokees.[32]

The 1750s and 1760s also bore witness to renewed rivalries among Native Southerners. For example, both the Cherokees and British vied for Creek support (or went to war against them), with Cherokees working to ensure that Chickasaw and Creek warriors did not pick up their war hatchets and go to war against them.

From a colonial perspective, the long-held British concern about Native peoples joining together and forming a pan-Indian alliance throughout eastern North America intensified. In their correspondence, British officials expressed anxiety about the possibility of a "general Indian war" and its consequences for British settler societies.[33] British officials hoped they could

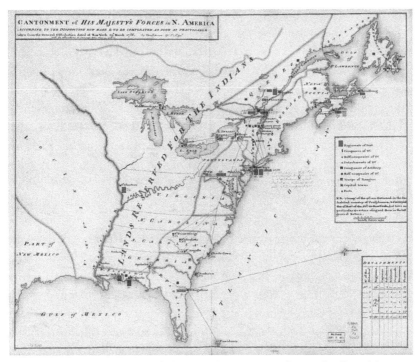

"Cantonment of His Majesty's forces in N. America according to the disposition now made & to be compleated as soon as practicable taken from the general distribution dated at New York 29th. March 1766." "Reserved for the Indians" indicates lands theoretically protected from settlers and speculators by the Proclamation Line of 1763. *Library of Congress, Rare Books and Special Collections Division, Washington, D.C.*

prevent inflaming the opinions of Native Southerners by slowing the growth of western settlements. The Proclamation Line of 1763, for example, was designed to stop settlement and land speculation west of the Appalachians. In theory, the western lands were reserved for Native Southerners.

In reality, British settlers and traders continued to stream into the Native South. Aware of the land hunger of settler populations, British colonial officials were eager to draft a peace agreement with chiefs throughout the Native South.

At Augusta, Georgia, on November 10, 1763, the British set about doing just that. Colonial officials invited chiefs from throughout the Native South to discuss and hopefully agree to peace terms in hopes of avoiding a general Indian war. These discussions, which the Creeks wanted to prevent

Choctaw chiefs Red Shoe and Shapohooma from attending (see chapter 4), were punctuated with signs that old rivalries among Native Southerners remained. Ultimately, though, talks resulted in the "Treaty of Peace and Friendship with the Head Men and Warriors of the Chickasaw, Upper & Lower Creeks, Chactaws, Cherokees and Catawbas."[34] But if the Seven Years' War taught the British anything, it was that military power was essential to both maintaining and expanding an empire. It was also a lesson that lived on in Native resistance to settler colonial expansion and one in which American settlers acted on when they declared their independence from Britain and ultimately formed a new republic.

◇◇◇◇◇◇◇◇◇◇◇◇◇◇◇◇◇◇◇◇◇◇◇◇

As we've seen, the violence and political instability that characterized the 1750s and 1760s throughout much of the Native South had ramifications for the social stability of Native polities. Native Southerners had a long history of social innovations and cultural adaptation by this time, and it was in the Gulf Coast region that a group whom the Spanish referred to as the *cimarrones*, or "wild ones," and Muscogee speakers called *isti semoli*, or "wild men," emerged.[35] We've come to know these Native Southerners as Seminoles.

The historian Claudio Saunt argues that the first reference to the Seminoles in English documents dates to 1765.[36] However, an earlier series of migrations into what is today Florida by the people who became the Seminoles dates to the period between 1702 and 1750. Subsequent migrations between 1750 and 1812, and 1812 and 1820, led to the establishment of additional Seminole villages in Florida.[37] This coalescence of people into Seminole villages involved the coming together of racially and ethnically diverse groups of people. These individuals formed communities that drew strength from their adaptive traditions and history of migration and resettlement throughout the Gulf Coast.[38]

Charting the history of Seminole origins is a complex story of ethnogenesis. The emergence of the Seminoles amounted to something much more than a group of Lower Creeks migrating out of the Creek Confederacy and settling in Florida in the hope of finding refuge from ethnocentric Muscogees and violent European settlers. The people who became the Seminoles lived in "permeable and constantly fluctuating" communities.[39] These dynamic communities had their ethnic origins among Oconees,

Miccosukees, Yamasees, and Indigenous peoples from Florida. It's also important to note that Creeks rejected the formation of a separate Seminole identity, insisting these migrant Indians remained Creeks. Such sentiments persisted well into the nineteenth century.[40]

The core of the early Seminole people who settled in Florida included the Miccosukees (also spelled Mikasukis) and the Oconees, Native Southerners who had formerly been part of the Lower Creek Confederacy but had exercised considerable regional autonomy.[41] According to the American naturalist and travel writer William Bartram, the "old Ocone Town" among the Lower Creek settlements was "evacuated" because of its proximity to white people.[42] The Oconees initially migrated toward the Upper Creek towns, but they found little comfort there. As a result, a large migration of Oconees headed toward the Gulf Coast and ultimately settled in what is today Florida.[43]

In Florida, Hitchiti-speaking migrants also attempted to form protective enclaves away from Muscogean peoples—who referred to them with the derogatory label "*istinko*"—and the growing number of aggressive white settlers.[44] Despite these tensions, some Mvskoke speakers, or people who spoke the language of the Muscogee Creeks, did coexist with Hitchiti-speaking people in the emerging Seminole communities. Additionally, runaway African slaves formed Maroon communities among the Seminoles and over time Africans and Seminoles blended their cultural and linguistic traditions.[45]

The people who migrated, resettled, and became known as the Seminoles did not move into a previously uninhabited land. In northern Florida and along the Gulf Coast, migrants from Lower Creek towns and runaway slaves began settling on lands once occupied by the people of the Apalachee and Timucuan chiefdoms. These migrating communities of Native Southerners also encountered Yamasees, Calusas, and Tekesats, Indigenous people who'd lived in small chiefdoms along Florida's southern peninsula for centuries.[46]

Seminole towns and communal identities nonetheless emerged where chiefdom societies once flourished. Seminole communities became sites of cooperation where each resident's needs were supported by principles of reciprocity. William Bartram observed of the typical Seminole town that its residents

> enjoy a superabundance of the necessaries and conveniences of life, with the security of person and property, the two great concerns of mankind.

The hides of deer, bears, tigers and wolves, together with honey, wax
and other productions of the country, purchase their clothing, equipage
and domestic utensils from the whites. They seem to be free from want
or desires. No cruel enemy to dread; nothing to give them disquietude,
but the gradual encroachments of the white people."[47]

Seminole life was not perfect, but the members of local communities did
strive to balance the needs of the population with the ability of the local
ecology to meet those needs. Bartram's observations might smack of hyper-
bole, but the Seminoles did indeed try to forge communal identities separate
from both settler and Creek encroachments.

By 1800, the Seminole population stood at about 1,500.[48] Within
Seminole communities, linguistic differences had the potential to shape
the contours of social distinctions. However, common religious beliefs and
ceremonies eased any tensions and brought people together in the fostering
of communal identities. Religious beliefs and ceremonies taught Seminole
people that they inhabited a world filled with powerful spirits. Seminoles
also learned that one's soul departed the body while they slept. If the soul
failed to return, Seminoles expected illness to follow and would require a
priest or priests to coax the soul back.[49]

Eighteenth-century Seminoles animated their beliefs through ceremonies,
oral traditions, and the routines of daily life. Seasonal ceremonies, such as
the Green Corn ceremony, brought tribal members together and reminded
people of the interconnected nature of Seminole life. Moreover, Seminoles
felt that ritual and ceremony had medicinal qualities. At the Green Corn
festival, for instance, a buckskin containing medicine bundles was presented
at the commencement of the ceremony. These bundles contained crystals,
ginseng, and white deer hair and were thought to possess both medicinal
and spiritual powers.[50]

Politically, chiefs and a council of elders helped to govern Seminole towns.
Towns and villages were largely autonomous, exercising independence in
decision-making.[51] Townspeople belonged to one of three language-based
bands, two of which were Miccosukee and one Muscogee. Each band had
its own chiefs and council of elders, with membership determined along
matrilineal lines. The prototype for the Seminole's kinship system was the
Creek *huti*, or extended kin group. The *huti* informed the matrilineal identity
and the arrangement of Seminole households.[52]

The implications of this system of kinship became clear when a man and woman married. After a couple married, the couple established a new household near the wife's former residence. All of the women who entered the couple's new household belonged to the wife's clan. The husband was the only household member not to share his wife's clan identity.

The Revolutionary War and the rise of the American Republic eventually posed new challenges to the Seminoles' way of life in Florida. Between 1780 and 1820, clan identities often appeared fractured in the face of revolutionary violence and settler expansion. Yet, in the context of revolutionary threats, Seminoles worked to reconnect to clan identities and secure their communities from external threats.

At the same time, a number of Seminoles emerged from the Revolutionary War as wealthy slave traders and slave owners. This proved the case for the Oconee chief Cowkeeper. Chief Cowkeeper actively sought ways to promote the autonomy of his people during an uncertain time. At the start of the Revolutionary War, Cowkeeper engaged in diplomacy and declared his loyalty to the British cause.[53] As the war raged on, and slaves absconded from plantations in Georgia and throughout the Gulf Coast region, runaway African and African American slaves found their quest for freedom curtailed. Cowkeeper appeared to have been one of the reasons for these circumscribed flights to freedom as he emerged from the war as one of the wealthier Seminole slave owners.[54]

◇◇◇◇◇◇◇◇◇◇◇◇◇◇◇◇◇◇◇◇◇◇◇◇

Cowkeeper's wealth and social standing did not typify economic life among the Seminoles. Seminoles rarely sold their slaves and African and Seminole communities were often bound together by principles of reciprocity and patronage.[55] The treatment of slaves in Seminole society traversed the spectrum of experiences and emotions, just as it did in other parts of the Southeast. However, historian Andrew Frank notes that non-Seminole outsiders observed, as a visiting Indian agent learned in the 1820s, that "people of color" in Seminole Country enjoy the "good life," having plenty to eat and work "without fear of punishment."[56]

In the broader regional economy, Seminole trade links with the British in East Florida meant that Seminole slave owners joined Cowkeeper in siding with the British when the Revolutionary War broke out. In fact, most Seminoles sided with the British during the war.[57] There remained, however,

Seminoles who crafted diplomatic alliances to meet specific local concerns. For example, the Mikausuki headman Senetahago (Kinagee) placed his allegiance with the Spanish, a decision that a number of other Seminoles also made.[58] The alliances that Seminoles forged during the Revolutionary War provide an example of how regional autonomy still governed the diplomatic and political decision-making of Native Southerners despite the war eventually spurring social and political changes that prompted a shift toward political centralization in the Native South. It also reveals the broader "layers of sovereignty" at play in Southeast North America. Western maps might designate the lands of the Upper and Lower Creeks and Seminoles as part of the Spanish empire, but the Spanish knew that these lands were still very much Indian Country.[59]

This is not to suggest that war didn't have an impact on the lives of Native Southerners; it did. Along the Gulf Coast, for example, enslaved people used Revolutionary-era violence to strike out for freedom and join Maroon communities. In other instances, Seminole warriors saw opportunities to protect their towns and villages from colonial expansion by launching counterattacks on settler communities.[60] Most Indigenous Southerners, however, saw the Revolutionary War between the British and the American colonists as a foreign war. Initially, Indian chiefs preferred to remain neutral, a diplomatic and military position that, as Seminole warriors had already concluded, proved increasingly difficult to maintain.

For Native Southerners, the decision on which side to align with and whom, if anyone, to fight alongside, was informed by regional political and economic calculations.[61] For the Catawbas, far to the north of the Seminoles and Gulf-region Indians, news of the outbreak of war was met with alarm.[62] Their Cherokee neighbors also expressed concern at the overflowing of violence.[63] While Cherokee chiefs such as Attakullakulla received assurances from local settler organizations that the British were determined to maintain "Our Mutual Friendship and Intercourse," such declarations did little to assuage the anxiety of Cherokee townspeople and their chiefs.[64]

Chiefs throughout the Native South were not without options. British, American, Spanish, and French agents all lobbied Indigenous leaders for their support.[65] The Catawbas, who'd relocated from North Carolina to reservation lands in South Carolina, worried about their lands being inundated by white settlers. As early as the 1740s and 1750s, South Carolina backcountry settlements pressed up against the heart of Catawba Country and its population of approximately 1,500 Catawbas and 200–300 warriors. Thus, by the 1770s, the Catawbas felt under siege. Approximately 300 settlers lived on Catawba reservation lands during this time and the chiefs became increasingly concerned about the possibility of Catawba women and children being abducted amid the Revolutionary violence.[66] Such fears led the Catawbas to conduct hastily arranged council meetings, at which they decided to side with the Americans. It proved a costly decision. As Catawba warriors did battle with British soldiers and their Cherokee allies, Catawba Country lay in ruins. When Catawbas began returning to their villages in 1781 they found "all was gone; cattle, hogs, fowls, etc. all gone."[67]

The Catawbas' neighbors, the Cherokees, took a different path. At the outbreak of the war, the memory of the Anglo–Cherokee War remained in the forefront of collective memory and gave shape to the stories Cherokees told about the white men. Still, more than a few Cherokees expressed concerns similar to those of their Catawba neighbors, worrying that "if any rupture should happen between them and the white people the [Cherokee] Women &c would run to the wood[s] and Starve."[68]

But some Cherokees proved eager for a fight and determined to reverse the outcome of the Anglo–Cherokee War. These Cherokees felt that they had good reasons to forge a military alliance with the British: they viewed American settlers as responsible for establishing settlements on Cherokee hunting grounds and making destructive incursions into Cherokee towns and villages. Chickamauga Cherokees, as they came to be known, found American settler expansion threatening to the sovereignty of Cherokee communities and a danger to Cherokee cultural traditions. Indeed, Chickamauga warriors continued their fight against American settlers well after the Revolutionary War ended, not putting down their war hatchets until 1794.

For Cherokees, the Revolutionary War proved particularly disruptive. American militias burned scores of Cherokee towns to the ground during the war and political divisions among the Cherokee war and peace chiefs became more pronounced. These political divides continued into the nineteenth century.[69] The Revolutionary War, though, left no portion of Cherokee Country untouched. Everyone experienced loss, but the suffering of Lower Town Cherokees proved particularly acute.[70] Like so many Lower Towns, the town of Keowee, located on the Lower Cherokee Trading Path in present-day South Carolina, was burned to the ground in August 1776.

Keowee's residents fled as their town burned, their cattle and hogs slaughtered by Georgia troops.[71]

In the decades after the American Revolutionary War, Cherokee people remade their society and reformed their political system. Wartime refugees sought out new homes and struggled to renew kinship ties. Politically, Cherokee chiefs disagreed over the diplomatic path to take in the post–Revolutionary War era, while a series of land cessions led to a considerable loss of Cherokee hunting grounds and lands used for residential and agricultural purposes east of the Appalachians.[72]

The Revolutionary War led to a disturbing contraction in Cherokee landholdings, disruption to communal identities, and ultimately gave rise to new diplomatic pressures on Cherokee sovereignty. For the Creeks, the Cherokees' neighbors and military combatants for much of the eighteenth century, the stakes proved no less serious. Creek headman faced some difficult decisions during the Revolutionary War. When the war came to Creek Country, and the death toll from wartime violence and disease began to mount, Creek leaders realized that neutrality was not a viable option. The vast territory that Creek Country encompassed meant that it became an important crossroads during the war. Given the economic and political importance of the Creeks' relationships with the Spanish and British in the region, a change in the balance of power had the potential to have profound consequences for the Creeks.[73] The Creeks needed to pick their allies carefully.

In this uncertain era, most Creek chiefs made the decision to align with the British. They hoped that such an alliance would help them safely navigate the violence of the war period.[74] Alexander McGillivray, an Upper Creek leader of mixed Creek and Scottish ancestry, emerged as one of the most prominent Creek chiefs to support the British.[75] McGillivray, who rose to the rank of "most beloved man," dreamed of establishing a Southern confederacy of Indians to halt the westward migration of American settler colonies. He also appealed to the Spanish for support and criticized Native Southerners who compromised his vision of a pan-Indian confederacy in the Native South. For example, McGillivray denounced Piomingo, a Chickasaw chief, as a leader who'd been "deluded" into ceding land to the Americans at the conclusion of hostilities. Piomingo's diplomatic decision-making, however, was not quite as simple as McGillivray portrayed it. Indeed, Piomingo was as likely concerned about Creek as American encroachments onto Chickasaw lands given that violence between Chickasaws and Creeks erupted once again in 1792 and 1793.[76] McGillivray's desire to create a pan-Indian identity—at least at a diplomatic level—to buttress the Native South against American expansion was in part driven by McGillivray's opportunism. McGillivray was by no means the only Creek to nurture a network of economic and political relationships, but his collection of stipends from both the Spaniards and Americans underscored his opportunistic tendencies. Thus, when Creeks began to see McGillivray as an "impostor" it reminded many within Creek towns and villages of the importance of maintaining coherent communal identities in a world punctuated by warfare and connected through overlapping webs of economic and diplomatic relationships.[77]

The Creeks nominally supported the British during the war, a position that spoke volumes for Creek concerns about American settlers from Georgia and South Carolina encroaching on their lands.[78] When the war finally ended, Creek concerns about their territorial sovereignty did not abate. Creek *micos* and headmen knew that they must devise new strategies if they hoped to protect the sovereignty of their lands. Using the footpaths and waterways that crisscrossed Creek Country, Creek leaders worked to recalibrate trade and diplomatic networks in the hope that new connections might advance the goal of preserving territorial sovereignty, matrilineal traditions, and cultural ceremonies.[79] The Creek story became one of change and renewal, a story that nonetheless remained attentive to the traditions that bound Creek families and communities together.

To the west of the Creeks, the Choctaws and Chickasaws felt the impact of the Revolutionary War as "imperial expansion" altered demography and prompted new diplomatic calculations.[80] Both attracted considerable attention from British, Spanish, French, and American diplomats.[81] The Choctaws, for example, gained the attention of imperial authorities during the American Revolutionary War. The Choctaws had experience engaging the Creeks and Chickasaws in war. That military experience, their population of approximately thirty thousand, and their strategically important location in the Lower Mississippi meant that both the British and Spanish lobbied hard to ally with them once the war broke out. This diplomatic attention provided Choctaw chiefs with important strategic leverage during the 1770s.[82]

The Choctaws tried to use that leverage to remain neutral during the war. However, Choctaw people did offer their support to different combatants—members of the Six Towns, for instance, offered aid to the Spanish, while other Choctaws remained "well disposed" to the British—at various times during the war. In general, though, the Choctaws didn't experience the type of factionalism that emerged in Cherokee politics.[83] Historian Greg O'Brien explains that the memory of the Choctaw Civil War (1746–1750) remained an object lesson in the dangers of factionalism. Thus, by the 1770s Choctaws did not allow "themselves to become so devoted to either the cause of Britain or Spain that they would spill the blood of other Choctaws."[84]

Choctaws did not escape wartime suffering. Food shortages and hunger impacted Choctaw people, many communities relying increasingly on food supplies from the Spanish. Due to trade routes being cut and hunting grounds lost, these supplies proved essential to the sustenance of many Choctaw communities. Still, it wasn't easy to find reliable European allies. For example, the Choctaw chief Franchumastabie expressed his displeasure at what he perceived to be the British not fighting as hard as Choctaw warriors who'd offered their support in combating the Patriot insurgents.[85]

For the Choctaws northern neighbors, the Chickasaws, the Revolutionary War presented chiefs with diplomatic pressures from the Spanish and British. As peace chiefs debated how best to maintain Chickasaw neutrality, Chickasaw warriors calculated how they'd respond to attacks by Abenaquis, Shawnees, Kickapoos, and other Native warriors.[86] The Chickasaws had a long diplomatic and military history directed at preserving their identity as a politically autonomous people. In the seventeenth and early eighteenth centuries, Chickasaws took refuge from slave-raiding parties by relocating to large, centralized towns protected by palisades. By the 1760s and the French defeat in the Seven Years' War, the growing prosperity of the Chickasaws meant that people "felt safe enough to expand their settlements" once again.[87] The Chickasaw story, in other words, involved a history of strategic decision-making designed to preserve their territorial sovereignty and collective identity. The era of the Revolutionary War therefore presented both new and old challenges to Chickasaw sovereignty and the safety of its towns and villages. For a time, leading Chickasaw headmen such as Payamataha worked to protect Chickasaw sovereignty by juggling diplomatic overtures from French, Spanish, British, and American representatives. At the same time, headmen strove to maintain peaceful diplomatic relations with Native polities throughout the Native South and Illinois Country.[88]

Despite all these challenges and uncertainties, Chickasaw communal identities remained fairly stable during the Revolutionary War and into the

1790s. There existed, however, exceptions. For instance, the Scottish loyalist and trader James Colbert, who fathered as many as six mixed-race Chickasaw children, neglected traditional Chickasaw diplomatic responsibilities and reportedly worked against Payamataha.[89] Chickasaws generally disliked Colbert and as such his betrayal of Payamataha might be viewed as a rare example of discord among the Chickasaws during this revolutionary age. Throughout the war, Chickasaws remained united in the cause of preserving their sovereignty.[90] In the 1790s, both the Spanish and Americans made diplomatic and trade overtures toward the Chickasaws, but those overtures proved no threat to Chickasaw sovereignty or communal identities.[91] While prominent Chickasaws like Mingo Houma and Payamataha died in 1784 and 1785, respectively, their steady leadership had laid the foundation for future Chickasaw efforts to balance diplomatic friendships with the United States and Spain while also guarding Chickasaw territorial sovereignty against "unauthorized surveyors" and land cessions to the Americans.[92]

Still, the Americans did ultimately win the war and form a new republic. And the citizens of that American republic quickly turned westward, looking greedily to lands beyond the thirteen original states—to the Ohio, the Native South, and beyond. Native Southerners knew this; it's why the Chickamauga Cherokees launched their war of resistance on the Cumberland and Tennessee River regions in a bid to defend their communal identities and territorial sovereignty. And it's why the Chickasaw *mico* Piomingo worried about how "the White people have Got a very bad Trick that when they go a hunting, as there are Many that follow it for a Livelyhood, and find A good piece of ground and they Make a station camp on it and the Next thing they go To Building houses, which I hope Will not be Allowed."[93]

Among the Chickasaws, as for Chickamauga Cherokees and Native Southerners generally, the late 1780s marked the opening of a new and uncertain era in their engagement with settler colonialism.[94]

◇◇◇◇◇◇◇◇◇◇◇◇◇◇◇◇◇◇◇◇◇◇◇◇◇◇◇

For Native Southerners, the rise of the American republic meant the need to recalibrate their foreign policy focus. In 1785 and 1786, that new settler colonial reality began crystallizing when the Cherokees, Choctaws, and Chickasaws signed the Treaty of Hopewell with the Continental Congress. Among its numerous provisions, the treaty formalized the process of Cherokees, Choctaws, and Chickasaws returning prisoners of war, establishing territorial boundaries with the United States, and formalizing trade between the sovereign peoples of the Native South and the new republic.[95]

The formation of the United States led to not only the rethinking of foreign and trade policies in the Native South but also reflection on the nature and meaning of town life and cultural identities. How would the rise of the United States impact the sovereign landholdings of Native Southerners? Would diplomatic friendships with the new United States destabilize relations with other Native polities? And what impact would all these changes have on kinship identities, cultural beliefs, and ceremonial practices in the Native South?

These were big questions, and they struck at the heart of what identity meant (and would mean) to Native Southerners. Native Southerners therefore took great interest in the Indian policy that George Washington's government began formulating at the end of the 1780s. Under the direction of secretary of war Henry Knox, the federal government worked to craft a policy that became known as "expansion with honor." With Americans eager to extend their territorial holdings westward, the federal government worked to balance the interests of its citizens with the determination of the Native South's chiefs to preserve their territorial sovereignty and communal identities.[96]

American attitudes toward Native Americans in the early republic ranged from crudely racist to patronizing. Where one group unabashedly articulated exterminationist or eliminationist views, the other offered patronizing descriptions of "the Indians'" racial "nature." American elites such as the Philadelphia physician Benjamin Rush expressed the latter position when referring to the "tyranny of custom" that prevailed among Indigenous peoples. Thomas Jefferson, who encouraged Native Americans to either amalgamate with whites or resettle on reservations west of the Mississippi River, straddled both perspectives. In 1803, Jefferson wrote about the future of Native Americans in the republic, declaring,

> In truth, the ultimate point of rest & happiness for them is to let our settlement and theirs meet and blend together, to intermix, and become one people. Incorporating themselves with us as citizens of the U.S., this is what the natural progress of things will of course bring on, and it will be better to promote than retard it.[97]

Jefferson supported efforts to extend the factory system throughout the Native South as a means of bringing trade and what he saw as the benefits of civilization to Indigenous communities. He also believed that Native leaders should recognize their precarious status as spokespeople for sovereign Indigenous nations in the context of the new republic, insisting that "our strength and their weakness is now so visible" that the American Indians "must see that we have only to shut our hand to crush them, and that all our liberalities toward them proceed from motives of pure humanity only."[98]

If this was expansion with honor then Native Southerners struggled to find much that was honorable in Jefferson's proposals. In the mid-1790s, the Chickasaw elder Ugulayacabé gave voice to Indigenous suspicions about U.S. policy when he quipped that American declarations of friendship were akin to "the rattlesnake that caresses the squirrel in order to devour it."[99] Still, as the U.S. government refined its "Indian policy" between the 1790s and 1810s, Native Southerners continued to work toward the rebuilding of their communities. Trade networks needed repair and the restructuring of social and political life slowly gathered momentum.[100] But just as Native Southerners moved toward nation-state models of governance (see the following chapter for more details), Nativist priests and war chiefs who aspired to the creation of pan-Indian alliances vied for Native loyalties from the Ohio River valley to the Native South.

<hr/>

The Seven Years' War and the era of the American Revolution provided the backdrop for the rekindling of Nativist revivals across eastern North America. Indigenous priests and war chiefs led these Nativist revivals. They hearkened back to Native cultural and religious beliefs and ceremonial practices in an attempt to refocus their followers' attention on the stories and cultural traditions that Nativist leaders believed once grounded communal identities. At the same time, more than a few Nativists were also interested in forging intertribal or pan-Indian alliances, as a means of countering the growing power of the American republic.[101]

Nativist priests and war chiefs felt deeply concerned about the social and cultural changes going on around them—changes that many associated with settler colonialism. They railed against alcohol consumption and distrusted an emerging generation of mission-educated mixed-race chiefs who led efforts to form tribal nations and accommodate Indigenous society to the American republic's social and economic structures. In response, Nativist prophets tried to stitch together interconnected networks to resist American territorial and cultural encroachments, thereby protecting Native territorial sovereignty and cultural identities.[102]

As we've seen, late-eighteenth- and early-nineteenth-century pan-Indian leaders were not a new phenomenon in North America. Nativist prophets had been preaching among Indigenous communities in the Ohio River valley since the 1730s.[103] By the 1760s, a new generation of prophets emerged in the Upper Susquehanna. These Nativist prophets insisted that all Indigenous people shared a common past and present. Native prophets taught their followers that they were an exceptional people, but they had become degenerate and needed to reconnect with traditional belief systems and ceremonial practices. For example, a female prophet from the Lenni Lenape tribe (or Delaware) instructed her followers to stop drinking alcohol and to remember that they were both separate from, and superior to, nearby whites and blacks. Such messages revealed how Nativist prophets used symbols, rituals, and ceremonies to unite Indigenous people; they also began articulating Western racial ideologies in their political and social discourse as a means of distinguishing among white, black, and Indian people.[104]

Nativist prophets existed among the Lenni Lenape, Shawnee, Creek, and Cherokee peoples during the late eighteenth century. These prophets took traditional oral storytelling and ceremonial practices and adapted them to a new type of pan-Indianism—a pan-Indianism rich in moral lessons and defined by heroism and ritual power.[105] At the same time, the emphasis on "sin" offered prophets a narrative device to inspire their followers to action. The Lenni Lenape prophet Neolin used this strategy to frame his concern about the loss of Indian hunting lands by emphasizing a message of Indigenous independence from white Americans. Neolin urged his followers to stop cooperating with the whites and live separately from them.[106]

Shawnee prophets increased their diplomatic outreach to other Native peoples following the Treaty of Paris of 1783. This treaty ended the Revolutionary War and left Natives angry because they had not been consulted during the peace negotiations. Native Southerners shared their anger. Among Cherokee prophets and war chiefs, Chickamauga Cherokees lifted their voices ever louder in council meetings in an effort to push for war against the whites and to restore what they understood to be traditional religious beliefs and cultural practices. Cherokees like Tsiyu-gansini, or Dragging Canoe, began attracting a loyal following by preaching a message of resistance to American settler colonialism.[107] Dragging Canoe therefore attempted to lead

Cherokee warriors from the Overhill Towns into an alliance with Shawnee prophets and warriors. Their goal was simple: build a massive pan-Indian military alliance and halt settler expansion into their lands, with force if necessary—something Chickamauga warriors did along the Cumberland and Tennessee River corridors until the mid-1790s.[108] Until his death in 1791, Dragging Canoe kept up his fight against the white Americans and their land hunger.[109]

Dragging Canoe's politics, and the outreach of Shawnee prophets in the Carolinas during the 1780s and 1790s, failed to unite Native Southerners with Indigenous people in the Mid-Atlantic and Ohio River valley. In the Southeast, scores of Indigenous communities focused instead on recovering from the ravages of the Revolutionary War. A growing number of Native communities in the Southeast restructured life around farmsteads instead of towns, and increasingly Indigenous communities relied on annuities from the federal government, or payments from the cession of land to the United States, just to survive the years immediately after the war.

There proved other forces at play in stymieing pan-Indianism. Tribal "nationalism" was on the rise, particularly among the Cherokees, Creeks, Choctaws, Chickasaws, and Seminoles. Leaders from these polities began working to unite the people they claimed to represent under a centralized form of government. Town and clan identities did not disappear nor did the influence of matrilineal traditions abate, but the movement toward a system of written laws and a nation-state framework proved inexorable by the opening of the nineteenth century.

Before Native Southerners formalized written constitutions and over-hauled their economies in the early nineteenth century, Native warriors persisted in their resistance to settler encroachments on their lands. In 1791, a battle that historians have come to call the "Victory with No Name" marked the high watermark for armed pan-Indian resistance against American settler expansion.[110] On a battlefield north of the Ohio River, in a portion of western Pennsylvania known as the Northwest Territory, Shawnee, Delaware, Miami, Ottawa, Ojibwa, Potawatomi, Wyandot, and Iroquois warriors came together in a successful armed defense of their homelands. President Washington, fearing Indian warriors might unite with the Spanish and impede the westward expansion of the American republic, sent American troops to the region under the command of Revolutionary War veteran Arthur St. Clair. For several years American troops had tried and failed to "quash Indian resistance." St. Clair and his 1,400 troops were meant to end this resistance once and for all. They failed spectacularly, with St. Clair's troops being wiped out by Native warriors.

◇◇◇◇◇◇◇◇◇◇◇◇◇◇◇◇◇◇◇◇◇◇◇◇◇◇◇◇◇◇

In the two decades following the "Victory with No Name," efforts to unite Native peoples in the Ohio River valley and the Native South failed to realize the lofty ambitions of pan-Indian prophets and warriors. In the Ohio River valley in 1794, the United States defeated Native warriors from the Western Confederacy at the Battle of Fallen Timbers, effectively ending coordinated Indigenous resistance to settler expansion until the emergence of the Shawnee warrior Tecumseh in the early nineteenth century. In the Native South that same year, Chickamauga Cherokees agreed to a cessation of attacks on settlers headed for Tennessee and Kentucky.

Military setbacks were not the only factors to blunt the drive for pan-Indian coalitions; the continued adherence of Native Southerners to regional communities and cultural traditions tended to trump pan-Indianism. For example, the Creek prophet Josiah Francis led a religious revival movement in the 1810s. Francis, who was also known as Hildis Hadjo, emerged less as a leader of a pan-Indian movement than as a leading figure among Red Stick Creeks, a group committed to maintaining Creek religious and cultural traditions in the face of settler colonial expansion.[111]

Nonetheless, efforts were made to coordinate some sort of Native resistance against an expansive United States. In September 1811, for example, a small group of Shawnee chiefs met with Choctaw, Cherokee, and Creek leaders (mainly Red Stick Creeks) at the Upper Creek town of Tuckabatchee, on the Tallapoosa River. Inspired by the Shawnee warrior Tecumseh, the gathering renewed efforts to forge a pan-Indian alliance to empower Indigenous people in the Ohio and the interior South in their resistance to the westward expansion of the United States.[112] It was a noble vision, but it proved no match for the building tidal wave of American violence and anti-Indian racism; it also proved out of step with the emergence of tribal nationalism in the Southeast.

As Native Southerners came to terms with the rise of the American republic, a new generation of Indigenous leaders began working to establish new political structures that eventually gave renewed meaning to Indigenous identities and redefined kinship and community. These political innovations overlapped with the work of Indigenous women. In communities across the Southeast, Native women remained committed to the principle of territorial sovereignty and the traditions of matrilineal culture. In other words, Native Southerners adapted, innovated, and changed. But just as these changes began to mature, a new series of wars, violence with settlers, and political challenges confronted them. The era of removal was about to dawn.

CHAPTER SIX

TRIBAL NATIONALISM, REMOVAL, AND DIASPORA

At noon on August 30, 1813, an event occurred that reverberated throughout the Native South. In southwestern Alabama, Red Stick warriors launched an attack on a stockaded dwelling owned by the planter Samuel Mims. In what became known as the "Fort Mims massacre," most of the soldiers stationed at the fort were killed.[1] But what truly sent shockwaves through settler communities in Georgia and the Mississippi Territory was the murder of women and children. "The fall of Fort Mims," one writer recalled, was compounded by the "butchery of so many women and children."[2]

The tremors of fear that swept over white Southerners immediately after the violent events at Fort Mims prompted a forceful response from the American military against the Red Sticks. The Red Sticks' attack, however, revealed the determination of the Creek warriors to resist the territorial expansion of the American Republic. How best to resist settler expansion into the sovereign domain of the Creek people became a question that all Native Southerners debated during the early nineteenth century. At Fort Mims, Red Stick warriors declared their position, targeting not only settler soldiers and white women and children but also Creeks from the town of Tensaw. The Tensaw Creeks had purportedly helped the Americans provision Fort Mims, an alliance that enraged Red Stick warriors.

The Fort Mims massacre, and what subsequently became known as the Red Stick War (1813–1814) highlights the halting and sometimes violent atmosphere in which tribal nationalism began to take root in the Native South during the early decades of the nineteenth century. As steady waves of white settlers migrated to the Old West and the western frontiers of the Southeast, Native Southerners continued working toward the reconstruction of communities, farmsteads, and built a new political order to help them confront the challenges posed by the rise of the United States. While Creeks, Cherokees, and Native Southerners throughout the Southeast searched for ways to rearticulate a cohesive and meaningful sense of community, peace and war chiefs sometimes clashed over how best to project a political identity that would buttress their claims to territorial sovereignty. Ultimately, these efforts came into conflict with the eliminationist logic of federal and state governments.[3]

◇◇◇◇◇◇◇◇◇◇◇◇◇◇◇◇◇◇◇◇◇◇◇◇◇◇

Efforts to re-embed systems of communal cohesion and tribal governance in the Native South were punctuated by frontier violence, war, and growing pressure from state and federal government officials during the early nineteenth century. Cherokees and Creeks, Yuchis and Yamasees, Choctaws, Caddos, Tunicas, Biloxis, and scores of other Native Southerners tried to both retain and rearticulate a sense of community and tradition in a world that grew increasingly hostile toward them.

The decades between the 1780s and 1810s witnessed rapid changes in the Native South. Trade networks were in constant flux and future government structures were debated vigorously in the Native South's council houses. For example, Alexander McGillivray, the prominent Creek leader, tried and failed to institute a centralized form of government among the Creeks during the late eighteenth century. While his efforts foundered, a growing body of Creek leaders recognized the need for laws and institutional structures that would halt settler intrusions onto Creek territory and prevent practices such as property theft. For instance, in the early nineteenth century, white Georgians engaged in the theft of Creek-owned cattle, and in retaliation Creeks stole cattle belonging to Georgians. As Creek leaders began passing laws to address this problem, the question of whether whites were subject to Creek laws became a serious legal and political debate.[4]

As Creeks and other southeastern Native polities began passing written laws to protect the communally owned property of their members, issues of territorial sovereignty came into focus like never before. Could Creeks prosecute a white citizen from Georgia if that Georgian stole cattle from Creek lands? Alternatively, could the Creeks' neighbors, the Cherokees, try a white frontiersman for murder if that individual killed a Cherokee within the borders of the Cherokee Nation? Among American lawmakers, such questions raised concerns about the United States' sovereignty and whether the existence of an *imperium in imperio*—a state within a state—jeopardized the future security of American citizens.[5]

These questions remained part of American political and cultural discourse throughout the early nineteenth century, culminating with the removal era of the 1820s and 1830s in the Southeast.[6] But questions of sovereignty, political authority, and cultural tradition gripped communities in the Native South both before and during these removal crises. The debates that emerged sometimes divided Native polities, bringing into question the meaning of collective identities and sometimes resulting in violence and civil war.

This proved the case among the Creeks and Seminoles. During the Revolutionary War, Americans looked to Spanish-held West Florida and British-controlled East Florida as logical spaces in which to expand the Republic. For Lower Creeks and Seminoles, the territorial ambitions of the Americans had implications for a sovereign Native land base and access to trade partners. Through much of the Gulf region, Panton, Leslie & Company dominated trade networks with Native Southerners. At the same time, American slave-trading and slave-owning interests looked for new markets and aspired to shore up the stability of racial slavery in the Gulf South. As a result, Native peoples such as the Hitchitis and Seminoles came under renewed pressure to return runaway slaves to their white American masters.[7]

Set against this historical backdrop, Red Stick warriors voiced their strong opposition to Creek land cessions and alliances with Americans. Historians have long considered the outbreak of the Red Stick War in 1813 as the beginning of a Creek civil war pitting those committed to rearticulating traditional cultural practices and ceremonial structures against Creeks (the so-called White Sticks) willing to institute political changes and open trade networks with the American Republic. This explanation only partly explains the outbreak of war. What was at stake in the Red Stick War was the meaning of Creek identity in the context of the aggressively expansive United States.

For Red Sticks, the maintenance of Creek sovereignty and communal identities—buttressed by matrilineally determined gender roles and lineages—meant the perpetuation of a way of life. This in turn involved the reaffirmation of a sense of place, or a connection to the lands and riverine

The Georgia militia under General Floyd attack Creek warriors at the Red Stick town of Autossee, on the Tallapoosa River. *Hargrett Rare Book and Manuscript Library, University of Georgia, Athens.*

worlds that gave meaning to cultural traditions, stories, and ceremonies. What Creeks didn't agree on in the early nineteenth century was how to achieve these objectives. Disagreements therefore meant that local political identities and economic interests had the potential to put Creeks at cross-purposes in the pursuit of a renewed collective identity.[8]

This proved true in the Red Sticks' attack on the Tensaw Creeks. In the early nineteenth century, Tensaw Creeks developed a fairly diversified economy, remained open to the possibility of trade with the Spanish, and began embracing what its headmen saw as the benefits of a European system of education. None of this meant that Tensaws abandoned traditional beliefs and culture as markers of identity. Well into the early nineteenth century, the Tensaws continued to organize themselves into a *talofa*, or daughter town, in relation to the nearby Alabama *talwas*. So, while the Tensaws remained in a reciprocal relationship with the Alabamas, a political relationship dating back to at least the seventeenth century, the appearance of Tensaws being disinterested in resisting the westward movement of white settlements put them at odds with the Red Sticks.[9]

Portrait of Creek war chief Menawa, 1838. *Library of Congress, Prints and Photographs Division, Washington, D.C.*

Red Stick Creeks were thus inspired to take arms by a desire to preserve their version of territorial and cultural sovereignty. They also found inspiration in the pan-Indianism of Tecumseh and Indian prophets throughout the Ohio Valley and interior portions of the Southeast. With these influences shaping their political thinking and sense of collective identity, the Red Sticks saw the Tensaws' growing web of relationships as a threat to the Creeks' collective ability to resist American settler expansion.[10] At the same time, the U.S. government saw violence among the Creeks as a danger to the Republic in the Southeast. Indeed, the Red Stick War overlapped with the War of 1812 (1812–1815), a war declared by the United States on Britain over major trade and diplomatic disagreements and perceptions that the British provided military support to North American Indians like the Red Sticks.[11]

The United States incorporated the Red Stick War into its larger war against the British and their Indian allies. At the Creek town of Tohopeka, in what is today central Alabama, Major General Andrew Jackson defeated Red Stick warriors in a battle that took on profound historical significance. Known to the Americans as the Battle of Horseshoe Bend, the fighting that took place on March 27, 1814, included the U.S. infantry and some six hundred allied warriors from among the Cherokees, Choctaws, and Lower Creeks. With the rallying cry of "Remember Fort Mims" ringing out among American troops, the Red Sticks were defeated and the town of Tohopeka destroyed. Of the one thousand Creek warriors who went into battle under war chiefs like Menawa of Tohopeka, between eight and nine hundred lost their lives.[12]

Among the Indigenous warriors at the Battle of Tohopeka and who fought alongside the Americans were prominent Cherokees such as Kahmungda-clageh (or The Ridge), Sequoyah (the inventor of the Cherokee syllabary), and a young Sam Houston, the adopted Cherokee son of Oolooteka (or John Jolly).[13] The Cherokees had a long history of conflict with the Creeks and may have seen the Red Stick War as an opportunity to align with the Americans as they worked to formalize a centralized form of government and reassert their territorial sovereignty.[14]

However, just as the Creeks lost twenty million acres of territory in the disastrous land cession at the Treaty of Fort Jackson in August 1814, pressure on the Cherokees to cede land to the United States led to two treaties in 1817 and 1819 that resulted in a considerable loss of land and the eventual migration of some Cherokees into Arkansas Territory and Spanish (and later Mexican) Texas.[15]

The steady loss of Creek and Cherokee territory through land cessions to the U.S. government became an unpleasant fact of life for Native leaders. In this historical context, Cherokee leaders attempted to articulate written laws and draft a constitution to define the sovereignty of the Cherokee Nation. They did all of this amid removal crises in 1806–1809, 1817–1819, 1824, and 1827. In the face of American land hunger, Cherokees established the Cherokee National Council in 1794, promulgated written laws in 1807–1808, passed a constitution in 1828, and established the first Indigenous newspaper in North America, the *Cherokee Phoenix*, in 1828. The founding of the *Phoenix* proved particularly important because it represented the most visible example of Cherokee cultural nationalism. Published in both English and the Cherokee writing system, or syllabary, the *Phoenix* promoted the interests of Cherokees and aimed to cultivate a cohesive sense of nationhood by telling the stories of disparate Cherokee communities.[16]

By the mid-1820s the leaders of the Cherokee Nation were as determined as they'd ever been to preserve their nation's sovereignty and protect the lands of their people from further settler encroachment. Recognizing the importance of a sovereign territorial base to the projection of a national Cherokee identity, Cherokee delegates intensified lobbying in Washington, D.C., or Washington City, as it was then known, in a bid to protect and preserve their lands during the latter half of the 1820s.

Not all Cherokees agreed with this diplomatic approach. As we've seen, the Chickamauga Cherokees placed pressure on peace chiefs in council meetings during the latter decades of the eighteenth century and argued that the Cherokees should take the fight to the Americans. The Chickamaugas also established communities among the Lower Towns in the hope of maintaining what they defined as traditional ways of life. Some, however, made the difficult decision to migrate west and join, in the words of one American observer in 1803, "a number of Vagabonds, emigrants from the Delawares, Shawnees, Miamis, Chicasaws, Cherokees, Piorias" in the territories of Louisiana and Arkansas.[17]

Other Cherokees decided to stay and fight. The charismatic elder Nunnatsunega (White Path) stayed and resisted the forces of removal. He also opposed a new generation of Cherokee leaders. These leaders were men educated at mission schools who seemed determined to undermine the matrilineal traditions of the Cherokees. Nunnatsunega also felt that these new leaders were undermining local political autonomy and the rich ceremonial and spiritual traditions of Cherokee towns. Nunnatsunega, who was from the Cherokee town of Ulun'yi (Turnip Town, located in present-day Georgia), therefore rejected the centralization of Cherokee government and the growing influence of Christian missionaries in Cherokee culture.[18]

Nunnatsunega's opposition to some of the changes occurring around him encountered challenges not only from a new generation of Cherokee leaders but ran headlong into the growing power of American settler colonialism. Territorial pressure from settlers, the westward march of the slave frontier, and the cultural chauvinism of Christian missionaries tended to magnify internal pressures (and visions) in both Creek and Cherokee societies during the early nineteenth century. As both the Creeks and Cherokees tried to establish new political structures and create a protected space within their tribal nations for the renewal of communal identities, racial attitudes began hardening. While some missionaries and members of the emerging abolitionist movement in the Northeast questioned arguments about the innate inferiority of American Indians, the growing consensus was that efforts to acculturate Native people into settler society had failed.[19] The Cherokees, like other Native Southerners, were viewed by the most vocal proponents of removal as weak, ignorant, lazy, improvident "savages."[20]

Racial stereotypes impacted Indigenous communities across the Native South. Combating them was not easy. Like the Creeks and Cherokees, the Choctaws and Chickasaws faced a series of overlapping challenges that included political rifts and the navigation of imposed racial labels such as "full-blood" and "half-breed." These culturally contrived labels had no scientific validity; indeed, when Native Southerners began adopting them they used them to refer as much to cultural and political alliances as to an imagined biology identity.[21]

In addition to sorting through the genealogies and political allegiances of one another, Native Southerners grappled with the presence of federally appointed Indian agents and the steady loss of territory. For the Choctaws and Chickasaws, colonial assaults on their lands and waterways accelerated after the United States and Spain signed the Treaty of San Lorenzo (also known as Pinckney's Treaty) in 1795. That Europeans and Americans spoke about both the Choctaws and Chickasaws as "nations" during this period reflected the enduring diplomatic and military power of these Native polities. It also reveals how the United States recognized, albeit grudgingly, the Choctaws and Chickasaws as sovereign peoples possessing collective legal and social identities that Western governments knew they could not ignore. While American leaders spoke about amalgamating Native peoples with the white population, or removing Indians west of the Mississippi, they also understood that they lacked the economic and military power to act decisively on these ideas. Not until the 1820s did this dynamic change in any meaningful way; until then, Choctaw and Chickasaw lands remained firmly within the orbit of Indian Country.[22]

To meet the challenges to their sovereignty in the 1820s the Chickasaws and Choctaws did as the Creeks and Cherokees did and formalized written laws and organized constitutional governments. In 1824, the Chickasaws established a tribal council and divided the nation into four districts—Pontotoc, Chesafaliah, Choquafaliah, and Big Town. By 1829 the Chickasaws had established their own system of written laws, thereby declaring to the world the formalization of their borders and sovereignty as an Indigenous nation.[23]

The Choctaws took similar measures to preserve their identity as a sovereign people. In 1826, Choctaws formed a constitutional government to more effectively address the United States government's challenges to the nation's sovereignty. Under the leadership of David Folsom and Greenwood LeFlore, written laws helped Choctaws prescribe everything from political districts—Moshulatubbee, Apukshunnubbee, and Pushmataha—to punishments for a variety of crimes.[24] A national government, the Choctaw lawmaker James McDonald argued, would enable Choctaws to present coordinated rebuttals to the "bitter and endless persecution" of the Choctaw people and the sovereignty of their nation. Choctaw leader Peter Pitchlynn made similar observations, arguing that the promulgation of written laws sent a message to those outside the Choctaw Nation that Choctaws spoke with a collective national voice in prescribing its laws and policing its territorial boundaries.[25]

Both Choctaw and Chickasaw leaders opposed territorial cessions to the Americans and expressed their displeasure about white settler intrusions on their lands. Having a formal set of laws and constitutional governments therefore aided diplomatic efforts to protect the sovereignty of these respective Indigenous nations. But political reform did not mean Choctaws and Chickasaws abandoned older cultural beliefs and practices. To the contrary, central government helped preserve Choctaw and Chickasaw worldviews. For example, the principles of matrilineality continued to shape kinship identities and gave meaning to the day-to-day operations of life.[26]

For the Choctaws—who numbered approximately twenty thousand and were dispersed in communities that stretched over what Americans called Mississippi and Alabama Territories—and the Chickasaws—whose population ranged from four to five thousand and included people with genealogies that stretched back to Yazoo River tribes—social, political, and economic life was in the midst of significant structural changes during the 1820s.[27]

Economically, life became more varied. A mix of cattle and farming, in addition to the presence of trading factories, precipitated changes in land use patterns and innovations in how people lived. As farmsteads and mule-and-plow agriculture replaced town clusters as the dominant living pattern, Choctaw men increasingly found employment working the land and in using horses to herd cattle while women spun and wove clothing.[28] Such divisions of labor had faint echoes of past specialization, but the nature of Choctaw employment was changing for men and women as the frontiers of American slavery and settler society pressed westward.[29]

Christianity also contributed to changes in daily life and added yet another cultural layer to debates about the meaning of Choctaw and Chickasaw identities. Native Southerners had long valued education, but during the 1790s missionaries moved into the Native South and established schools, churches, and plantations with the goal of lifting "clouds of heathenish darkness."[30] In the process these Christian outsiders began changing the type of education that Choctaws and Chickasaws, Creeks and Cherokees, Seminoles and Shawnees received, encouraged a shift away from matrilineality, and urged men to perform agricultural labor—the very same labor that was once a key factor in women's political power. In Choctaw communities, for example, Presbyterian missionaries taught lessons in dependency and subjection, messages at odds with an ethos of "personal freedom and autonomy" coveted by Choctaws.[31]

For a small but increasingly powerful group of Native Southerners, territorial sovereignty, cultural independence, and socioeconomic autonomy became explicitly tied to racial slavery. Cowkeeper, the Seminole leader discussed in chapter 5, rose to become a prominent slave owner and played a significant role in redefining Seminole identity (at least for wealthy, slave-owning Seminoles). Like other prominent eighteenth-century Seminoles, such as Brims, Cowkeeper's involvement in slavery—and trade networks more generally—highlighted how some Seminoles had no intention of living in isolation from the outside world. By the early nineteenth century, Seminoles continued nurturing trade networks and incorporating outsiders on terms of their choosing.[32]

The Seminoles' determination to protect their autonomy was evident in three wars (1817–1818, 1835–1842, 1855–1858), in which they fought to retain their homelands in what is today Florida. This also happened to be territory that the United States purchased from Spain in 1819. However, the so-called Seminole Wars did not mean that Seminole political and economic leaders rejected the network of trade that existed throughout the Gulf region.[33] In fact, Seminole leaders such as Osceola, who made a name for himself during the Second Seminole War, devoted his adult life to engaging in diplomacy and forming coalitions among Seminoles and runaway slaves. These alliances gave Osceola access to vast networks of intelligence that helped him and his supporters resist settler colonial expansion into Seminole Country.[34]

Trade and diplomatic networks connected Seminole communities, most of which remained based on small-scale agricultural production, to the outside world. For a few Seminoles, the presence of slave labor helped augment their wealth. That said, Maroon communities, or communities of runaway slaves, continued to coexist alongside Seminole towns.[35] Throughout the Gulf Coast region and into the interior of the Southeast, Native Southerners lived alongside and enslaved people of African ancestry.

The shift away from captivity practices to racial slavery underscored how Native Southerners remained enmeshed in broader cultural, economic, and diplomatic networks. These networks had an impact on how Native Southerners articulated difference. The vocabulary of race—of "red," "black," and "white" people—became as much a part of Indigenous culture as it did for Euroamericans during the early nineteenth century.

The adoption of racial slavery in the Native South was by no means smooth; at times it was halting, and it did encounter opposition from elders who insisted on maintaining traditional social and cultural practices. For example, amid the turmoil of the American Revolutionary War, Nancy Ward (or Nanye'hi), the Cherokee War Woman of Chota, urged fellow Cherokees not to disregard traditional adoption and marriage practices in preference for the racial violence that appeared to be engulfing the Native South.[36]

Such warnings help to explain the uneven adoption of racial understandings of "blood" and kinship throughout the Native South. Still, the trajectory toward racial slavery proved unmistakable. Take, for instance, the case of an African American slave named Molly. Just prior to the American Revolution, a white man by the name of Sam Dent beat and killed his Cherokee wife. Fearful that he'd become the victim of Cherokee "blood law"—a system of justice that required members from the victim's clan to seek retributive justice on the perpetrator of his or her clan to restore balance and harmony between the clans—Dent fled Cherokee Country and took refuge in Augusta, Georgia. There he purchased a slave named Molly. Dent returned to Cherokee Country and offered Molly to his now deceased wife's clan—the Deer clan—a transaction that the Cherokees evidently accepted. Molly, however, was not sacrificed and put to death; instead, Cherokees gave her a new name—"Chickaw"—and adopted her into Cherokee kinship networks.[37]

Molly's unlikely journey reveals to us an aspect of Cherokee society and culture in transition. The implications of interracial marriage, of competing understandings of justice, and of the Cherokee adoption of a racialized slave highlights how Cherokees navigated traditional and Euroamerican worldviews on a daily basis. Race loomed large in the lives of all southerners by the early nineteenth century, but its application to the daily lives of Cherokees—as for Native Southerners generally—only made sense when contextualized in reference to older cultural systems and social conventions.

The lives of Native Southerners and African Americans intersected on an increasing basis during the early nineteenth centuries. Cases of famous Cherokee leaders like John Ridge and Elias Boudinot marrying and starting families with white women scandalized large segments of American society, while racially mixed families involving Cherokees and African Americans had implications for the meaning of Cherokee identity that continue to reverberate into our own time (as the Cherokee Nation's efforts to strip the descendants of Cherokee freedpeople in 2007 reveals).[38]

The case of the prominent Cherokee slave owner, Shoe Boots, highlights just how entangled Cherokee–white–African American lives had become by the 1790s. In the 1790s, Shoe Boots lived with Clarinda Ellington, a white captive from Kentucky, as man and wife. The couple had at least two children before Clarinda absconded and returned to Kentucky with her children. In the ensuing years, Cherokees came to know a teenage slave, "Black Doll," as Shoe Boot's "wife." Together Shoe Boots and Black Doll had five Afro-Cherokee children, although the racial identity of those children remained a point of contention among Cherokees well into the nineteenth century.[39]

The increasingly poisonous nature of antiblack racism throughout North America tested the adaptability of Cherokee kinship and adoption practices. Could biracial people be Cherokee in an era when the status of a slave in both the white and Native South was reserved for people of African descent? Some Cherokees believed they could, but they found it difficult to have their voices heard as educated, slave-owning Cherokees—men such as John Ross, John Ridge, and James and Joseph Vann—dominated political discourse and attempted to redefine the Cherokee Nation in racialized and patriarchal terms that were recognizable to the United States' political elites.[40]

Slave plantations in the Native South became sites of both extreme brutality and mind-numbing discipline. Slaves rarely found any kindness from their Indian masters, turning instead to the unstable family and social networks that they cobbled together in the emotionally and physically violent world of racial slavery. The Vann family plantations in the Cherokee Nation were infamous for the brutal discipline meted out to slaves. Similarly, the Chickamauga warrior White Man Killer and the Creek slave owner Alex Cornells earned reputations for being particularly brutal slave owners. Creek slave owners, such as Jack Kinnard, also kept a close watch over their slaves. While Native Southerners like Kinnard placed slave populations outside the traditional protections of kinship, they jealously guarded their property rights. When, for example, the self-styled "Chief of the Embassy for Creek and Cherokee Nations," William Augustus Bowles (who was born in Maryland to English parents), attempted to meddle in Creek slavery by aiding runaways, Kinnard became enraged and insisted that Bowles was fast losing the respect of the Creeks.[41]

Racial slavery added a potentially explosive dimension to the changing social dynamics in the Native South. Slave catchers policed the Native South for runaway slaves, and masters and overseers surveilled the company that slaves kept. In the Creek Nation, for example, slave owners clashed with slaves over religion. As Christian missionaries made their presence felt throughout the Native South, some of those missionaries attempted to proselytize among the enslaved. With large numbers of Native Southerners refusing to send their children to missionary schools or attend their churches, missionaries often turned their attention to slaves owned by Creeks, Cherokees, Choctaws, and Chickasaws.

Just as it incurred the ire of white slave owners, Native slave masters often expressed anger toward missionary preaching among (or in the vicinity of) slaves. For example, in 1828 twenty-five Creek men violently interrupted a religious ceremony among slaves owned by Creek slave masters. The slaves were tied up with cords and, according to one eyewitness, beaten unmercifully. Such examples underscore the discipline and control that Indigenous slave owners exercised over enslaved people. And while it was the case that some Native slave owners made space for Christian missionaries on their farms and plantations, from the perspective of the enslaved, the violence and emotional terror of slavery meant that it mattered little whether one was enslaved in the white or Native South.[42]

◇◇◇◇◇◇◇◇◇◇◇◇◇◇◇◇◇◇◇◇◇◇◇◇

By the 1820s, some very dark political storm clouds began to threaten not only the wealth of slave owners in the Native South but the livelihoods of all Native Southerners. The westward expansion of slavery and the growing political gulf between North and South meant that Indigenous nations in the Southeast were about to encounter their sternest test since the American Republic's founding.

For most Americans, Andrew Jackson embodies the excesses of a brand of American settler colonial expansion that led to the forced removal of seventy to one hundred thousand Native Americans from the eastern half of the United States.[43] Jackson, however, was by no means the first to espouse Indian removal. In correspondence with the Indian agent Benjamin Hawkins in 1803, President Thomas Jefferson wrote about the importance of American Indians assimilating with white America, lest they be crushed under the tidal wave of settler civilization.[44] In 1808 and 1809, Jefferson wrote to a number of prominent Cherokee leaders, simultaneously urging them to adopt the political structures of the American Republic and to accept federal assistance in relocating to the Trans-Mississippi West.[45]

Long before Jackson won the presidency in 1829, then, a movement to break the sovereignty of tribal nations by allotting land to individual Native Southerners in the South or relocating Native communities west of the Mississippi River gathered momentum. And it was not only the expansion of slavery that fueled this shift in Indian policy. A growing American nationalism began sweeping through American popular and political culture. American nationalism, or the belief that the United States was exceptional among nations, shaped white American perceptions of Native Southerners. The secretary of war, John C. Calhoun, gave voice to such sentiments in 1818. Calhoun, a South Carolinian, declared of Native Southerners that "the neighboring tribes are becoming daily less warlike, and more helpless and dependent on us. . . . They have in great measure ceased to be an object of terror, and have become that of commiseration." According to Calhoun, a "vigilant administration" using a "combination of force and persuasion" would bring them within the "pale of civilization." If necessary, and given their enfeebled condition, Calhoun felt that it would take little to remove these tribes and segregate them on lands far from the vital centers of American civilization.[46]

The steady shift away from a federal Indian policy that emphasized expansion with honor to removal was driven by a number of powerful socioeconomic and political forces in early nineteenth-century America. For millions of white southerners, removal presented a solution to the problem of much needed arable land for an expansive, and increasingly profitable, slave economy. The Louisiana Purchase of 1803 opened not only new frontiers of opportunity for white settlers but also offered the possibility of carving out a small area of the Trans-Mississippi West on which to confine American Indians. President James Monroe (1817–1825) responded to these shifts in public sentiment. Monroe openly supported the acquisition of natural resources owned by Native people, and championed Indian removal by 1825.[47]

Through treaties with the United States government, Native Southerners lost hundreds-of-thousands of acres of land between 1789 and 1829. As Thomas Jefferson's correspondence reminds us, efforts to acquire Native lands were underway long before either Monroe or Jackson was elected to the presidency. For example, in the two decades after the Louisiana Purchase in 1803, Creek chiefs signed six treaties that saw their land holdings dramatically reduced. The Red Stick War, which ultimately led to a massive loss of Creek territory, reminded Creek leaders of the importance of centralized government if they hoped to speak with one persuasive voice against land cessions and removal.

Despite this, local political concerns and individual ambition stymied a coherent Creek response to the growing removal crisis. On February 12, 1825, for instance, the Coweta headman William McIntosh signed the Treaty of Indian Springs. This treaty opened the removal era for the Creeks. In return for a $200,000 payment and land in the newly created Indian Territory, located in what is today eastern Oklahoma, McIntosh ceded lands communally owned by the Lower Creeks in Georgia. The Treaty of Indian Springs was later nullified and a new treaty signed by a Creek delegation that included the Upper Creek chief and slave owner Opothle Yoholo. The Second Treaty of Washington (1826) therefore led to the removal of thousands of Creeks from Georgia with the federal government agreeing to pay $33.33 per person to defray the cost of emigration to the west.[48] For McIntosh, the damage to his reputation among fellow Creeks was beyond repair. On a crisp April evening, Creek law officers—known as "lawmenders"—"duly executed" McIntosh for his role in ceding communal lands.[49]

McIntosh would not be the last Indigenous leader executed by his own people for selling tribal land. As the pressure from state and federal officials to disregard Native assertions of sovereignty and to remove Indigenous communities to free up land for settlements and plantations intensified, chiefs encountered growing pressures. Those pressures were exacerbated in 1829 when the discovery of gold in the Georgia hills sparked the United States' first gold rush. And when President John Quincy Adams (1825–1829) did not immediately accede to white demands for the removal of Native Southerners from Georgia, the stage was set for Andrew Jackson and his anti-Indian policies.[50]

Jackson won the presidency at the end of 1829, sweeping every region of the country except New England. Jackson, a Tennessee slave owner who billed himself a champion of the common man, promptly set to work on Indian removal. On December 8, 1829, Jackson delivered a speech that framed removal as a humanitarian policy. Jackson declared, "This emigration should be voluntary, for it would be as cruel as unjust to compel the aborigines to abandon the graves of their fathers, and seek a home in a distant land." Native people should trust the federal government, Jackson insisted, because "our conduct toward these people" would reflect on "our national character."[51]

Jackson's "grammar of good intentions" strove to mollify opposition from northern lawmakers—led by New Jersey's Theodore Frelinghuysen—who opposed removal while at the same time trying to satisfy southern demands for Indian removal.[52] As the rhetoric of states' rights intensified—coalescing around the issue of racial slavery—Jackson, who'd supported the idea of Indian removal as early as the War of 1812, settled on an Indian policy that reflected his sympathies for the white South.[53]

Southern lawmakers eagerly embraced Jackson's removal policy and increased their calls for the removal of Native Southerners in overtly racist ways. Focusing on Cherokee removal, the proponents of removal insisted that the racial qualities and lifestyle choices of Native Southerners set them at odds with white civilization. Picking up on this idea, Thomas McKenney, the federal government's superintendent of Indian affairs, framed removal as a policy in the best interests of American Indians. McKenney maintained that if the Indians did not relocate to the West, "the extermination of the race" was almost guaranteed.[54] Therefore, "the welfare of the Indians, and the prosperity and happiness of their race" demanded removal.[55]

The racial prejudices of southern lawmakers also took on much harsher tones during the 1820s and 1830s. For example, Georgia senator John Forsyth expressed the views of his constituents when he declared that the Cherokees "were a race not admitted to be equal to the rest of the community."[56]

As Congressional debates about the Indian removal bill gripped the public consciousness in 1829 and 1830, President Jackson remained acutely aware that even if the bill passed through Congress he could not use force to compel Native people to relocate. Section 7 of the bill prohibited the federal government from using force to remove Native nations, stating that "nothing in this act contained shall be construed as authorizing or directing the violation of any existing treaty between the United States and any of the Indian tribes."[57] Lawmakers—particularly southern lawmakers—may have spoken about Indian removal as if Native sovereignty was of little concern, but the law being discussed suggested that the sovereignty of the Indigenous nations of the Native South was real and valid.

Jackson administration officials wasted few opportunities highlighting the voluntary nature of what became the Indian Removal Act. Secretary of War John Henry Eaton assured skeptical lawmakers that "nothing of a compulsory nature to effect the removal of this unfortunate race of people has ever been thought of by the President, despite assertions to the contrary."[58]

Following the passage of the Indian Removal Act in 1830, federal agents traveled to the Native South with the task of convincing chiefs and headmen to sign removal treaties and to emigrate west. True to the "grammar of good intentions," federal agents insisted that removal to the Trans-Mississippi West would provide Native Southerners with refuge from prejudice back East. While many federal and state lawmakers longed for the dissolution of tribal sovereignty, some chiefs came to believe that a life in diaspora was preferable to persecution in the Southeast if it meant preserving some sense of sovereignty and communal identity.

Such motives inspired Creek chiefs to open negotiations with the federal government. In March 1832, chiefs from the Upper and Lower Creeks met with secretary of war Lewis Cass to sign the Treaty of Cusseta. The treaty ceded 5.2 million acres of land to Alabama. Of that land, the federal government promised to survey a little over 2.1 million acres for the allotment of land to Creeks on an individual basis. The treaty also provided Creeks with lands in the Trans-Mississippi West and made provision for an annuity of $210,000 over twenty years.[59]

The Treaty of Cusseta was technically not a removal treaty. In practice, however, it displaced 14,609 Alabama Creeks, undermined Creek sovereignty, and eventually sparked the Second Creek War in 1836.[60] In the immediate aftermath of the treaty's signing, whites flooded into Creek Country and speculators acquired assets owned by Creeks. For the Creeks, widespread impoverishment and territorial displacement ensued. In the white South, by contrast, the 1830s were flush times; the "cotton kingdom" expanded westward and Creek land became prime real estate.[61] The Creeks therefore found themselves "without friends and surrounded by enemies." Federal government promises of protection rang hollow at this time as land speculators and intruders made "stealing . . . the order of the day."[62]

◇◇◇◇◇◇◇◇◇◇◇◇◇◇◇◇◇◇◇◇◇◇◇◇

The Creeks were not the first Native Southerners to lose their ancient homelands and suffer greatly on the forced relocation to Indian Territory.[63] The Choctaws faced political pressure for their removal throughout the 1820s as their leaders worked to remake Choctaw government. As noted above, the Choctaws passed written laws and brought to life a national government in 1826. These changes, however, underlined factional disagreements within the Choctaw Nation. On one side of this emerging political divide were the supporters of Nittucachee and the elderly war chief Mushulatubbee. Nittucachee and Mushulatubbee opposed the centralized vision of Choctaw sovereignty supported by Choctaws such as David Folsom and Greenwood LeFlore, the later styling himself the "chief of the Choctaw Nation." Despite their political differences, all of these men owned slaves and were integrated into broader market economies; but LeFlore's and Folsom's vision for bringing previously autonomous regions together under a national council modeled on the United States did not sit well with their Choctaw opponents.[64]

The factionalism associated with Choctaw political identities during the 1820s and early 1830s had the potential to turn violent very quickly. In 1830, shortly after Mushulatubbee referred to LeFlore and his supporters as "yanke Coalitionists," Mushulatubbee supporter Peter Pitchlynn arranged to have LeFlore assassinated.[65] Given the political assassinations that marred

Portrait of Choctaw leader Peter Pitchlynn. *Library of Congress, Prints and Photographs Division, Washington, D.C.*

Creek, and, ultimately, Cherokee politics, Pitchlynn's threat was by no means an idle one. In spite of the tense political atmosphere, moderate political reforms did, as noted above, occur.[66]

Choctaw leaders such as LeFlore, Nittucachee, and Mushulatubbee ultimately succumbed to the diplomatic pressure of the U.S. government and agreed to sign a removal treaty. The Treaty of Dancing Rabbit Creek was proclaimed in February 1831. It followed a failed attempt to remove the Choctaws in 1818–1819, and a subsequent effort at removal with the Treaty of Doak's Stand in 1820 (which saw half the Choctaw homeland ceded to the United States). The Treaty of Dancing Rabbit Creek abrogated all previous agreements between the United States and the Choctaws. The treaty ceded Choctaw lands to the United States and called for the removal of all Choctaws from their remaining ancestral lands. Over the following years, the Choctaws experienced the first large-scale relocation to Indian Territory, with close to twenty thousand Choctaws making the melancholy journey to lands reserved for them in Indian Territory.[67]

These unwilling Choctaw migrants joined a small number of fellow Choctaws, Creeks, and Cherokees who had already migrated west. However, not all Choctaws left their homelands. Approximately 1,600 Choctaws remained in the Southeast, including the now hugely unpopular LeFlore.[68] In the coming decades, Mississippi Choctaws and their kin in the Trans-Mississippi West tried to put old divisions behind them and worked to rebuild communities beyond the political gaze of federal and state government officials.

A similar set of challenges faced the Choctaws' northern neighbors, the Chickasaws. At the beginning of the nineteenth century, local *iksas*, or kin groups, continued to determine political representation among the Chickasaws. Their leaders, such as the *minko*, or chief, Ishtehotopa, and the head warrior, Tishomingo, rose to their positions of authority through a combination of heredity and accomplishment.[69]

The Chickasaws' continued adherence to regional political and kinship systems reveals a deep commitment to traditional understandings of communal identity. However, Chickasaw culture and politics was by no means static; Chickasaws did innovate in an effort to meet the challenges of the removal era. Mixed-race families, such as the Colbert family, played an active role in facilitating Chickasaw political innovation.

The Colberts enjoyed increasing economic and political influence during the early nineteenth century. In 1812, Levi Colbert became counselor to Minko Chehopistee, a position that launched Colbert into greater political prominence in the 1820s. Colbert used his growing political status to lead treaty negotiations with the federal government, negotiations that resulted in land cessions in 1816 and 1818. In 1828, the Chickasaw selected Levi Colbert to lead an exploration party into the Trans-Mississippi West to survey sites for a possible Chickasaw relocation.[70]

Despite federal officials rejecting Colbert's suggestion to relocate Chickasaw communities to Caddo and Osage lands, the federal government increased removal pressure on the Chickasaws. This pressure eventually got the better of the aging Colbert. In 1830, he placed his signature on the Franklin Treaty and ceded yet more land to the United States. Further land cessions came in the ensuing years. In 1834, Chickasaw leaders signed

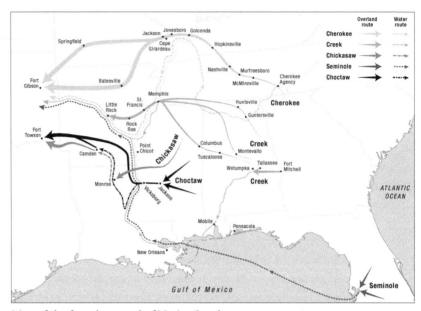

Map of the forced removal of Native Southerners. *Erin Greb Cartography.*

the Treaty of Washington. The 1834 treaty constituted a supplement to the 1832 Treaty of Pontotoc. Together, these treaties set out the terms for the sale of Chickasaw lands and made provision for the protection of Chickasaws who relocated to Indian Territory. The 1834 treaty, however, failed to set out where in Indian Territory Chickasaw communities would resettle.[71]

Chickasaw dispossession and removal was therefore a gradual process. Although small parties of Chickasaws began making the dreaded trek west during the 1830s, the vast majority of Chickasaw people did not relocate to Indian Territory until 1837. In that year, Chickasaw and Choctaw leaders signed the Treaty of Doaksville. The treaty gave the Chickasaws the right to settle in the western part of the Choctaw lands in southeast Indian Territory. Instead of purchasing the land, the Chickasaw leaders agreed to lease the Choctaw tract for $530,000. Chickasaws also received political representation in the Choctaw Council, something they held until 1856 when Chickasaw leaders established their own constitution and settled on lands separate from the Choctaws in Indian Territory.[72]

In 1837, approximately four thousand Chickasaws were coerced into making the emotionally and physically traumatic journey to Indian Territory. The "Great Removal," as Chickasaws referred to their relocation, began in

Memphis and involved a riverboat journey west. The journey was fraught, with scores dying due to disease, suffering from malnutrition, and on one tragic occasion three hundred Chickasaws drowned after their boat, the *Monmouth*, sank.[73]

Not all Chickasaws joined the Choctaws in Indian Territory. At least 450 Chickasaws remained in the Southeast, and many more tried to find refuge in a desperate attempt to avoid removal.[74] Although Jackson administration officials insisted that removal was not intended to be coercive, federal forces routinely hunted down Chickasaws, just as state militias and federal troops tracked down Creeks, Cherokees, and Choctaws.[75]

◇◇◇◇◇◇◇◇◇◇◇◇◇◇◇◇◇◇◇◇◇◇◇◇◇

Native Southerners fought to preserve the sovereignty of their nations and to resist removal by crafting written laws and asserting the importance of their national governments. However, the most protracted attempt to resist removal was mounted by the Cherokee Nation.

The Cherokees focused their legal and diplomatic energies on resisting removal during the 1820s and 1830s. The implementation of centralized structures of government, written laws, and a detailed understanding of the American legal system helped Cherokees to both rebuild their communities after the Revolutionary War and sustain their opposition to the forces of removal in the early nineteenth century.[76]

Despite all of the political changes adopted by the Cherokees, a series of removal crises during the first two decades of the nineteenth century and the signing of nine treaties with the United States squeezed Cherokee landholdings and saw some Cherokees migrate and resettle on lands beyond the western banks of the Mississippi River. In June 1819, for example, the Cherokee leader Charles Hicks reported to the Cherokee agent in Tennessee that twenty-two "families of Cherokee emigrants" received "boats and provisions [from the federal government] to proceed to Arkansas river by water [,] sending the stocks of horses by land."[77] Many of these Cherokee migrants desperately wanted to preserve what they understood to be a traditional way of life free from federal government interference and saw migration and resettlement as the best way to achieve that goal.[78]

Under the leadership of principal chief John Ross, the majority of Cherokees steeled themselves to resist removal. Cherokee leaders understood the arguments in favor of their removal, from the racially motivated claims that they would fall in the face of a superior civilization to the assertions from government officials that relocation would protect Cherokees from white aggression.[79] Cherokee leaders and their white supporters had an answer to these claims. As one opponent of Cherokee removal wrote, "A desire has been professed for the removal of the Indians, founded on an apprehension, that they may suffer intolerable aggressions from the neighboring whites. But it is for them to say when the evil, of being surrounded by Christian white men, shall be greater than those which they may expect, among heathen savages, and the wild beasts of the wilderness."[80]

Cherokees might have been united in their resistance to removal during the 1820s and early 1830s, but they did not agree on strategy. Factions emerged, and disagreements grew increasingly fraught during the latter part of the 1820s as mixed-race, wealthy, slave-owning elites tightened their grip on political power. For all the divisions, though, the Cherokee National Council agreed to make the ceding of Cherokee land a capital offense. Such a law constituted a rearticulation of the Cherokee principle of communal property ownership. No individual had a right to sell what belonged to the nation. To reinforce the collective determination of Cherokees to resist removal, the editors of the *Cherokee Phoenix* worked to unite Cherokees by outlining the logic for opposing removal and reasons to celebrate the accomplishments of the nation. Leading Cherokee intellectuals such as Elijah Hicks and Elias Boudinot, the editor of the *Phoenix,* highlighted the social, economic, and cultural accomplishments of Cherokee people.[81]

In the pages of the *Phoenix* in 1828, Boudinot made it clear that the Cherokees had a sovereign right to their southeastern homeland. He editorialized that "all mankind have an equal right to the things that have not yet fallen into the possession of anyone: and these things belong to the first possessor." Applying this Western conception of land rights to the early-nineteenth-century Cherokees, Boudinot concluded that "the Cherokees were settled in towns over this territory, before a white man ever appeared on these shores, and when he did appear and made discovery, he only discovered the Cherokees in peaceable possession of a country, given them by the Almighty."[82] The Cherokees, to use nineteenth-century legal jargon, possessed "preemptive rights."[83]

Despite publicizing Cherokee economic and political accomplishments, the implementation of written laws to police intruders into the Cherokee Nation, and laying out the legal rationale for Cherokee sovereignty, momentum for removal proved relentless. The discovery of gold in Georgia in 1829 and the state of Georgia's constant agitation for the suspension of Cherokee sovereignty reinforced the settler colonial drive to eliminate the Cherokees from the Southeast. In the early months of 1830, the state of Georgia successfully tested its sovereignty over the Cherokee Nation when it convicted a Cherokee man named Tassel for murdering a fellow Cherokee. Tassel's eventual hanging, coupled with the 1830 passage of the Indian Removal Act, placed the Cherokee Nation on a legal collision course with both the state of Georgia and the federal government.[84]

Principal chief John Ross led the Cherokee defense of their national sovereignty. However, even Ross recognized the magnitude of what awaited the Cherokees. He confided to a colleague that "we are fated to be wretched," not because the Cherokees were incapable of improving or governing their own affairs, but because "of the mountains of prejudice entertained against us by the Anglo Americans."[85]

The "mountains of prejudice" that Ross perceived may have rationalized the push for Cherokee removal but it also reinforced the commitment of the Cherokee Nation to defend its national sovereignty following the passage of the Indian Removal Act.[86] The Cherokee homeland, its sacred places, ancient fires, and the communities that gave Cherokee life its meaning were all under assault like never before. As Cherokees looked on in horror as other Native Southerners reluctantly signed treaties that led to their forced relocation, the Cherokee Nation launched a coordinated legal attack on the logic of removal.[87]

That assault began when the Cherokee Nation hired the prominent lawyer William Wirt to challenge the Tassel conviction. Wirt, a former U.S. attorney general, argued before the U.S. Supreme Court in *Cherokee Nation v. Georgia* (1831) that the Cherokee Nation's sovereignty and treaties with the United States meant that the state of Georgia had no legal authority over the Cherokee Nation. The Supreme Court's chief justice, John Marshall, was sympathetic to the case presented on behalf of the Cherokee Nation. However, he ruled that the Cherokee Nation had no right to sue the state of Georgia, declaring instead that it constituted a "domestic dependent nation."[88]

In the immediate aftermath of the Supreme Court's decision, the state of Georgia continued to make life as miserable as possible for the Cherokees. Georgia militiamen and frontiersmen used violence to intimidate Cherokee communities. Then, in 1832, Georgia law enforcement officers arrested the missionary Samuel Worcester while he resided in the Cherokee Nation. A Georgia court tried Worcester and sentenced him to five years of hard labor. Worcester and a fellow missionary had resided in the Cherokee Nation where they worked to assist antiremoval efforts. Their support for the Cherokees proved unwavering, even refusing to swear an oath of loyalty to Georgia when pressed by state officials.

Then, in an even more dramatic turn, Worcester's case made its way to the U.S. Supreme Court. In *Worcester v. Georgia,* Chief Justice Marshall ruled in 1832 that the Cherokees had constituted a sovereign nation at the time of the United States' founding. The Cherokee Nation's treaties with the United States meant the federal government was obliged to recognize Cherokee sovereignty, making the state of Georgia's arrest of Worcester on Cherokee land an explicitly unconstitutional act.[89]

Cherokee leaders celebrated the *Worcester* decision as a victory for the sovereignty of their nation. Their celebrations, however, proved short-lived. President Jackson scoffed at Chief Justice Marshall's decision, and the state of Georgia moved ahead with efforts to survey Cherokee lands and divvy them up among settlers by means of a land lottery. Over the coming years, the authoritarian nature of American democracy in relation to American Indians was on full display. State and federal officials either willingly broke, or simply disregarded, treaties and trade laws pertaining to the Cherokee Nation. Both state and federal officials engaged in fraud, corruption, and intimidation to compel Cherokee leaders to accept removal. As President Jackson warned the Cherokees in April 1835, "You cannot remain where you now are. Circumstances that cannot be controlled, and which are beyond the reach of human laws, render it impossible that you can flourish in the midst of a civilized community. . . . Deceive yourselves no longer. . . . Shut your ears to bad counsels."[90]

Jackson's ominous words had their desired effect. That summer, the Reverend John F. Schermerhorn—whom Ross called Skaynooyaunah, or "The Devil's Horn"—worked to persuade Cherokee leaders of the dire nature of their predicament. Schermerhorn urged removal and resettlement in Indian Territory.[91] With the Choctaws, Chickasaws, Creeks, and thousands of other Native peoples having already been pressed to relocate, a small group of Cherokee leaders decided the time had come to agree to a removal treaty with the federal government. In December 1835, members of the Treaty Party met at the Cherokee town of New Echota to sign what became known as the New Echota Treaty. Among the Cherokee signatories to that treaty were Major Ridge, John Ridge, and Elias Boudinot. These men were among the most prominent members of the Treaty Party, a party comprised overwhelmingly of wealthy slave-owning Cherokees. Principal chief John Ross denounced the Treaty Party's decision to sign the Treaty of New Echota, referring to it as unrepresentative of the Cherokee peoples' will. Ross was not alone in harboring such sentiments. Cherokees eventually executed Major Ridge, his son John Ridge, and Elias Boudinot for ceding communal lands without consulting and gaining the consent of the majority of the Cherokees.[92]

The Ross Party continued to fight removal over the coming years. These efforts failed, culminating in the forced emigration of between twelve and sixteen thousand Cherokees in 1838 and 1839. Several thousand, including principal chief Ross's wife, died en route to Indian Territory. The overland and river routes taken by the Cherokees became embedded in the popular consciousness of Cherokee people. The trauma of Cherokees being ripped from their homes caused emotional scars that continue to shape Cherokee historical consciousness into the present.[93]

For Native Southerners, the era of removal was characterized by major internal political changes, the abuse of power on the part of state and federal governments, and violence. This proved as true for the Seminoles as it did for the Cherokees. Through two Seminole Wars, between 1817–1818 and 1835–1842, and a third war between 1855 and 1858 that's referred to as the Billy Bowlegs War, Seminoles fought to retain their land. And yet despite armed resistance to relocation, Seminoles were far from united on how to approach removal.[94]

Two important treaties help to frame the era of removal for the Seminoles. The first, the Treaty of Moultrie Creek (1823), gave Seminoles brief respite from removal pressures by setting out reservation lands for them in central Florida. But this respite proved short-lived. In 1832 the Treaty of Payne's Landing ceded large swaths of Seminole lands to the United States.[95]

As in the Cherokee Nation after the Treaty of New Echota, political violence followed the Treaty of Moultrie Creek. Most Seminoles denounced the treaty, and warriors loyal to Osceola assassinated Charley Emathla, a prominent Seminole signatory to the Moultrie Creek treaty. Emathla's death sparked the Second Seminole War, a war that proved costly to the

United States. Over the coming years, the federal Indian agent to the Seminoles was murdered and the United States military lost over 1,500 men in fighting against Seminole warriors. The Seminoles' armed resistance lasted until 1842. For the United States, the Second Seminole War was the most expensive war it fought until the American Civil War. Over forty thousand American troops saw action, with the war costing the United States over $30 million dollars. At its conclusion, however, federal officials estimated that they'd rounded up all but five hundred Seminoles and relocated them to Indian Territory.[96]

◇◇◇◇◇◇◇◇◇◇◇◇◇◇◇◇◇◇◇◇◇◇◇◇

The Second Seminole War highlighted the U.S. government's commitment to eliminating Native American people from the eastern half of the republic. Such a commitment was matched only by the graft and corruption of private and public sector actors as American citizens exploited the forced removal of Native Southerners for their own financial and territorial gain. Tales of fraud thus followed Native Southerners as they made their unwelcome march toward the setting sun and attempted to rebuild communities that resembled those they'd been forced to leave behind.[97]

For Native Southerners who avoided removal, exposure to fraudulent behavior became a fact of life. In Georgia, unscrupulous land speculators defrauded Creeks out of lands once communally owned.[98] In Mississippi, the corrosiveness of capitalism and land speculation combined in an unholy alliance between the private and public sector. During the 1830s the value of Choctaw and Chickasaw lands skyrocketed as state lawmakers passed legislation approving road construction from Martin's Bluff to the Tombigbee River.[99] On the bones of Choctaw and Chickasaw ancestors, American settler societies continued to rise.

Native Southerners and their allies, however, did not submit meekly to the economic and political corruption of the removal and postremoval eras. Instead, they fought, enabling some Choctaws to remain in the Southeast. For example, Choctaws and their legal representatives invoked Article 14 of the Treaty of Dancing Rabbit Creek in a bid to claim individual allotments on lands that the state of Mississippi asserted sovereignty over. A little over 1,400 heads of household claimed allotments, of which only a fraction were granted. Indeed, the commitment to removing Choctaws from Mississippi continued throughout the 1840s (federal legislation in 1842 called for the removal of the remaining Choctaw population), and eventually into the Civil War and Jim Crow eras.[100]

Choctaw historian Clara Sue Kidwell argues that the "issue of land and identity is a very important one for the Choctaw."[101] This remains true for Choctaws today. This is despite the fact that in the decades between the end of the removal era and the allotment era of the late nineteenth and early twentieth centuries, the federal government managed to identify and transport 290 Choctaws from Mississippi and Louisiana to Indian Territory in 1903. In 1907 an even larger relocation occurred with 1,462 Choctaws relocated to the Trans-Mississippi West by the federal government. According to the commissioner of Indian affairs, 1,072 Choctaws remained east of the Mississippi to preserve what Kidwell identifies in her analysis as the important link between land and Choctaw identity.[102]

Native Southerners from formerly large and small polities confronted challenges similar to those of the Choctaws. Despite the legal defense of their sovereignty in the 1830s, this, as we've seen, proved the case for the Cherokees. Whole communities of Cherokees were rounded up and placed into concentration camps to await transportation to Indian Territory. Some Cherokees, such as Tsali, a former Chickamauga warrior, attempted to resist the U.S. military's relocation of Cherokee communities. Other Cherokees managed to evade the removal process and made homes for themselves and their families in Virginia, Georgia, Tennessee, Alabama, and other parts of the eastern United States.[103] Of approximately one thousand Cherokees who remained in the Southeast immediately after removal, the majority lived in the mountains of North Carolina. These Cherokees relied heavily on William H. Thomas, the attorney for the North Carolina Cherokees. With Thomas's legal assistance, this small Cherokee population managed to acquire title to lands in North Carolina. These land purchases became the basis for what is today the core of the Eastern Band of Cherokees Reservation in North Carolina.[104]

Like the Cherokees in North Carolina, several hundred Creek Indians avoided federal government efforts to coerce them into migrating to Indian Territory. Coerced removal certainly had some devastating consequences for Creek kinship bonds and community cohesion. One scholar estimates that as many as four thousand Creek people died—either en route to Indian Territory or within a year of arriving in the West—as a result of removal.[105] In Alabama, however, a small number of Creeks avoided removal and worked to keep their families together. The "eastern Creeks," as social scientists referred to them in the early twentieth century, remained in the Southeast despite their population dipping to as low as 160 (including slaves) during the 1840s. The Alabama Creeks claimed patents to lands under the first article of the Fort Jackson Treaty (1814). Article 1 outlined land provisions for Creeks and their descendants who allied with the United States during the Red Stick War. These land grants remained in Creek hands through removal, the American Civil War, and Jim Crow segregation. Today they are the territorial foundation for the Poarch Band of Creek Indians.[106]

Native Southerners did not disappear after removal.[107] While it's true that many who remained in the South kept a low profile through the Jim Crow era and beyond, Native Southerners were not eliminated. But through the postremoval decades, the Native Southerners who remained in the southeastern United States quietly forged new lives for themselves and rearticulated what it meant to be a Choctaw or Creek, Cherokee, Catawba, Yamasee, or many other Indigenous identities that continue to call the southeastern portion of North America home. Despite Jim Crow laws that attempted to sever Native Southerners from their lands, inhibit access to education, and imposed bureaucratic forms of genocide that included legal attempts to redefine Native Southerners as black or "colored" (and thus define indigeneity out of existence), Native Southerners held on to their traditions, nurtured family bonds, and to this day remain in the South.[108]

◇◇◇◇◇◇◇◇◇◇◇◇◇◇◇◇◇◇◇◇◇◇◇◇

Native Southerners found themselves caught in the crosshairs of an aggressively expansive settler colonial republic during the early nineteenth century. When the nineteenth century opened, few could have anticipated just how destructive their engagement with state and federal governments would become during the 1820s and 1830s. As white Americans moved assertively to build a continental empire, the sovereignty of the Native South was abused, degraded, and ignored by federal and state officials.

In the 1840s and beyond, Native Southerners worked to rebuild their lives. Most did so in diaspora, as tens of thousands attempted to reconnect the frayed threads of kinship and reestablish institutions of law and government, culture and education that had once bound Indigenous communities together in the Southeast. Their task in diaspora wasn't going to be easy; the expanding frontiers of American settlement quickly caught up with them and ultimately brought a bloody civil war between North and South to Native land in Indian Territory.

For those Native Southerners who evaded removal and remained in the Southeast, a precious connection to sacred sites and what they understood as traditional culture enabled people to renew their Native identities. Renewing these connections during the 1840s and beyond proved a challenge in a region dominated by the slave economy and defined by white supremacy. It was also challenging because the federal government made periodic attempts to remove what lawmakers referred to as the "remnant" populations of both large and small tribes—such as the Cherokees, Seminoles, Tunicas, and Waccamaws—in the latter half of the nineteenth century and throughout the twentieth.

EPILOGUE

This book covers a vast chronology in which we've seen Native Southerners crafting many identities and telling both old and new stories about themselves and their communities. Time and place helped to shape Native identities, but at no time was the Native South a cultural or political monolith. Such a place would be dreary and rather uninteresting. Instead, the history covered in this book tells the stories of Native Southerners who actively shaped and reshaped their worlds. This remains true today just as it did a century ago, or two centuries ago, or five centuries ago. In other words, Native identities are dynamic, innovative, and responsive to the needs of community members. Native Southerners may point to a common core of values, cultural practices, or set of stories, but their identities are alive with meaning because they make them so.

Lynette Allston, the chief of the Nottoway Tribe of Virginia, reflected on the Native South's cultural richness and diversity of its people when I spoke to her by phone.[1] Allston is all too aware of the complex web of relationships that her Nottoway ancestors negotiated throughout the Native South and beyond. She's also conscious of the history of settler colonial practices and structures of power that dispossessed the Nottoway people of so much of their ancestral homelands. History is therefore important to Allston, but it's not the only factor that gives her Nottoway identity meaning.

Food also helps Allston tell the story of her identity and feelings of connectivity with her Nottoway ancestors. Growing up in southern Virginia, Allston recalls the cooperative farming and bartering practices that both sustained Nottoway people and buttressed a tight-knit community. Nottoway people tried to live quiet lives throughout the twentieth century, out of the racial gaze of segregationist Virginia authorities. In spite of, or perhaps because of, institutional and popular racism in Virginia, Nottoways maintained a keen sense of their collective identity through family and community cohesiveness.

Food—whether in the form of its cooperative farming or when consumed at meals—brings families together to reinforce that sense of community. Meals with family members and friends were (and remain) more than opportunities to nourish one's body; they're social rituals that deepen family and community bonds. Allston remembers childhood meals in this light; she also recalls the cooking practices of her mother and grandmother and how her family ate meals prepared "from really old recipes." Food provided Nottoways like Allston with nourishment, but it also offered a tangible connection to the knowledge and traditions of her forebears.

Beverly Payne, a member of the Occaneechi Band of the Saponi Nation located in Alamance County, North Carolina, shared a similar set of stories with me. For Payne, identity is multifaceted. Some in her tribe feel that church membership is vital to community identity. For others it's recovering Occaneechi traditions. Payne knows that "a lot of traditions are lost," but she works hard to keep those traditions alive. "Some of us," Payne insists, "try to speak the language," and in doing so provide a linguistic connection to the traditions of her Occaneechi ancestors.[2]

Payne is all too aware of the impact that European and American colonialism had, and continues to have, on how Native Southerners understand their identities. Kelly Fayard, a member of the Poarch Band of Creek Indians, also recognizes the historical dimensions of identity formation and reformation among Native Southerners.[3] The Poarch Creeks evaded removal in the early nineteenth century and today maintain a reservation about eight miles north of Atmore, Alabama. Fayard observes that the historical identity of the Poarch Band is complex. The ancestors of modern-day Poarch people worked, for example, as agents and interpreters for settler colonists and fought against the Red Stick Creeks at the Battle of Fort Mims.

Historically, Creeks formed vast trade networks and diplomatic alliances with outsiders. In fact, this was common throughout the Native South during the eighteenth and early nineteenth centuries. Today, however, knowledge of this history leads to some good-natured ribbing from other Native people who refer to the Poarch Creeks as "collaborators."

Humor, though, is a form of storytelling that sometimes has an edge to it that forces people to reflect on the broader realities of their existence. For

Poarch Creeks, that means being highly conscious of how outsiders perceive them. In Alabama, members of the Poarch community recognize the stereotypes—"Indians don't pay taxes," or "Indians want federal recognition so they can build casinos." These stereotypes, Fayard reminds me, had political implications in 2016 as gubernatorial candidates fought to win over Poarch voters and state legislators debated the efficacy of a statewide lottery. One opinion writer sarcastically suggested that the Poarch Band has so much tax-free money "from three casinos in the gambling meccas of Atmore, Wetumpka and Montgomery," that lawmakers should give Alabama back to the Poarch Creeks.[4]

Fayard notes that the Poarch Creeks work hard to dispel racial stereotypes. With a professional-looking website, the Poarch Band emphasizes that they are good neighbors who pose no political challenge to the wider Alabama community.[5] As Fayard puts it, "We want everyone to know the Poarch story but we also want to have the opportunity to foster economic opportunity."

Talk to Native Southerners today, and the desire to see their communities have economic opportunities and flourish in twenty-first-century society emerges as a common theme. But to access these opportunities means navigating some persistent racial stereotypes. Harold "Buster" Hatcher, the chief of the Waccamaw Indians in North Carolina, made this point when I spoke with him. "The only people who have to be recognized," Hatcher insists, "are Indians." Chief Hatcher would know; he's been at the forefront of Waccamaw politics for several decades and worked on federal recognition applications on behalf of the tribe.[6]

Hatcher, a Vietnam veteran and recipient of the Purple Heart, knows what it is to sacrifice. He's also felt the sting of southern racism, recalling how whites in the South routinely called Native Americans "brass niggers" during his childhood. Unsurprisingly, Hatcher expresses frustration toward the federal government's bureaucratization of Indigenous identity and the racial slights he's experienced during his lifetime. "We fight the wars of this country," Hatcher tells me, "but don't enjoy its privileges." Beverly Payne expressed similar sentiments when I spoke with her. Of her Indigenous identity she says, "I'm proud," but observes that "the Constitution wasn't written for anybody but white people."

◇◇◇◇◇◇◇◇◇◇◇◇◇◇◇◇◇◇◇◇◇◇◇◇◇

These are just some of conversations that I've been fortunate to have with Native Southerners in recent years. They reflect the different ways in which

Native Southerners form individual and collective identities in the twenty-first century. What they have in common, however, is a deep historical awareness of how European and American settler societies impacted, and continue to impact, their lives. In this way, the stories that Native Southerners tell about their identities are formed in opposition to settler colonialism.

This oppositional component of Native identity formation is historically logical and politically necessary. Through the American Civil War, Jim Crow segregation, Cold War America, and federal government and private campaigns of terror and disruption, Native communities throughout the United States have needed to remain vigilant if they hope to keep the eliminationists and exploitative forces of colonialism at bay.[7]

And yet Native Southerners are not "extinct" or confined solely to reservations. Indigenous people who can chart their identities back to Lumbees, Saponis, Tuscaroras, Nottoways, Catawbas, Waccamaws, Cherokees, Choctaws, Chickasaws, Creeks, Seminoles, Caddos, Biloxis, Yamasees, and many others live to retain a connection to the lands and worldviews of their ancestors. Settler colonialism has circumscribed the physical connection to these ancestral homelands, stories, and cultural traditions, but the emotional bonds remain. Indeed, stories about Native ghosts haunting the settler colonial landscape of the American South persist to this day. Such stories create a narrative connection to the trauma caused by coerced removal in the early nineteenth century, provide Native Southerners with a spiritual link to their ancestors, and serve to remind non-Indigenous Americans that they live and work on lands taken from Indigenous people.[8]

If time has tested the durability of Native storytelling, rituals, and ceremonies, space has also impacted how Native Southerners and their descendants define their identities. As we've seen, by the time Europeans arrived in North America, Native Southerners had already developed complex social, cultural, and religious identities that reflected their particular histories of migration, resettlement patterns, and attachment to place. Historical events such as colonial invasion and warfare, disease epidemics, the coerced migrations of the early nineteenth century, and the assimilationist policies that followed during the nineteenth and twentieth centuries all tested the durability of Native identities.

For the vast majority of early nineteenth-century Native Southerners, a life in diaspora was forced upon them by a violent and aggressively expansionist

American republic. "Diaspora" is not a term usually associated with Native American history. Instead, ethnohistorians tend to emphasize the importance of land and a sense of place in Native identity formations. But if the history of the Native South (and Native Southerners) teaches us anything, it is that if we're to fully understand the worldviews of Native Southerners, their politics and evolving traditions, families and communities, to say nothing of the violence that so often characterized American settler colonialism and the Trail of Tears, then coming to terms with diasporic identities will need to remain part of future research and teaching. This will ensure that we do justice to the totality of the historical experiences of Native Southerners.[9]

The concept of diaspora isn't new.[10] It's a concept more commonly linked to people of Jewish or African descent whose forebears experienced a traumatic—usually violent—separation from their homelands. Over decades and centuries, the descendants of these unwilling migrants strive to reproduce their social, cultural, and religious identities in lands previously foreign to them. In essence, diasporic peoples forge new homes for themselves while also striving to reconnect (at least emotionally) with their ancestral homelands by nurturing stories about a long-lost spiritual home, culture, or worldview. This was a conceptualization of identity that Lynette Allston put to me. Given the constant pressures of settler colonialism, Native Southerners often found their communities forced into migrations they'd never wanted to take. With heavy hearts, they undertook these migrations and formed what Allston refers to as "isolate communities." In other words, Native Southerners like Allston's Nottoway ancestors not only survived but they strove to maintain a sense of community that American settler colonialism tried to destroy.

Diasporic people therefore develop a multisited sense of home that is both physical and emotional in nature. They forge ahead with the creation of a renewed sense of belonging in a space their ancestors unwillingly came to, and work to deepen (if only historically and psychologically) the cultural and kinship traditions with an ancestral home that over generations becomes physically foreign. In the decades that have elapsed since the coerced removals of the 1820s and 1830s and allotment and termination policies at the end of the nineteenth and early twentieth centuries, Native Southerners forced into exile from their ancestral homelands have grappled with the reality of diaspora in the settler colonial world that surrounds them.

To begin to empathize with how Native Southerners began forming diasporic identities during the Trail of Tears and subsequent decades it's essential to understand the trauma associated with the act of removal. Removal was a series of events made possible by acts of state-sanctioned violence. In a world where most black people were enslaved (and subsequently segregated), and in which Indigenous people existed outside the body politic of the settler republic, Indian removals constituted acts in keeping with the white supremacist sympathies of the majority of its citizens and institutional structures at the core of the Republic's Enlightenment-era founding.[11]

For those Native Southerners removed to Indian Territory during the 1820s and 1830s, renewing cultural traditions and reconnecting kinship ties proved an immense challenge. Viewed in its totality, removal constituted a violent tear in the fabric of Native societies. Families and communities were separated, ancient knowledge lost, and the future uncertain. Stitching those families and communities, their worldviews, and their connections to ancestral homelands back together proves an ongoing and painful process.

The trauma of removal began in the Native South. In the chaos of the preremoval years, hunger, disease, and extreme levels of anxiety shrouded communities with uncertainty and fear. Among the Cherokees, for example, the seizure of property and the confinement of large numbers of people in forts as they awaited orders to leave for the West meant that physical and emotional deprivation was commonplace.[12] So profound was the suffering in these hastily constructed camps that outsiders felt compelled to comment on it. In 1837, the physician G. S. Townsend reported from Tennessee that "disease brought on by excessive fatigue and exposure from hunting" had become all too common among the Cherokees.[13]

Once that unwanted journey west began, emotional suffering stalked Native Southerners and their descendants. For some, the emotional darkness of removal amounted to an acute sense of spiritual loss as people mourned the separation from the lands and rivers that sustained them and their ancestors. These local ecosystems were alive with deep wells of meaning that enriched communal identities. The places of the Native South were teeming with physical and spiritual life; being removed from them constituted an emotional and physical wound of immense pain.

Forced removal also made death a very real physical possibility. U.S. military officers reported on the grim scenes of hunger, illness, and death. No one was immune. The young and old, men and women, all ran the gauntlet of illness and death on the forced march to Indian Territory. Malnutrition was the norm, while mumps, measles, and whooping cough were among the common killers.[14] The Cherokee leader Charles Hicks reflected on these hardships as he waited to cross the Mississippi River in January 1839. Hicks described the cold and ice that greeted the Cherokee emigrants. Despite the suffering already endured by his party, Hicks knew that "a great deal of hardship and exposure" remained as they journeyed to Indian Territory.[15]

Sickness, hunger, and death also followed African American slaves forced to make the trek to Indian Territory with their Native masters.[16] Some Native slave owners, however, sold their slaves before being forced to leave the South. For example, James Watson, a Georgia slave trader, purchased a number of slaves from Creek slave owners.[17] In other instances, Native slave owners used their wealth to arrange for the transportation of their slaves to Indian Territory. That's what Benjamin Marshall, a biracial Creek who owned hundreds of slaves, did in 1835. Marshall used his wealth and connections to arrange an emigration party of 511 people, including his slaves, to start the journey to Indian Territory from a ferry stop on the Tallapoosa River.[18]

Acknowledging the suffering of African Americans during the removal era does not diminish the experiences of Native Southerners. Native and African Americans endured great hardships and loss, and exploring the complex ways in which removal was experienced only adds to our understanding of this dark chapter in American history. That said, it remains true that for Native Southerners the unwanted migration west forced people to confront an uncertain future, an anxiety compounded by cultural understandings of the West as the "darkening lands," or a place of death.[19] Was it even possible to survive in such a place?

There existed no easy answer to that question during the 1830s and 1840s. When Native Southerners arrived in Indian Territory, most families had few resources with which to rebuild their lives.[20] Additionally, social and political institutions needed rebuilding, a task made all the more difficult by political factionalism and the need to adjust to new neighbors—such as the Quapaws, Osages, Kiowas, and Comanches.[21]

But rebuild Native Southerners did in Indian Territory. The Creek people rebuilt their economy, government, and sense of communal identity by dividing themselves into two main regions. One group comprised mainly of Lower Creeks. They recreated Creek plantations and small farms in the Arkansas River valley. Another group built communities along the Canadian River. The Canadian River communities came overwhelmingly from the old

Upper Creek region in the Southeast and followed charismatic leaders such as Opothle Yoholo and Tukabatchee. These two groups governed separately until 1840. Thereafter, Creek leaders worked to bring people together under a single constitution. These attempts to forge Creek national unity failed to bear fruit prior to the outbreak of the American Civil War in 1861, reflecting both the gulf between the two groups and the continued importance of regional political identities among Creek people.[22]

The Cherokees also struggled to bring people together under a single, unified government. Tensions between the Ross Party and Treaty Party carried over into Indian Territory, while Cherokee settlers who'd been in the West for a decade or longer—the so-called Old Settlers—resented the efforts of the Ross Party to undercut what they insisted were well-established laws and political structures. Violence and political assassinations punctuated life in Indian Territory for the Cherokees during the late 1830s and early 1840s. While old factional disputes reemerged during the American Civil War, Cherokees did manage to adopt a new constitution in 1839 and signed the Act of Union in 1840 that united the factions. With a lid placed on simmering partisan tensions for the time being, Cherokees built their farms and plantations, and developed such an enriching social and economic life by the 1850s that some referred to the decade before the Civil War as a "golden age" for Cherokees living in diaspora.[23]

Creating new political homelands was a difficult task for Native Southerners still reeling from the traumas of removal. This proved especially true for the Chickasaws who arrived in Indian Territory with no land base of their own. The Chickasaws shared land with the Choctaws in one of the more fertile regions of Indian Territory. The Choctaws' diasporic homeland was bound by the Red River to the south and the Arkansas and Canadian Rivers to the north. Here the Choctaws developed a comprehensive system of government, education, and expanded an economy that included profitable slave plantations. In contrast, the Chickasaws struggled. Most remained in emigrant camps in fear of attack from Apache, Comanche, and Kiowa warriors. Still, the Chickasaws persisted, and in 1855 they made a payment of $150,000 to the Choctaw Nation for land on which they could build their own political homeland in diaspora.[24]

The Seminoles, forced into removal after fighting a long resistance war in Florida, also arrived in Indian Territory with no discrete land base to call their own. Additionally, the removal treaty that laid out the parameters of Seminole removal meant that the autonomous African American communities living among the Seminoles became pawns in a crude attempt by Creek slave owners to claim black Seminoles as their slaves. Forced into diaspora, relocated on Creek lands in Indian Territory, the Seminoles faced an uncertain future.

Feelings of uncertainty and anxiety gripped all Native Southerners in Indian Territory in 1861. When news of the outbreak of the American Civil War reached Indian Territory, Native leaders tried to chart a path of neutrality. Such positions quickly dissolved, as debate over the war reopened old factional disputes and ultimately saw many Indigenous leaders align with the Confederacy and the Southern cause. A significant and influential number of Choctaw, Chickasaw, Creek, and Cherokee leaders had a vested interest in seeing the South triumph given their ties to slavery.[25] Moreover, antiblack racism was as strong in many parts of Indian Territory as it was in the American South. Peter P. Pitchlynn, the principal chief of the Choctaw Nation, articulated the views of many who supported the Confederacy in Indian Territory when he declared in 1863 that "what confidence can a Choctaw have in that [federal] government whose perverted or unnatural will, reverses the social order, and arrays brother in deadly conflict against brother for negro freedom and equality."[26] Almost half a century later, some Native Southerners living in diaspora still expressed antiblack sentiments. Smarting at the federal government for "compelling the Indians to free the slaves and *give them equal rights in land in the Indian Territory*," Minda G. Hardon, a Muscogee-Creek woman, complained that these events were "unjust to the Indians."[27]

◇◇◇◇◇◇◇◇◇◇◇◇◇◇◇◇◇◇◇◇◇◇◇◇◇◇

Historical studies of the Civil War, Jim Crow segregation, and the allotment era in Indian Territory continue to grow and expand our knowledge of Native Southerners living in diaspora. Studies of Native Southerners who remained in the American South and navigated the Civil War, Jim Crow racism, allotment, and termination in the twentieth century have also expanded. These studies have proven instrumental in reminding readers that Native Southerners continue to nurture communal identities. In Alabama, for instance, Kelly Fayard's research reveals that American Indian identities remain "extremely strong and present in the contemporary community."[28]

For much of the late nineteenth and first half of the twentieth century, the survival of Native communities in the Southeast was no guarantee. Economically squeezed, forced to navigate the politics of termination and allotment, battered by racism, and in some cases struggling to reverse declining populations, Native Southerners took some drastic steps to preserve their identities. Some banned interracial marriage with African Americans, others adopted the simplistic historical tropes of American popular culture, and still others migrated to the cities in search of economic opportunities.

In Jim Crow America, therefore, Native Southerners had a choice to make. Some kept their Native identity quiet in the hope that if they "passed" in white society they might make a decent living that enabled them to support their families. Others, like the Nottoways, worked quietly but cooperatively in hopes of maintaining their communities. Still other Native Southerners passed racially restrictive laws to prove to white supremacist lawmakers in the South that they were not "colored" or "Negro," but in fact "Indians." In Jim Crow America, there was no perfect choice.[29]

Native Southerners made it through the long, dark era of Jim Crow segregation just as their ancestors survived and thrived after the removal era. For those Native Southerners whose forebears evaded the American military, remained in the South, and made it through this racially charged era, they could take heart in a new storehouse of stories about heroes who resisted removal or took refuge in mountain hideouts where Native families banded together in the postremoval decades.[30]

Having survived the removal era, the American Civil War, Jim Crow segregation, the Great Depression, and the assimilation and termination eras, those Native Southerners who remained would in time reassert their political, cultural, and social identities for the world to see in the late twentieth century.[31]

Today, they continue to do so, meeting their diasporic brothers and sisters in council meetings or at powwows.[32] My, how the architects of removal and assimilation failed. In our digital age, the identities of Native Southerners have never been so far-flung and yet seemingly so close. The stories that Native Southerners still tell about their identities are as alive with meaning as they've ever been.

NOTES

◇◇

INTRODUCTION

1. Cronon, "Place for Stories," 1347–76; Tuan, *Space and Place*, 6, 9, 12, 34, 75; Lankford, "Some Cosmological Motifs," 14–15.

2. Atleo, *Tsawalk*, 1–3; Conley, *Cherokee Thoughts*, 15–16. The members of the Haliwa-Saponi community in North Carolina, like scores of Native Southerners, have had their Indigenous origins and identities questioned by white Americans since at least the 1870s. While colonial records trace Saponi identities back to the eighteenth century, Haliwa-Saponi origins are often connected back to a mixture of African American, Cherokee, and Tuscarora ethnic roots. For further discussion of this point, see and Richardson, "Ethnicity Affirmed," 51–71.

3. Ewen, *Bering Strait Theory*. See also Weaver, *Other Words*, 5–6; Womack, *Red on Red*, 41–42, 205; and Zellar, *African Creeks*, vii, 5, 140.

4. Duncan, *Living Stories of the Cherokee*, 32.

5. For a recent overview of sources and methods in Native American history and studies, see Anderson and O'Brien, *Sources and Methods in Indigenous Studies*; and Fixico, *"That's What They Used to Say."*

6. Charles Hudson, *Knights of Spain, Warriors of the Sun*, 186–92; Peter N. Moore, *World of Toil and Strife*, 13; Joseph M. Hall, *Zamumo's Gifts*, 90; Reynolds, *Cherokee Struggle to Maintain Identity*, 26.

7. Historian Claudio Saunt contends that as many as one hundred thousand Native Americans were removed from their homes in the eastern half of the United States and forcibly relocated to lands west of the Mississippi River. Scott Freeman, "Preview: UGA's Claudio Saunt to Speak on the Long-lasting Impact of Georgia's Indian Removal," November 6, 2015, http://artsatl.com/preview-ugas-claudio -saunt-indian-removal/.

8. F. Todd Smith, *From Dominance to Disappearance*. Recent synthetic studies emphasize the importance of exchange economies across Native North America. See essays by Guy Bibbon and Barbara Mills in Pauketat, *Oxford Handbook of North*

American Archaeology; Bonvillain, *Native Nations*, 11–12. For more specialized studies, see Anderson, *Indian Southwest*; and Usner, *Indians, Settlers, and Slaves*.

9. For discussion of the geographical boundaries of the Native South, see Charles Hudson, *Southeastern Indians*, 6–7. See also Swanton, *Indians of the Southeastern United States*, 3–7; Gallay, *Indian Slave Trade*, 30.

10. Rees and Livingood, "Introduction and Historical Overview," in *Plaquemine Archaeology*, 1–19; Bowne, *Mound Sites of the Ancient South*.

11. To understand the changes in life for Native Southerners, historians and anthropologists differentiate among the Native peoples from regions as geographically and ecologically diverse as the Mississippi Valley, the Gulf Coast, and the "interior Southeast" (what are today southern Kentucky, Tennessee, Alabama, inland portions of North and South Carolina, and southwestern Virginia). See Perdue and Green, *Columbia Guide to American Indians of the Southeast*, 29; Minnis, *People and Plants in Ancient North America*, 87–88; Marvin T. Smith, "Aboriginal Population Movements," 43–56.

12. Wunder, *Native American Sovereignty*; Vine Deloria Jr., "American Indians in Historical Perspective,"123–33; David E. Wilkins and Lomawaima, *Uneven Ground*, chap. 1.

13. See Fogelson's introduction to *Handbook of North American Indians*. See also Garrison and O'Brien, *Native South*.

14. Pritzker, *Native American Encyclopedia*, chaps. 7 and 8.

15. Peterken, *Natural Woodland*, 45–47.

16. Walthall, *Prehistoric Indians of the Southeast*, 104.

17. CO, South Carolina, Journal of Council, May 25, 1752, CO 5/467, and CO, Board of Trade, Folio 1, John Stuart, "Talk to the Cherokees," February 1, 1766, CO 5/67, National Archives of Great Britain; Dowd, *War under Heaven*, 263; Owens, *Red Dreams, White Nightmares*, 81.

18. CO, South Carolina, Journal of Council, March 20, 1752, CO 5/467; National Archives of Great Britain. See also Smithers, "Our Hands and Hearts are Joined Together," 609–29.

19. John Stuart to Board of Trade, March 9, 1764, CO 323/17/240; Bloustein, *Deerskin Diplomacy*, 24, Hatley, *Dividing Paths*, 81; Ethridge, *Creek Country*; Matthew C. Ward, *Breaking the Backcountry*; Juricek, *Colonial Georgia and the Creeks*.

20. The study of Indigenous societies using the "chiefdom" framework owes much to the pioneering anthropological research of Marshall Sahlins. See his *Social Stratification in Polynesia* and "Poor Man, Rich Man, Big Man, Chief," 285–303.

21. Hämäläinen, "Shapes of Power," 64.

22. Glezakos, "Words Gone Sour?," 396.

CHAPTER ONE ORIGINS

1. Grantham, *Creation Myths and Legends of the Creek Indians*, 14.

2. Steponaitis, "Contrasting Patterns of Mississippian Development," 193–228.

3. Charles Hudson, *Southeastern Indians*, 97; Merrell, *Indians' New World*; Kowalewski, "Coalescent Societies," 95.

4. Archaeologists analyze material artifacts and try to make sense of them in conjunction with ethnographic sources, a process requiring scholars to read "up and down" a variety of sources that help to give meaning to human behavior and different types of communal organizations. Kehoe, *North America Before the European Invasions*, 5–7.

5. Fogelson, introduction to *Handbook*, 10.

6. The origin traditions of the Native South were, and remain, dynamic. The dialogic nature of oral narratives, the use of mnemonic devices to help structure narrative meaning, and the cultural innovativeness of Native Southerners means that Indigenous oral traditions belong to a store of knowledge that might be termed experiential history. Merrell, *Into the American Woods*, 43–49; Philip J. Deloria, "What is the Middle Ground, Anyway?," 81–96; Wildcat, *Red Alert*, 15, 31, 56–57.

7. Leeming, *Creation Myths of the World*. Vol. 1, pts. 1–2, p. 2; Leeming and Page, *Mythology of Native North America*, 77–78; Leeming, *Oxford Companion to World Mythology*, 19.

8. Swanton, *Myths and Tales of the Southeastern Indians*, 269; Lankford, *Native American Legends of the Southeast*, 107–12; Jason Baird Jackson, *Yuchi Folklore*, 21.

9. Milne, "Picking up the Pieces," 391.

10. Milne, *Natchez Country*, 40.

11. Charles Hudson, *Catawba Nation*, 115.

12. "The Catawba—A Small Nation Defeated," IV (18E9), n.d., MS Coll. 126, Speck Papers, American Philosophical Society. For further analysis see Douglas S. Brown, *Catawba Indian Peoples*; Merrell, *Indians' New World*, 114, 271; Beck, *Chiefdoms, Collapse, and Coalescence*, 260.

13. Charles Hudson, *Catawba Nation*, 115–16, 124.

14. H. Thomas Foster II, *Archaeology of the Lower Muskogee Creek Indians*, xv–xvii, 1–2; Fitts, "Mapping Catawba Coalescence," 1–59.

15. A similar origin narrative among the Cherokees replaces the crawfish with a water beetle. Mooney, *James Mooney's History, Myths, and Sacred Formulas*, 239–40.

16. Grantham, *Creation Myths and Legends*, 14, 16; Swanton, *Myths and Tales*, 269; Speck, *Ceremonial Songs of the Creek and Yuchi Indians*, 103, 138.

17. Grantham, *Creation Myths*, 16.

18. Grantham, *Creation Myths*, 17; Gatschet, *Migration Legend of the Creek Indians*; Atkinson, *Splendid Land, Splendid People*, 19.

19. Bartram, *Travels* (1794), 463.

20. Mails, *Cherokee People*, 19; Thornton, *Cherokees*, 1.

21. Conley, *Cherokee Nation*, 17; Fogelson, "Who Were the Aní-Kutáni?," 255–63.

22. Ywahoo, *Voices of Our Ancestors*, 29–30; Erdoes and Aritz, *American Indian Myths and Legends*, 105–7; Stookey, *Thematic Guide to World Mythology*, 74.

23. Ellen R. Emerson, *Indian Myths*, 393; Grantham, *Creation Myths*, 26; Leeming and Page, *Mythology of Native North America*, 88.

24. McLoughlin, *Cherokees and Christianity*, 171.

25. Wells, *Searching for Red Eagle*, 62; Mould, *Choctaw Tales*, 77–78.

26. McClinton, "Cherokee and Christian Expressions of Spirituality," 70–71.

27. Camuto, *Another Country*, 27–28.

28. Perdue, *Cherokee Women*, 14–15; Johnson, *Cherokee Women in Crisis*, 25.

29. Swanton, *Source Material*, 79; O'Brien, "Supplying Our Wants," Brown, 61.

30. Mould, *Choctaw Tales*, xxxix, 64; Barnett, *Mississippi's American Indians*, 90.

31. Swanton, *Source Material*, 33; Halbert, "Choctaw Migration Legend," 215–16; Brescia, "Choctaw Oral Tradition Relating to Tribal Origin," 3–16.

32. Swanton, *Source Material*, 33–34; McNeese, *Myths of Native America*, 77; Galloway, *Choctaw Genesis*, 336–37; Mould, "'Chahta Siyah Okih,'" 224–25.

33. Arrell M. Gibson, *Chickasaws*, 18; Ethridge, *From Chicaza to Chickasaw*, 191–92.

34. Barnett, *Mississippi's American Indians*, 99.

35. Swanton, *Chickasaw Society and Religion*, 26–27; Arrell M. Gibson, *Chickasaws*, 8–9; Atkinson, *Splendid Land, Splendid People*, 1.

36. Crawford, *Origins of Native Americans*, 2.

37. See Ewen, *Bering Strait Theory*.

38. Barton to Thomas Pennant, September 12, 1792, Series 1, BD284, Barton Papers, American Philosophical Society.

39. Barton's reference to the "first visitors" to the New World incorrectly identifies those visitors as the English. Barton to Pennant, September 12, 1792, Barton Papers, American Philosophical Society. From the late nineteenth century and well into the twentieth, public school children in the United States were introduced to American Indians with this question in history primers. See for example Tuttle, *Boy's Book about Indians*, 13; Scudder, *History of the United States of America*, 89; Susan Pendleton Lee, *New Primary History of the United States*, 35; and Kidd, *Forging of Races*, 228–29.

40. "Archaeology," 528; Philip J. Deloria, "Historiography," 11.

41. Silverberg, *Mound Builders*, 58–59; Johansen, *Native Peoples of North America*, 31–32.

42. Charles Hudson, *Southeastern Indians*, 36–37.

43. Acosta, *Natural and Moral History of the Indies*, 63; Pagden, *Fall of Natural Man*, 194–95; McNiven and Russell, *Appropriated Pasts*, 94–95.

44. O'Neill, *Mystery of the Bering Land Bridge*, 6–7.

45. Robert G. Martin, *Twilight of the Mammoths*, 51.

46. J. M. Adovasio points out that the "Clovis Man" theory rested on an overly masculine interpretation of archeological evidence, with "Clovis Woman" being notably absent from many studies. See Adovasio, *First Americans*, xvii.

47. Paul S. Martin, *Last 10,000 Years*; Mithen, *After the Ice*, 213–14.

48. Tuniz, Gillespie, and Jones, *Bone Reader*, 132.

49. Fiedel, *Prehistory of the Americas*, 60; McManamon, *Archaeology in America*, 22.

50. Madsden, "Colonization of the Americas before the Last Glacial Maximum," 1–4; Schmitz, "Review of Bioarchaeological Thought on the Peopling of the New World," 71–72; Nelson, *Quetico*, 67–68. Hendrix, *Down and Dirty*, 15.

51. Reich et al., "Reconstructing Native American Population History," 373.

52. Reich et al., "Reconstructing Native American Population History," 370–74, esp. 373.

53. See for example Simon Moya-Smith, "Harvard Professor Confirms Bering Strait Theory Is Not Fact," *Indian Country Today Media Network*, July 31, 2012, http://indiancountrytodaymedianetwork.com/2012/07/31/harvard-professor -confirms-bering-strait-theory-not-fact; Ragavan et al., "Upper Palaeolithic Siberian Genome Reveals Dual Ancestry of Native Americans," 87–91.

54. Meltzer, *First Peoples in a New World*, 170; Charles E. Homes, "The Beringian and Transitional Periods in Alaska," 188.

55. Tamm et al., "Beringian Standstill and Spread of Native American Founders," e829. See also Kitchen, Miyamoto, and Mulligan, "Three-Stage Colonization Model," e1596; Perego et al., "Distinctive Paleo-Indian Migration Routes," 1–8.

56. Straus, Meltzer, and Goebel, "Ice Age Atlantis?," 507–32; Hranicky, *Prehistoric Projectile Points*, 19–20; O'Hara, *Cave Art and Climate Change*, 17.

57. Stanford and Bradley, *Across Atlantic Ice*, 14.

58. A good example of the tenor of this debate can be found in Straus, Meltzer, and Goebel, "Ice Age Atlantis?," 507–32; Bruce Bradley and Dennis Stanford, "Solutrean-Clovis Connection," 704–14; and Shea, "Solutrean-Clovis Connection," 293–95.

59. Stanford and Bradley, *Across Atlantic Ice*, 5, 14, 68.

60. Fladmark, "Routes," 510–28; Fladmark, "Feasibility of the Northwest Coast as a Migration Route," 119–28; Fladmark, "Times and Places," 13–43.

61. Rogers, "Glacial Geography," 130–37; Gruhn, "Linguistic Evidence," 77–100; Gruhn, "Pacific Coast Route," 249–56.

62. Olsen, *Sacred Places*, 21; E. James Dixon, *Bones, Boats, and Bison*, 31; Erlandson and Braje, "Foundations for the Far West," 157; Aron, *Mysteries in History*, 12; Powell, *First Americans*, 120–22.

63. Ruth Hopkins, "Clovis vs. Beringia: Europe or Siberia? A Review of *Across Atlantic Ice*," *Indian Country Today Media Network*, July 8, 2012, http://indiancountry todaymedianetwork.com/2012/07/08/clovis-vs-beringia-europe-or-siberia-review -across-atlantic-ice-121018.

64. Ewen, *Bering Strait Theory*.

65. Vine Deloria Jr., *Red Earth, White Lies*, 70.

66. Vine Deloria Jr., *Red Earth, White Lies*, 34.

67. Jack Forbes, *American Discovery of Europe*, 88.

68. Frederick H. West, "Late Paleolithic Cultures in Alaska," 161–87; Delcourt and Delcourt, *Prehistoric Native Americans*, 62.

69. Bousman and Oksanen, "Protoarchaic in Central Texas and Surrounding Areas," 211; Kehoe, *North America Before the European Invasions*, 21.

70. Joe W. Saunders, "Middle Archaic and Watson Brake," Kehoe, *North America Before the European Invasions*, 28–30.

71. Archaeologists date the Woodland period from ca. 1000 BCE to 1000 CE.

72. Ellerbe and Greenlee, *Poverty Point*, 83, 86; Jon L. Gibson, *Ancient Mounds of Poverty Point*, 162.

73. Webb, *Poverty Point Culture*, 34–35; Bense, *Archaeology of the Southeastern United States*, chaps. 5–6; Jon L. Gibson, *Ancient Mounds of Poverty Point*, 20, 24, 49, 48, 164–65, 215. Archaeologists have uncovered similar artifacts in North Carolina and Georgia. See Ward and Davis, *Time Before History*, 64.

74. Kehoe, *North America before the European Invasions*, 34, 87.

75. Kehoe, *North America Before the European Invasions*, 34–36.

76. Blitz, "Adoption of the Bow," 123–45, esp. 127, 131–32; Klotter and Klotter, *Concise History of Kentucky*.

77. Stockel, *Lightning Stick*, 3.

CHAPTER TWO THE CHIEFDOM ERA

1. Confer, *Daily Life in Pre-Columbian Native America*, 14, 32–33; Shaffer and Reilly, *Native Americans Before 1492*, 36, 54; Richard I. Ford, "Human Disturbance and Biodiversity," 215; Vavilov, *Origins and Geography*, 210.

2. Other important Ohio mound-building sites include Fort Ancient, Serpent Mound, Marietta Mound, and Fort Hill. See Snow, *Archaeology of Native North America*.

3. Shaffer and Reilly, *Native Americans Before 1492*, chap. 2; Susan L. Woodward and McDonald, *Indian Mounds of the Middle Ohio Valley*.

4. Marvin T. Smith, *Archaeology of Aboriginal Culture Change*, 3.

5. Readers should note that when doing further reading on this period they will find that some archaeological works refer to this era as occurring between ca. 500 and 1200, while others date it to ca. 500 to 1000.

6. Bruce D. Smith, *Mississippian Emergence*, xxiv

7. William C. Foster, *Climate and Culture Change in North America*, 155.

8. William C. Foster, *Historic Native Peoples of Texas*, 5. On the broader hemispheric and global impacts of climate change, see Earle, "Evolution of Chiefdoms," 2; William C. Foster, *Climate and Culture Change in North America*, 155; Summerhayes, *Earth's Climate Evolution*, 352–54; and Rodning and Mehta, "Resilience and Persistent Places," 349–50.

9. Krupp, *Echoes of the Ancient Skies*, xi, 43, 220, 229; Earle, "Property Rights and the Evolution of Chiefdoms," 96; Blitz and Lorenz, *Chattahoochee Chiefdoms*, 12.

10. Earle, "Evolution of Chiefdoms," 1–15.

11. Pauketat, *Ascent of Chiefs*, 174.

12. Timothy R. Pauketat, "Politicization and Community in the Pre-Columbian Mississippi Valley," 27–29; Gregory D. Wilson, *Archaeology of Everyday Life*, 49–52.

13. John F. Scarry, *Political Structure and Change*; Ethridge, *From Chicaza to Chickasaw*, 17.

14. Charles Hudson, *Knights of Spain*, 425; Hahn, *Invention of the Creek Nation*, 14–15; Ethridge, *From Chicaza to Chickasaw*, 17.

15. Reginer, *Reconstructing Tuscalusa's Chiefdom*, 24; Blitz, "Mississippian Chiefdoms and the Fission-Fusion Process," 577–92.

16. Dean H. Smith, *Modern Tribal Development*, 25.

17. Pauketat, *Ascent of Chiefs*, 5; Thomas E. Emerson, *Cahokia and the Archaeology of Power*, 44; Nass and Yerkes, "Social Differentiation in Mississippian and Fort Ancient Societies," 58.

18. Thomas E. Emerson, *Cahokia and the Archaeology of Power*, 148; Mehrer, *Cahokia's Countryside*, 122.

19. Pauketat, *Ascent of Chiefs*, 42–3; 17–18; Robert L. Hall, "Cahokia Identity and Interaction Models," 17–18; Kelly, "Emergence of Mississippian Culture," 142.

20. Dean H. Smith, *Modern Tribal Development*, 25; Weatherford, *Native Roots*, 13–14; Pauketat, *Archaeology of Downtown Cahokia*, 3; Civitello, *Cuisine and Culture*, 101; Gallay, *Indian Slave Trade*, 26.

21. Iseminger, *Cahokia Mounds*, 13, 137.

22. Dalan, "Construction of Mississippian Cahokia," 89; Young and Fowler, *Cahokia*, 301–2.

23. Pauketat, *Ascent of Chiefs*, 40.

24. Pauketat, *Ascent of Chiefs*, 20. On this point see also Kang, "Exogamy and Peace Relations of Social Units," 85–99.

25. King, *Etowah*, 2–3.

26. Oberg, "Types of Social Structure," 472–87; Beck, *Chiefdoms, Collapse, and Coalescence*, 29–30. For a case study that provides an instructive point of comparison, see La Vere, *Caddo Chiefdoms*.

27. King, *Etowah*, 5.

28. Charles Hudson, *Southeastern Indians*, 39–40, 44, 51, 55.

29. Worth, *Timucuan Chiefdoms of Spanish Florida*, 5–6. See also Milanich, *Timucua*.

30. Widmer, *Evolution of Calusa*.

31. Worth, *Timucuan Chiefdoms of Spanish Florida*, 4, 25. See also Perdue and Green, *Columbia Guide*, 61; Kenneth Coleman, *History of Georgia*, 3; Hally, *King: Social Archaeology*, 9, 17, 505; Blitz and Lorenz, *The Chattahoochee Chiefdoms*, 6, 132, 140.

32. Charles R. Cobb, "Mississippian Chiefdoms," 67.

33. Worth, *Timucuan Chiefdoms*, 18.

34. Hally, Smith, and Langford, "Archaeological Reality of de Soto's Coosa," 121–38; King, *Etowah*, 6; Ethridge, *Creek Country*, 26–27.

35. Blitz, *Ancient Chiefdoms of the Tombigbee*; Charles R. Cobb, "Mississippian Chiefdoms," 67–68; Shuck-Hall, *Journey to the West*, 15–24; Ethridge, *From Chicaza to Chickasaw*, 31.

36. Beck, "Consolidation and Hierarchy," 641–61.

37. On the process of cycling, see David G. Anderson, *Chiefdoms*, 12–14.

38. Welch, *Moundville's Economy*, 31; Welch, "Outlying Sites," 162.

39. Barnett, *Mississippi's American Indians*, 37, 90–91.

40. Scarry, "Domestic Life on the Northwest Riverbanks," 45, 72.

41. Welch, *Moundville's Economy*, 180–81.

42. There's very limited evidence to suggest that items manufactured within the Moundville chiefdom were exchanged with Indigenous people from other polities. See Welch, *Moundville's Economy*, 184–85.

43. Atkinson, "De Soto Expedition," 67–73. For further analysis of de Soto's expedition through the Southeast, see Galloway, *Hernando de Soto Expedition*.

44. Shuck-Hall, "Alabama and Coushatta Diaspora and Coalescence," 251–52.

45. Gallay, *Indian Slave Trade*, 7, 31.

46. Lankford, "Some Cosmological Motifs," 12.

47. Lankford, "Some Cosmological Motifs," 16–17.

48. Chappell, *Cahokia*, 60; Dye, "Snaring Life from the Stars and the Sun," 239.

49. Cambron and Waters, "Petroglyphs and Pictographs," 27–51; Simek et al., "Sacred Landscapes," 430–46; Deter-Wolf and Diaz-Granados, *Drawing With Great Needles*, xxi, 85, 175; Diaz-Granados and Duncan, *Petroglyphs and Pictographs of Missouri*, 80, 111, 241; Dubin, *North American Indian Jewelry and Adornment*, 11; Kehoe, *North America Before the European Invasions*, 134–35; DuVal, "Mississippian Peoples' Worldview," 89–107.

50. Frank, *Routledge Historical Atlas*, 17. For "scalloped stone discs and copper symbol badges," see Power, *Early Art of the Southeastern Indians*, 96.

51. David G. Moore, *Catawba Valley Mississippian*, 47; Barnett, *Mississippi's American Indians*, 43; Regnier, *Reconstructing Tascalusa's Chiefdom*, 87–88.

52. Fiedel, *Prehistory of the Americas*, 137; Snyder, *Slavery in Indian Country*, 17.

53. Perdue, "Writing the Ethnohistory of Native Women," Fixico, 78.

54. Johansen and Pritzker, *Encyclopedia of American Indian History*, 2:432.

55. Perdue, *Cherokee Women*, 9; Carson, "Dollars Never Fail to Melt Their Hearts," 17.

56. Hally, *King: Social Archaeology*, 18; Ethridge, *From Chicaza to Chickasaw*, 53; Bowne, *Sites of the Ancient South*, 24.

57. On the issues of wealth in Native American history, see Harmon, *Rich Indians*.

58. Blitz and Lorenz, *Chattahoochee Chiefdoms*, chap. 2; Kehoe, *North America Before the European Invasions*, 140–41. Similar observations have been made of the architecture and town planning in Central and South America. See for example Scott C. Smith, *Landscapes and Politics*.

59. Silverberg, *Mound Builders*, 179; Kehoe, *North America Before the European Invasions*, 112.

60. Milner, *Moundbuilders*, 124–25.

61. Powers, *Early Art of the Southeastern Indians*, 23; Milner, *Moundbuilders*, 106–8. A list of the different types of mounds can be found in the "Museums and

Sites" section of Perdue and Green, *Columbia Guide to American Indians of the Southeast*. For a broader discussion of effigy mounds and material culture, see Walthall, *Prehistoric Indians of the Southeast*.

62. Perdue and Green, *American Indians of the Southeast*, 31.

63. Shipp, *History of Hernando de Soto and Florida*, 5; Hopkins, *Greatest Killer*, 208.

64. Kowalewski, "Coalescent Societies," 118.

65. Burns, *Science and Technology in Colonial America*, 107.

66. Martire d'Anghiera, *De Orbe Novo*, 1:284–85; Stannard, *American Holocaust*, 73, 83; Kessell, *Spain in the Southwest*, 7–8.

67. Hogner, *Our American Horse*, 35; Peterson, *Arms and Armor*, 106–7, 125; Bennett, *Conquerors*, 345–46.

68. Gallay, *Indian Slave Trade*, 26.

69. David J. Hally, "Platform-Mound Construction," 92–93.

70. Galloway, *La Salle and His Legacy*, 179; Barnett, *Natchez Indians*, 20, 21–23; Ian W. Brown and Steponaitis, "Grand Village of the Natchez Indians," 182.

71. On early weaponry among American Indians, see Otis Tufton Mason, *North American Bows, Arrows, and Quivers*; Browne, "Projectile Points," 209–13; Lynott, "Identification of Attribute Variability," 189–211. See also Knecht, *Projectile Technology*.

72. Driver, *Indians of North America*, chap. 17.

73. Richter, *Ordeal of the Longhouse*, 7, 60; William E. Engelbrecht, "New York Iroquois Political Development," 229.

74. Snyder, *Slavery in Indian Country*, 14.

75. Pauline Turner Strong, "Transforming Outsiders," 339.

76. Galloway, *Practicing Ethnohistory*, 147; H. Thomas Foster II, "Identification and Significance of Apalachicola," 1–13.

77. Perdue, *Cherokee Women*, 69–70. See also Beck, *Chiefdoms, Collapse, and Coalescence*, 233.

78. I have borrowed the phrase "new worlds for all" from Calloway, *New Worlds for All*.

CHAPTER THREE CAPTIVITY, COLONIALISM, AND COALESCENCE

1. Alvord and Bidgood, *First Explorations*, 80; Bowne, *Westo Indians*, 24, 53. See also Hann, *Native American World Beyond Apalachee*.

2. Crane, *Southern Frontier*, 16; Bowne, *Westo Indians*, 89; Gallay, *Indian Slave Trade*, 56. The Spanish referred to the Westos as the Chichimecos. Like the English, they were also willing to exchange firearms for the Indian slaves the Westos brought with them. See Gallay, *Indian Slave Trade*, 56; Grady, *Anglo-Spanish Rivalry in Colonial South-East America*; Mason, *Archaeology of Ocmulgee Old Fields*, 9; and Warren, *Worlds the Shawnee Made*, 86–87.

3. Gallay, *Indian Slave Trade*, 38; Ben Ford, "Shoreline As a Bridge," 73; Carlisle and Golson, *Native America*, 166; Morris, *Bringing of Wonder*, 5. For an account

of winged and horned water serpents in Native oral traditions in the Southeast, see Lankford, "Great Serpent in Eastern North America," 107–35. For fascinating accounts of Native peoples meeting Europeans and engaging with them on the coastline of North Carolina, see Stick, *Outer Banks Reader*, 3–6.

4. Boyd, "Fort San Luis," 1–19; Bushnell, "Patricio de Hinachuba," 1–21; Covington, "Apalachee Indians Move West," 221–25; Hixson, *American Settler Colonialism*, 40; Dubcovsky, "'All of Us Will Have to Pay for These Activities,'" 1–18.

5. Meyers, "From Refugees to Slave Traders," 81–103; DuVal, *Independence Lost*, 13; Dubcovsky, "Defying Indian Slavery," 295–322.

6. Swanton, *Early History of the Creek Indians*, 66.

7. This is a vast historiography. Some classic titles and useful case studies include Lyon, *Enterprise of Florida*; Lockhart, *Nahuas and Spaniards*; Gutiérrez, *When Jesus Came, the Corn Mothers Went Away*; Barrett, *Spanish Colonial Settlement*; Lamana, *Domination with Dominance*; Larson, *Bioarchaeology of Spanish Florida*; Restall, *Seven Myths of the Spanish Conquest*; Martínez, *Genealogical Fictions*; and Horn, "Indigenous Identities in Mesoamerica," 31–78.

8. For an overview of recent historical research about Indian slavery, see Bossy, "South's Other Slavery," 27–53.

9. On the Haudenosaunees, see Richter, *Ordeal of the Longhouse*; Toba Pato Tucker, *Haudenosaunee*; and Susan M. Hill, *Clay We Are Made of*.

10. Bowne, *Westo Indians*, 49.

11. This and the previous paragraph are based on the research of Swanton, *Early History of the Creek Indians*, 305; Gallay, *Indian Slave Trade*, 56, 146; Jason Baird Jackson, "Introduction: On Studying Yuchi History," xxii.

12. Lederer, *Discoveries*, 14; Alvord and Bidgood, *First Explorations*, 155–56; Swanton, *Early History of the Creek Indians*, 296.

13. On ethnogenesis in the Americas, see for example Jonathan D. Hill, *History, Power, and Identity*.

14. "Indians of Louisiana, Their Number and the Commerce That Carried on with Them," in Rowland and Sanders, *Mississippi Provincial Archives*, 3:537. (Hereafter cited as *MPA*.) See also Gallay, *Indian Slave Trade*; Ethridge, "Introduction: Mapping," 23; and Ethridge, "Contact Era Studies and the Southeastern Indians," 63–77

15. Kowalewski, "Coalescent Societies," 122; McDonnell, *Masters of Empire*, 10.

16. Carl F. Miller, "Reevaluation of the Eastern Siouan Problem," 115–211; DeMallie, "Tutelo and Neighboring Groups," 14:286–300. See also Ethridge, "The European Invasion and the Transformation of Tennessee," 3–34.

17. Ethridge and Charles Hudson, "Early Historic Transformation of the Southeastern Indians," 34–50, esp. 40; Ethridge, *Creek Country*, 23; Kowalewski, "Coalescent Societies," 106; Worth, *Struggle for the Georgia Coast*, xiv; Rodning, *Center Places and Cherokee Towns*, 159; Wright, *Only Land They Knew*, 108–9; Bowne, "Rise and Fall of the Westo Indians," 56–78; Hoffman, *Florida's Frontiers*, 145–46; Lenman, *Britain's Colonial Wars*, 56; Reff, *Disease, Depopulation, and Cultural*

Change, 30, 52; Bossy, "Indian Slavery in Southeastern Indian and British Societies," 219; McCandless, *Slavery, Disease, and Suffering*, 174; Reséndez, *Other Slavery*, 14, 16, 217; Fitts, *Fit for War*.

18. Ethridge, "Introduction: Mapping the Mississippian Shatter Zone," 19; Perttula, "Social Changes among the Caddo Indians," 249–70; La Vere, *Caddo Chiefdoms*, chap. 8; Thornton, *American Indian Holocaust and Survival*, 67. For a discussion of the Savano Town refugees, see Ramsey, *Yamasee War*, 16, 117–18.

19. Ethridge, "Introduction: Mapping," 1–24.

20. Ethridge, "Introduction: Mapping," 1.

21. Ethridge, "Introduction: Mapping," 8.

22. Hämäläinen, "Shapes of Power," 31–68.

23. Usner, *Indians, Settlers, and Slaves*, 84–85; Taylor, *American Colonies*, 389.

24. Starkey, *European and Native American Warfare*; Milner, "Warfare, Population, and Food Production," 182–201; Kristofer Ray, "Constructing a Discourse of Indigenous Slavery, Freedom and Sovereignty in Anglo-Virginia, 19–39.

25. Juster, *Sacred Violence in Early America*, 35. See also Slotkin, *Regeneration through Violence*; Schaafsma, "Head Trophies and Scalping," 90–123; DuVal, *Native Ground*, 127; Smithers, *Cherokee Diaspora*, 50–51; Thrasher, *Fight Sports and American Masculinity*, 6.

26. Snow, "Iroquois-Huron Warfare," 149–59; Richter, *Ordeal of the Longhouse*, 31–32; Wayne E. Lee, *Barbarians and Brothers*, 154–55.

27. Clayton, Knight, and Moore, *De Soto Chronicles*, 1, 211, 395, 401; Covington, "Relations between the Eastern Timucuan Indians and the French and Spanish," 13; Craig Morris, "Signs of Division, Symbols of Unity," 530; Gallay, *Colonial Wars*, 665; Beck, *Chiefdoms, Collapse, and Coalescence*, 42; Oatis, *Colonial Complex*, 49; Raab, *Spain, Britain and the American Revolution in Florida*, 9.

28. Laubin, *American Indian Archery*, 16; Malone, *Skulking Way of War*, 17.

29. Dickson, "Yanomamo of the Mississippi Valley?," 75–133; Dye, "Warfare in the Sixteenth-Century Southeast," 211–22; Starkey, "European-Native American Warfare in North America," 237–62; Jones, *Native North American Armor, Shields, and Fortifications*, 136–38.

30. Otis Tufton, Mason, *North American Bows, Arrows, and Quivers*, 645.

31. Trigger, "Inequality and Communication in Early Civilization," 27–52; Trigger, *Children of Aataentsic*, 416; Rushforth, *Bonds of Alliance*, 35–37; Salafia, *Slavery's Borderland*, 33; Cameron, *Captives*, 22–27; For comparison with the Trans-Mississippi West, see Brill, "Technology of Violence and Cultural Evolution in the Santa Barbara Channel Region," 314–32, esp. 327; Stodder et al., "Cultural Longevity and Biological Stress in the American Southwest," 481–505, esp. 496.

32. O'Brien, *Choctaws in a Revolutionary Age*, 27.

33. Beck, "Catawba Coalescence and the Shattering of the Carolina Piedmont," 134; Bowne, *Westo*, 62, 73; Ramsey, *Yamasee War*, 107–11.

34. Gallay, *Indian Slave Trade*, 186; Snyder, *Slavery in Indian Country*, 13, 65, 104. For a study of slavery in southwestern North America and an excellent point of

comparison with the Native South, see Brooks, *Captives and Cousins*. For a recent synthetic history of slavery in the Americas, see Reséndez, *Other Slavery*.

35. Strong, "Transforming Outsiders," 339.

36. Snyder, *Slavery in Indian Country*, 128.

37. Perdue, *Slavery and the Evolution of Cherokee Society*, 4; Stevenson, *What is Slavery?*, 21.

38. Bienville to Maurepas, September 30, 1741, in Rowland and Sanders, *MPA*, 3:755–56; Usner, *Indians, Settlers, and Slaves*, 19; Ethridge, *From Chicaza to Chickasaw*, 53, 91, 97, 138; Snyder, *Slavery in Indian Country*.

39. Atkinson, *Splendid Land, Splendid People*, 29; Kelton, *Epidemics and Enslavement*, 154; Ethridge, *From Chicaza to Chickasaw*; Snyder, *Slavery in Indian Country*, 60; Spear, *Race, Sex, and Social Order*, 20.

40. Fortescue, *Calendar of State Papers*, 509.

41. Arrell M. Gibson, *Chickasaws*, 7, 17, 21, 46; Snyder, *Slavery in Indian Country*, 63.

42. Mr. de Perier to the Abbe Raguet, May 12, 1728, in Rowland and Sanders, *MPA*, 2:573; Lambert, *Choctaw Nation*, 23; Stubbs, "Chickasaw Contact with the La Salle Expedition," Galloway, 47.

43. Snyder, *Slavery in Indian Country*, 85; Arrell M. Gibson, *Chickasaws*, 30.

44. Ethridge, "Emergence of the Colonial South," 47–64, esp. 60–61; Snyder, *Slavery in Indian Country*, 59.

45. Mulcahy, *Hubs of Empire*, 94.

46. Memoir of the King to Serve as Instruction for Sieur de Bienville, the Governor of the Provence of Louisiana, February 2, 1732, in Rowland and Sanders, *MPA*, 3:543.

47. Crosby, *Columbian Exchange*, 44–52, 64–66.

48. Duran, Duran, and Brave Heart, "Native Americans and the Trauma of History," 62; Axtell, *Indians' New South*, 22–24.

49. Wood, "Changing Population of the Colonial South," 57–132, esp. 82–84; Kelton, "Great Southeastern Smallpox Epidemic," 21–37.

50. Adair, *History of the American Indians*, 253. See also Axtell, *Natives and Newcomers*; and Kelton, *Cherokee Medicine*, 11.

51. Thornton, *American Indian Holocaust*, 79.

52. Kowalewski, "Coalescent Societies," 119; Bragdon, *Columbia Guide*, 153; Warren, "Reconsidering Coalescence," Baird, 164; Lakomäki, *Gathering Together*, 17.

53. Ethridge, *Creek Country*, 158–61; Angela Pulley Hudson, *Creek Paths and Federal Roads*, 26; Carson, "Horses and the Economy," 495–513; Boulware, "'Skilful Jockies' and 'Good Saddlers,'" 68–95. See also Paulett, *Empire of Small Places*.

54. Braund, *Deerskins and Duffels*, 100, 132; 10–13, 15, 20, 148; Usner, "American Indians on the Cotton Frontier," 297–317; Hudson, *Creek Paths*, 21, 25, 27; Pesantubbee, *Choctaw Women*, 134–38; Barnett, *Mississippi's American Indians*, chap. 4; Harmon, *Rich Indians*, 62–64. On the deerskin trade and rising tensions between men and women in the Native South, see "'Domestick . . . Quiet being broke,'" 151–74, esp. 157–59.

55. The Carolina colony was founded as a proprietary colony and designed to be a bulwark against Spanish colonial expansion. Proprietary governance ended in 1729, when North and South Carolina each became royal colonies. See William L. Saunders, *Colonial Records of North Carolina*, 2:3, and Roper, *Conceiving Carolina*, 155.

56. Hahn, *Invention of the Creek Nation*, 73–74; Oatis, *Colonial Complex*, 69–70.

57. Ocheses warriors also saw action against the Tuscaroras, the most powerful Native society in eastern North Carolina. Hahn, *Invention of the Creek Nation*, 73–74.

58. Oatis, *Colonial Complex*, 70; Smith, *Louisiana and the Gulf South Frontier*, 65. Some estimates put the number of Creek warriors as high as 1,300. See Corkran, *Creek Frontier*, 56.

59. Corkran, *Creek Frontier*, 106; Braund, *Deerskins and Duffels*, 133–35; Barnett, *Mississippi's American Indians*, 153; O'Brien, *Choctaws in a Revolutionary Age*, 27–28, 35–39; O'Brien, "Protecting Trade through War," 103–22; Spencer C. Tucker, *Encyclopedia of North American Indian Wars*, 209; F. Todd Smith, *Louisiana and the Gulf South Frontier*, 138–39.

60. Carson, *Searching for the Bright Path*, 30–35; Pesantubbee, *Choctaw Women*, 105–6. See also Galloway, "Choctaw Factionalism and Civil War," 70–102; Wells, *Native Land*, chap. 16; and Warren, *Worlds the Shawnees Made*, 217.

61. Corkran, *Creek Frontier*, 59, 108; Crane, *Southern Frontier*, 187, 263, 266; Hatley, *Dividing Path*, 44–45.

62. Corkran, *Creek Frontier*, 108; Hahn, *Invention of the Creek Nation*, 131; Oatis, *Colonial Complex*, 252–54; Joseph M. Hall, *Zamumo's Gifts*, 154. For further analysis, see Braund, *Deerskins and Duffels*, esp. chap. 7; Snyder, *Slavery in Indian Country*; Ivers, *This Torrent of Indians*.

63. Vaughan, *Early American Indian Documents*, 13:42; Bragdon, *Columbia Guide*, 30–31; Boyce, "'As the Wind Scatters the Smoke,'" 153; La Vere, *Tuscarora War*, 199; Sider, *Living Indian Histories*, 225; Woodward, "Indian Land Sales and Allotment in Antebellum Virginia," 161–81, esp. 162–63.

64. La Vere, *Tuscarora War*, 6–7; Abraham Gibson, *Feral Animals in the American South*, 40.

65. Note that North Carolina officially became a separate colony in 1712, though the process began much earlier.

66. The 1710 population figure includes both black and white people in North Carolina. La Vere, *Tuscarora War*, 11–12.

67. La Vere, *Tuscarora War*, 15.

68. Vaughan, *Early American Indian Documents*, 13:43; La Vere, *Tuscarora War*, 16; Ready, *Tar Heel State*, 30, 32.

69. Boyce, "'As the Wind Scatters the Smoke,'" 152.

70. Both quotations are found in Fenn and Wood, *Natives and Newcomers*, 45.

71. Wright, *Only Land They Knew*, 118; Powell, *North Carolina through Four Centuries*, 77.

72. La Vere, *Tuscarora War*, 18.

73. La Vere, *Tuscarora War*, 66–7; Weidensaul, *First Frontier*, 241; Beck, *Chiefdoms, Collapse, and Coalescence*, 17.

74. Carson, "Histories," 195–98.

75. Powell, *North Carolina through Four Centuries*, 79.

76. See La Vere, *Tuscarora War*, and Wallace, 67–70. During the war, colonial officials negotiated with the Tuscarora leader of the upper towns, Tom Blount, in an effort to keep them peaceable and out of the conflict. Wallace, *Tuscarora*, 69.

77. McDowell, *Journal of the Commissioners of the Indian Trade*, 1:262; Vaughan, *Early American Indian Documents*, 13:317; Wallace, *Tuscarora*, 71–72; Fenton, *Great Law and the Longhouse*, 390; Boyce, "'As the Wind Scatters the Smoke,'" 151–63.

78. Swanton, *Indians of Southeastern United States*, 208–11; Grenier, *First Way of War*, 44–6; Ramsey, *Yamasee War*, 16–19.

79. Fortescue, *Calendar of State Papers*, 6; Norton, *Journal*, 140.

80. McDowell, *Journal of the Commissioners of the Indian Trade*, 1:53, 55, 72; Crane, *Southern Frontier*; Kulikoff, *From British Peasants to Colonial American Farmers*, 100; Gallay, *Indian Slave Trade*, 249; Taylor, *American Colonies*, 234; Ramsey, *Yamasee War*, 21, 24.

81. Mulcahy, *Hubs of Empire*, 86; Weidensaul, *First Frontier*, 248.

82. Oatis, *Colonial Complex*, 117; Sider, *Living Indian Histories*, 199, 236; Ivers, *This Torrent of Indians*; Carpenter, *"Times Are Altered with Us,"* 99.

83. Usner, *Indians, Settler, and Slaves*, 14; Ramsey, *Yamasee War*, 21, 62–67; Dubcovsky, *Informed Power*, 180–81.

84. Leach, "Colonial Indian Wars," 4:140.

85. Ramsey, *Yamasee War*, 89–91.

86. Ramsey, *Yamasee War*, 91–2.

87. Charles Rodd to his Employer (Forwarded by Him to the King), May 8, 1714, in Fortescue, *Calendar of State Papers, August 1714–December 1715*, 28:168; Oatis, *Colonial Complex*, 1; Warren, *Worlds the Shawnees Made*, 104.

88. Charles Rodd to his Employer (Forwarded by Him to the King, May 8, 1714, in Fortescue, *Calendar of State Papers, August 1714–December 1715*, 28:167.

89. Charles Rodd to his Employer (Forwarded by Him to the King, May 8, 1714, in Fortescue, *Calendar of State Papers, August 1714–December 1715*, 28:169.

90. Thornton, *The Cherokees*, 35; Kelton, *Epidemics and Enslavement*, 202; O'Brien, "Quieting the Ghosts," 51–52. Historian Alan Gallay reminds us that Native people had a tradition of building forts long before Europeans arrived in North America. Gallay, *Indian Slave Trade*, 272. For analysis of Native negotiations with the British about the location of forts see Ingram, *Indians and Outposts*.

91. Samuel Eveleigh to Messrs. Boon and Berresford, October 2, 1715, in Fortescue, *Calendar of State Papers, August 1714–December 1715*, 28:296–97; David Crawley to William Byrd, July 30, 1715, in Fortescue, *Calendar of State Papers, August 1714–December 1715*, 28:247.

92. On pan-Indianism see Dowd, *Spirited Resistance*.

93. Samuel Eveleigh to Messrs. Boon and Berresford, October 2, 1715, in Forte-

scue, *Calendar of State Papers, August 1714–December 1715*, 28:299; F. Todd Smith, *Louisiana and the Gulf South Frontier*, 76.

94. Quoted in Kelton, *Epidemics and Enslavement*, 202. See also Snyder, *Slavery in Indian Country*, 94; Richter, *Before the Revolution*, 323–24.

95. An Act for the Payment of the Sum of Five Hundred Pounds, Current Money, Unto Maria, the Wife of John Charlton, Late of this Province, Vinter, in Case she Procures the Huspaw King, now at St. Augustine, and His People, to Return, and be Subject Again to this Government, in Cooper, *Statutes at Large of South Carolina*, 2:695; Crane, *Southern Frontier*, 236; Gallay, *Indian Slave Trade*, 341–42.

96. Col. Nicholson to Mr. Popple, August 13, 1715, in Fortescue, *Calendar of State Papers, August 1714–December 1715*, 28:261.

97. Lt. Governor Spotswood to the Council of Trade and Plantations, August 29, 1717, in Fortescue, *Calendar of State Papers, August 1717–December 1718*, 30:18–19; Lt. Governor Spotswood to the Council of Trade and Plantations, February 27, 1717, in Fortescue, *Calendar of State Papers, August 1717–December 1718*, 30:193–96.

98. Lt. Governor Spotswood to the Council of Trade and Plantations, August 14, 1718, in Fortescue, *Calendar of State Papers, August 1717–December 1718*, 30:332–334.

99. Lt. Governor Spotswood to the Council of Trade and Plantations, December 22, 1718, in Fortescue, *Calendar of State Papers, August 1717–December 1718*, 30:433.

100. Rowland and Sanders, *MPA*, 2:125.

101. Lee, *Barbarians and Brothers*, 150–51; Swanton, *Indians of the Southeast*, 203; Lerch, *Waccamaw Legacy*, 11. Historian Alan Gallay notes that an English source that explains Waccamaw aggression against South Carolina as the product of black agitation. See Gallay, *Indian Slave Trade*, 348. Waccamaws had good reason for taking this hostile position against the English as Waccamaws were often carried off into slavery by privateers. See Blanck, *Tyrannicide*, 89.

CHAPTER FOUR *PETITE NATIONS, TOWNS, AND CLANS*

1. Harrell, *Tomo-Chi-Chi*, 31–34; Sweet, *Negotiating for Georgia*, 19–22.

2. Sweet, *Negotiating for Georgia*, 19.

3. See discussion of the Coweta Resolution later in chapter, on pp. 95–96.

4. Sweet, *Negotiating for Georgia*, 21–22; Hahn, *Invention of the Creek Nation*, 149; Weaver, *Red Atlantic*, 20.

5. McElrath, Emerson, and Fortier, "Social Evolution or Social Response?," 23–24; Kowalewski, "Coalescent Societies," 110–11.

6. Kowalewski, "Large-Scale Ecology in Aboriginal Eastern North America," 159; Block, *Rape and Sexual Power in Early America*, 224–29. To place the Native South in a broader context, see Alice Nash, "'None of the Women Were Abused.'"

7. Braund, *Deerskins and Duffels*, 3.

8. Harmon, *Rich Indians*, 66.

9. "Caddo" is a shortened form of the French abbreviation *Kadohadacho*.

10. Sabo, "Terán Map and Caddo Cosmology," 439, 443.

11. Swanton, *Source Material*, 10, 12–13; La Vere, *Caddo Chiefdoms*, 45–46, 51.

12. Europeans believed that the exogamous marriage practices of Native Americans produced a strong taboo against incest and rape. See for example John McQueen to Enrique White, February 22, 1802, East Florida Papers, Bundle 137G11, reel 56, pt. 2, 137–39, MSS 19398, Manuscripts Division, Library of Congress.

13. Swanton, *Caddo Indians*, 160–61, 164–65; Barr, *Peace Came in the Form of a Woman*, 43.

14. Bolton, *Hasinais*, 104; Cecile Elkins Carter, *Caddo Indians*, 73; Perttula, "Social Changes among the Caddo Indians, 252.

15. Perttula, *"Caddo Nation,"* 45, 79–80; Girard, Perttula, and Trubitt, *Caddo Connections*, 110–11.

16. Muller, *Mississippian Political Economy*, 63; Barnett, *Natchez Indians*, 68; Milne, *Natchez Country*, 8.

17. Milne, *Natchez Country*, 6.

18. Barnett, *Mississippi's American Indians*, xvi.

19. Carson, "Sacred Circles and Dangerous People," 75; Usner, *Indians, Settlers, and Slaves*, 16; Schlotterbeck, *Daily Life in the Colonial South*, 22.

20. Carson, "Sacred Circles and Dangerous People," 73.

21. Sayre, *Indian Chief as Tragic Hero*, 235; Arnold, *Rumble of a Distant Drum*, 23–24.

22. Gaillardet and Shepherd, *Sketches*, 100–101.

23. DuVal, *Independence Lost*, 59.

24. Milne, *Natchez Country*, 2; Barnett, *Natchez Indians*, 66–68; Charles A. Weeks, *Paths to a Middle Ground*, 177.

25. Cushman, *History of the Choctaw, Chickasaw, and Natchez Indians*, 367–68; Onofrio, *Dictionary of Indian Tribes of the Americas*, 1:669.

26. Galloway, *Choctaw Genesis*, 203.

27. Carson, "Greenwood LeFlore," 226; Galloway, *Choctaw Genesis*, 109, 118, 124.

28. Swanton, *Source Material*, 55; Raeschelle J. Potter-Deimel, "A Wounded Eagle Soars over the Hills of Mississippi!," 323; Lambert, *Choctaw Nation*, 30; O'Brien, "Coming of Age of Choctaw History," 11.

29. Swanton, *Source Material*, 58; Searcy, "Choctaw Subsistence," 35; Faiman-Silva, *Choctaws at the Crossroads*, 7–8; Galloway, *Choctaw Genesis*, 193; Lambert, *Choctaw Nation*, 25.

30. DeRosier, *Removal of the Choctaw Indians*, 9–10; Carson, *Searching for the Bright Path*, 78–80.

31. Bartram, *Travels* (1794), 515.

32. Rodning, "Reconstructing the Coalescence of Cherokee Communities," 159.

33. Galloway, *Choctaw Genesis*, 31, 33–36, 54; Jeff Crane, *Environment in American History*, 9.

34. Carson, "Native Americans, the Market Revolution, and Culture Change," 191.

35. Searcy, "Choctaw Subsistence," 35.

36. Pesantubbee, *Choctaw Women in a Chaotic World*, 131.

37. Braund, *Deerskins and Duffels*, 90; Ethridge, "European Invasion and the Transformation of the Indians of Tennessee," 4, 19.

38. Swanton, *Chickasaw Society and Religion*, 31.

39. Wilson, *Archaeology of Everyday Life*, 12; Ethridge, *From Chicaza to Chickasaw*, 225; Barnett, *Mississippi's American Indians*, 99.

40. Arrell M. Gibson, *Chickasaws*, 39; Snyder, *Slavery in Indian Country*, 56; St. Jean, *Remaining Chickasaw in Indian Territory*, 10–13.

41. Arrell M. Gibson, *Chickasaws*, 18; Ethridge, *From Chicaza to Chickasaw*, 224.

42. Barnett, *Mississippi's American Indians*, 100; Arrell M. Gibson, *Chickasaws*, 6.

43. Arrell M. Gibson, *Chickasaws*, 9; Amanda J. Cobb, *Listening to our Grandmothers' Stories*, 23.

44. Collection 985, Quarles Papers, Southern Historical Collection, University of North Carolina; Arrell M. Gibson, *Chickasaws*, 8.

45. Adair, *History of the American Indians*, ed. Williams, 146.

46. Collection 792, Subseries 3.4, Series 4, Box 5, Wills Papers, Southern Historical Collection, University of North Carolina.

47. Swanton, *Early History of the Creek Indians*, 215; Verner Crane, *Southern Frontier*, 36–37; J. Leitch Wright, *Creeks and Seminoles*, 5; Spalding and Jackson, *Oglethorpe in Perspective*, 24–25; Ethridge, *Creek Country*, 28; Hahn, *Invention of the Creek Nation*, 243; Oatis, *Colonial Complex*, 56.

48. Swanton, *Early History of the Creek Indians*, 215–82; Jenkins, "Tracing the Origins of the Early Creeks," 236.

49. Braund, *Deerskins and Duffels*, 5–6; Hahn, *Invention of the Creek Nation*, 49–50; Frank, *Creeks and Southerners*, 11; Ivers, *This Torrent of Indians*.

50. Angela Pulley Hudson, *Creek Paths and Federal Roads*, 9–10; Silverman, *Thundersticks*.

51. Piker, *Okfuskee*, 166; Lankford, *Native American Legends*, 114.

52. Piker, *Okfuskee*, 166.

53. Green, *Politics of Indian Removal*, 7; Piker, *Okfuskee*, 211; Hahn, *Invention of the Creek Nation*, 21; Lewis and Jordan, *Creek Indian Medicine Ways*, 6; Waselkov, *Conquering Spirit*, 6.

54. In his classic study of the Creeks, Swanton contended that Creeks paid particular attention to the mother and father of children in order to preserve matrilineal identities. See Swanton, *Early History of the Creek Indians*, 369.

55. Ethridge, *Creek Country*, 110; Hahn, *Invention of the Creek Nation*, 25; Frank, *Creeks and Southerners*, 21; Piker, *Four Deaths of Acorn Whistler*.

56. Green, *Politics of Indian Removal*, 5; Ethridge, *Creek Country*, 231; Hahn, *Invention of the Creek Nation*, 22–23.

57. Piker, *Okfuskee*, 10.

58. Ethridge, *Creek Country*, 87; Hahn, *Invention of the Creek Nation*, 241; Piker, *Okfuskee*, 10; H. Thomas Foster II, *Archaeology of the Lower Muskogee Creek Indians*, 262; Rindfleisch, "'Owner of the Town Ground,'" 54–88.

59. Piker, *Okfuskee*, 116.

60. Downes, "Creek-American Relations," 142–43; Boyd and Latorre, "Spanish Interest in British Florida," 92–130; Sturtevant, "Spanish-Indian Relations," 41–94; Deagan, "Spanish-Indian Interaction," 281–318, esp. 286–89; Weber, *Spanish Frontier in North America*, 104, 143–44, 278.

61. Corkran, *Creek Frontier*, 51; Weber, *Spanish Frontier in North America*, 144; Braund, *Deerskins and Duffels*, 31–32.

62. Gallay, *Indian Slave Trade*, 17.

63. DuVal, *Independence Lost*, 13.

64. Hahn, *Invention of the Creek Nation*, 4, 110; Ethridge, *Creek Country*, 58; Denise I. Bossy, "Indian Slavery in Southeastern Indian and British Societies," 239; Hall, *Zamumo's Gifts*, 133.

65. Hahn, *Invention of the Creek Nation*, 4; Bossy, "Indian Slavery in Southeastern Indian and British Societies," 229.

66. Corkran, *Creek Frontier*, 83; Temple and Coleman, *Georgia Journeys*, 19; Hahn, "Cussita Migration Legend," 79.

67. Hahn, "Cussita Migration Legend," 79–80; Perdue and Green, *Columbia Guide*, 207; Vaughan, *Transatlantic Encounters*, 161; Shoemaker, "Wonder and Repulsion," 185; Weaver, *Red Atlantic*, 20–21; Thrush, *Indigenous London*, 83–85.

68. Georgia settlers honored Tomochichi at his funeral in 1739, sparking the legend that Tomochichi was the Indian friend who helped establish the colony of Georgia. Such mythmaking should be viewed with caution. See Shoemaker, *Strange Likeness*, 34–35, and Sweet, *Negotiating for Georgia*, 128.

69. Sweet, *Negotiating for Georgia*, 23; Cashin, "Oglethorpe's Contest for the Backcountry," 101.

70. McDowell, *Documents Relating to Indian Affairs*, ser. 2, 2:7.

71. Clark, *State Records of North Carolina*, 11:179–205; Carson, *Searching for the Bright Path*, 35–36; O'Brien, *Choctaws in a Revolutionary Age*, Calloway, *Scratch of a Pen*, 102–3.

72. "Creek," in Gallay, *Colonial Wars of North America*, 152–53. The French wondered openly about engagement with Native polities in the Carolinas, worrying about the gamble—"en faire parrier a la Caroline"—associated with the forging of such relations. Comte de Maurepas to Pierre de Rigaud, marquis de Vaudreuil, January 2, 1749, Pierre de Rigaud, marquis de Box 4, Folio 160, Vaudreuil Papers, Huntington Library; Pierre Francois de Rigaud, marquis de Vaudreuil to Comte de Jouy Antoine Louis Rouille, September 22, 1749, Box 4, Folio 185, Loudoun Papers, Huntington Library.

73. Wood, "Changing Population of the Colonial South," 85–86.

74. Charles Hudson, *Catawba Nation*, 5; Fitts, "Mapping Catawba Coalescence," 1–59.

75. Kroeber, *Cultural and Natural Areas*, 94; Douglas Summers Brown, *Catawba Indians*, 86–91.

76. See for example Coe, *Formative Cultures of the Carolina Piedmont*; Coe,

Town Creek Indian Mound, 276–77; Merrell, *Indians' New World*, 9, 47, 94; Fitts, *Fit for War*, 9, 12, 18, 117.

77. Lawson, *New Voyage to Carolina*, 37; Merrell, *Indians' New World*, 3, 10.

78. David G. Moore, *Catawba Valley Mississippian*, 1–2; Swanton, *Indian Tribes of North America*, 91.

79. Charles Hudson, *Catawba Nation*, 12; Merrell, *Indians' New World*, 8–10; Fitts, *Fit for War*, 10.

80. Theresa E. McReynolds, "Catawba Population Dynamics," 43–44.

81. Wood, "Changing Population of the Colonial South," 67; Wallace, *Tuscarora*, xiii; La Vere, *Tuscarora War*, 12.

82. Merrell, *Indians' New World*, chap. 1; Padget, "Lost Indians of the Lost Colony," 391–424.

83. Mark E. Miller, *Claiming Tribal Identity*, 325.

84. Lowery, *Lumbee Indians*, 4. See also Blu, *Lumbee Problem*, and Sider, *Lumbee Indian Histories*, for a scholarly meditations on Lumbee identity.

85. Croom, "Herbal Medicine among the Lumbee Indians," 144. See also Sider, *Living Indian Histories*, 186.

86. The Catawbas appear to have developed a reputation as feared warriors among the Native communities of the Ohio Valley, one Ohio Indian reputedly referring to the Catawbas as "all one Devil." See McConnell, *A Country Between*, 50. On French efforts to woo the Catawbas, see McDonnell, *Masters of Empire*, 172.

87. Archaeologists suggest that these practices didn't change greatly until the 1760s, when Catawbas began eating portioned meals in more individualistic ways. See Plane, "Catawba Ethnicity," 65.

88. Fitts and Heath, "'Indians Refusing to Carry Burdens,'" 145–46.

89. Fitts and Heath, "'Indians Refusing to Carry Burdens,'" 147; Plane, "Catawba Militarism," 80–120.

90. Proposition made by His Excellency Brigadier Hunter to Governor in Cheiffe to ye 5 Nations, June 16, 1717, in Brodhead and O'Callaghan, *Documents Relative to the Colonial History of the State of New-York*, 5:490; Conference Between Governor Burnet and the Indians, in Vaughan, *Early American Indian Documents*, 9:161–63; Mulkeam, *George Mercer Papers*, 493.

91. "William Burnet," *American Quarterly Register* 13 (1841): 291; McIlwain, *Abridgement to the Indian Affairs*, 141–42; Dubcovsky, *Informed Power*, 159–83.

92. Hanna, *Wilderness Trail*, 1:85.

93. McDowell, *Documents Relating to Indian Affairs*, ser. 2, 3:420–21.

94. Merrell, *Indians' New World*, 136, 139; Charles Hudson, *Catawba Nation*, 46; Marvin T. Smith, "Aboriginal Depopulation in the Postcontact Southeast; 259; Kraut, *Silent Travelers*, 14; McCandless, *Slavery, Disease, and Suffering*, 207–8; Theresa E. McReynolds, "Catawba Population Dynamics," 44.

95. Mails, *Cherokee People*, 19.

96. Thornton, *Cherokees*, 1; Hatley, *Dividing Paths*, 3, 13.

97. Swanton, *Final Report of the United States De Soto Expedition Commission*, 327; John Witthoft, "Notes on a Cherokee Migration Story," 305.

98. Adair, *History of the American Indians*, ed. Williams, 237.

99. Mooney, *Myths of the Cherokee*, 15–19; Conley, *Cherokee Nation*, 17; Fogelson, "Who Were the Aní-Kutánî?," 255–63; Smithers, *Cherokee Diaspora*, 75.

100. Thornton, *Cherokees*, 16–18; Kelton, *Cherokee Medicine*, 56–8.

101. Boulware, *Deconstructing the Cherokee Nation*, 6.

102. Drake, *Book of the Indians*, 27; Samuel Cole Williams, *Early Travels in the Tennessee Country*, 122; Henry T. Malone, *Cherokees of the Old South*, 24; Garrison, *Legal Ideology of Removal*, 44.

103. Strickland, *Fire and the Spirits*, 25–7; McLoughlin, *Cherokee Renascence*, 11; Perdue, *Cherokee Women*, 42; Conley, *Cherokee Nation*, 7.

104. Perdue, *Cherokee Women*, 17–20; Hatley, "Cherokee Women Farmers Hold Their Ground," 305–35.

105. Perdue, *Slavery and the Evolution of Cherokee Society*, 3–4, 13; Dunaway, "Incorporation as an Interactive Process," 455–70; Dunaway, *Women, Work, and Family*, 53, 58–60

106. Young Gentleman, *New Voyage to Georgia*, 59; Corkran, *Cherokee Frontier*, 11–12; Hatley, *Dividing Paths*, chap. 9; Robert A. Williams Jr., *Linking Arms Together*, 76–77; Oliphant, *Peace and War on the Anglo-Cherokee Frontier*, xiv, 12, 47, 109; Smithers, *Cherokee Diaspora*, 33.

107. Alliances, or diplomatic friendships, were key to Native Southerners working to preserve peace in their towns and among neighbors. See for example McDowell, *Documents Relating to Indian Affairs*, ser. 2, 3:266.

108. Boulware, *Deconstructing the Cherokee Nation*, 6; Ray, "Introduction: Understanding the Tennessee Corridor," ix–x.

CHAPTER FIVE WAR, REVOLUTION, AND PAN-INDIANISM

1. *South-Carolina Gazette*, August 4–8, 1759, col. 1, p. 2.

2. Fred Anderson, *Crucible of War*, 457; Baugh, *Global Seven Years War*, 358–60; Boulware, *Deconstructing the Cherokee Nation*, 75.

3. John Buckles, Journal, May 7, 1757, in McDowell, *Documents*, Colonial Records of South Carolina: Series 2, p. 459; Jacobs, *Appalachian Indian Frontier*, 49–52; Dowd, "Panic of 1751," 527–60; Wayne E. Lee, "Fortify, Fight, or Flee," 713–70.

4. John Buckles, Journal, May 7, 1757, in McDowell, *Documents*, Colonial Records of South Carolina, Series 2, p. 459; Jacobs, *Appalachian Indian Frontier*, 49–52; Dowd, "Panic of 1751," 527–60; Wayne E. Lee, "Fortify, Fight, or Flee," 713–70.

5. Fred Anderson, *War that Made America*, 165–67.

6. *South-Carolina Gazette*, August 8–11, 1759, col. 2, p. 2. For "Keep the Indians in proper subjugation," see Extract of a Letter from Sir Jeffrey Amherst to the Secretary of War, April 26, 1763, pt. 1, CO, Colonies, CO 323/17, National Archives of Great Britain.

7. Hatley, *Dividing Paths*, 111–13; Boulware, "Effects of the Seven Years' War on the Cherokee Nation," 395–426; Boback, "Indian Warfare, Household Competency," 83; Boulware, *Deconstructing the Cherokee Nation*, 67–68.

8. The above analysis is based on McDowell, *Documents Relating to Indian Affairs*, 2:170–71, 270–71, 275–79, 391–95, 403–6, McDowell, *Documents Relating to Indian Affairs*, 3:9–10, 56–57; Corkran, *Creek Frontier*, 114–20, 125–140; Paulett, *Empire of Small Places*, 102–3, 115–17; Shuck-Hall, *Journey to the West*, 71–72; Cashin, *Governor Henry Ellis*, 79; Cashin, *Lachlan McGillvray*, 85–92; Cashin, *Guardians of the Valley*, 86; Piker, *Four Deaths of Acorn Whistler*; Michael P. Morris, *George Galphin*, 31–37; Tortora, *Carolina in Crisis*, chap. 1.

9. Mapp, "French Geographic Conceptions of the Unexplored West," 166; Kelly L. Watson, *Insatiable Appetites*, 178; Herrera, *Juan Bautista de Anza*, 147; Hämäläinen, *Comanche Empire*, 68; Doolen, *Territories of Empire*, 58.

10. LeMaster, *Brothers Born of One Mother*, 115–16; Ingram, *Indians and British Outposts*, chap. 1; Tortora, *Carolina in Crisis*, 23–24; Nichols, *Engines of Diplomacy*, 20–21; Inman, *Brothers and Friends*, 17, 28–29; Stern, *Lives in Objects*, 49–50, 51, 147–48.

11. Piker, *Okfuskee*, 7, 9; Boulware, *Deconstructing the Cherokee Nation*, 76–77; Boulware, "'Our Mad Young Men,'" 80–98; DeVorsey, "Indian Boundaries in Colonial Georgia," 63–78; Galloway, "Choctaw Factionalism and Civil War," 120–56; Carson, *Searching for the Bright Path*, 31–3; Wayne E. Lee, "Peace Chiefs and Blood Revenge," 701–41; Marcoux, "Cherokee Households and Communities," 70.

12. Bond, *Mississippi*, 4–8; Galloway, "Henri de Tonti du des Cacta,"155–57.

13. Usner, *Indians, Settlers, and Slaves*, 15–17; Carson, "Sacred Circles and Dangerous People," 65–82.

14. Seck, "Relationship between St. Louis of Senegal, Its Hinterlands, and Colonial Louisiana," 268–69; Rushforth, *Bonds of Alliance*, 238.

15. Busbee, *Mississippi*, 31.

16. Usner, *Indians, Settlers, and Slaves*, 95.

17. Milne, *Natchez Country*, 54.

18. James Glen, South Carolina, Answer to Queries, 30 September 1849, 45:79, Shelburne Papers, William L. Clements Library, Manuscripts Division, University of Michigan; Taylor, *American Revolutions*, 255; Smithers, "Our Hands and Hearts Are Joined Together," 609–29.

19. As the British cultivated diplomatic friendships with the Cherokees, French agents sent agents for "talks" with Cherokee chiefs, something that troubled British colonial officials in the southern colonies. See for example, McDowell, *Documents Relating to Indian Affairs*, 2:54. Cherokee chiefs such as Old Hopp rejected French overtures and remained loyal British allies. See Paul Demere to Lyttelton, October 11, 1757, Box 6; Usteneka to Lyttelton, March 2, 1759, Box 10; Little Carpenters Talk to His Excellency the Governor of South Carolina, March 20, 1759, Box 10, Lyttelton Papers, Manuscripts Division, William L. Clements Library, University of Michigan, Ann Arbor.

20. George Clarke, "State of the British Provinces on the Continent of America, with Respect to the French who surround them," 1743, Box 9, Ser. 4, Vaudreuil Papers, Huntington Library.

21. Violence between Native warriors occurred on both a small and large scale. For example, colonists reported skirmishes and violence among Native warriors in the early 1750s, in one instance violence being sparked after a Cherokee hunting party left their camp and absconded with Chickasaw trade goods. See "State of the Chickesaw and Chactaw Nations," in McDowell, *Documents Relating to Indian Affairs*, 2:38.

22. Carpenter, *"Times Are Altered with Us,"* 173.

23. McDowell, *Documents Relating to Indian Affairs*, 2:11; Corkran, *Cherokee Frontier*, 25; Axtell, *Indians' New South*, 48.

24. South Carolina, Journal of Council, September 1, 1752, CO 5/467, National Archives of Great Britain; Memorial of James Glen to George Grenville, Folder 8, Glen Papers, South Caroliniana Library, University of South Carolina; Labaree, *Royal Instructions*, 544; "Considerations on a Future Peace &c. as It Relates to Great Britain Only," October 1759, MS North b.6, North Family Papers, Bodleian Library, Oxford University.

25. CO, South Carolina, Journal of Council, April 7, 1752, CO 5/467, National Archives of Great Britain.

26. Attakullakulla, quoted in Rozema, *Cherokee Voices*, 21. See also Tortora, *Carolina in Crisis*, 177–79. See also Old Hopp, Attakullakulla, & Demere, Summary of Talks, August 30, 1757, Box 5, Lyttelton Papers, William L. Clements Library, Manuscripts Division, University of Michigan.

27. A Talk from Tistoe and the Wolf of Keowee to his Excellency the Governor of South Carolina, March 5, 1759, Box 10, Lyttelton Papers, William L. Clements Library, Manuscripts Division, University of Michigan.

28. Preston, *Texture of Contact*, 153. For two documents that reveal British uncertainty and anxiety about the French and their Indian allies, and Indian chiefs working to assuage British concerns, see "Talk of Caesar to Captain Raymond Demere, December 21, 1756, 3:279–80, and "Old Hopp to Captain Raymond Demere," 3:234–37, both in McDowell, *Documents Relating to Indian Affairs*.

29. Anderson, *Crucible of War*, 213–15; Taylor, *American Colonies*, 430.

30. British officials continued to express concern about the Spanish presence at St. Augustine, worrying that if left unchecked the Spanish would threaten the infant colony of Georgia. See for example P. Collinson to the Earl of Bute, February 5, 1762, MS North b.6, North Family Papers, Bodleian Library, Oxford University; John Stuart, August 8, 1766, Folio 102, CO, Board of Trade and Secretaries of State, CO 5/67.

31. July 18, 1759, Treaty at Waulyhatchez with the Chactaws, Documents Related to Royal Scots, WO 34/40, RH 2/4/561, National Archives of Scotland; Corkran, *Cherokee Frontier*, 191.

32. Grace Steele Woodward, *Cherokees*, 80–81; Tortora, *Carolina in Crisis*, 178–79; Inman, *Brothers and Friends*, 27.

33. Owens, *Red Dreams, White Nightmares*, 3–5.

34. At a Congress held in Augusta on the 10th November 1763, a "Treaty of Peace and Friendship with the Head Men and Warriors of the Chickasaw, Upper & Lower Creeks, Chactaws, Cherokees and Catawbas," CO, Colonies, General, Folio 203, pt. 2 of CO 323/17, National Archives of Great Britain.

35. Sturtevant, "Creek into Seminole," 92–128; Snyder, *Slavery in Indian Country*, 214; F. Todd Smith, *Louisiana and the Gulf South Frontier*, chap. 5.

36. Saunt, *New Order of Things*, 34–36.

37. Covington, "Migration of the Seminoles into Florida," 340–57; Hahn, "Cussita Migration Legend," 67.

38. Angela Pulley Hudson, *Creek Paths and Federal Roads*, 5.

39. Frank, "Red, Black, and Seminole," 50.

40. Wasserman, *People's History of Florida*, 110; Edwin C. McReynolds, *Seminoles*, 140; Shire, *Threshold of Manifest Destiny*, 110; Rosen, *Border Law*, 126.

41. Michael D. Green, *Politics of Indian Removal*, 23; Sattler, "Remnants, Renegades, and Runaways," 52.

42. Waselkov and Braund, *William Bartram*, 89; H. Thomas Foster II, *Archaeology of the Lower Muskogee Creek Indians*, 65; Ramsey, *Yamasee War*, 109.

43. Weer, "Muskhogean Indians," 21.

44. Wright, *Only Land They Knew*, 183; Buffalo Tiger and Kersey, *Buffalo Tiger*, 7; H. Thomas Foster II, *Archaeology of the Lower Muskogee Creek Indians*, 10.

45. Innes, Alexander, and Tilkens, *Beginning Creek*, 14; Mulroy, *Seminole Freedmen*, 139–40.

46. Heard, *Handbook of the American Frontier*, 76–77; Wood, "Changing Population of the Colonial South," 78; Snyder, "The South," 315–33, esp. 319–21.

47. Bartram, *Travels of William Bartram*, 210.

48. Pritzker, *Native American Encyclopedia*, 389.

49. Weisman, *Like Beads on a String*, 49–52; Mulroy, *Freedom on the Border*, 9, 22.

50. Capron, *Medicine Bundles*, 175–85; Sturtevant, "Medicine Bundles and Busks," 31–70; J. Leitch Wright, *Creeks and & Seminoles*, 22; Grantham, *Creation Myths*, 51–52.

51. Kersey, "Those Left Behind," 175; Shire, *Threshold of Manifest Destiny*, 130.

52. Edwin C. McReynolds, *Seminoles*, 24; 96–97; J. Leitch Wright, *Creeks and Seminoles*, 16–17; Ethridge, *Creek Country*, 74; H. Thomas Foster II, *Archaeology of the Lower Muskogee Creek Indians*, 12–13.

53. Alfred Clarke to Governor Tonyn, May 4, 1781, Cornwallis Papers, PRO 30/11/6, National Archives of Great Britain.

54. Porter, *Black Seminoles*, 5; Paisley, *Red Hills of Florida*, 39; Landers, "Nation Divided?," 102; Raab, *Spain, Britain and the American Revolution in Florida*, 86; Landers, *Atlantic Creoles in the Age of Revolutions*, 179–81; Snyder, *Slavery in Indian Country*, 214–17.

55. Frank, "Red, Black, and Seminole," 56–57.

56. Frank, "Red, Black, and Seminole," 59.

57. Gallay, *Formation of the Planter Elite*, 152.

58. Louis Leclerc de Milford to Lt. White, October 19, 1793, in Kinnaird, *Spain in the Mississippi Valley*, 3:222; Raab, *Spain, Britain, and the American Revolution in Florida*, 86; Paisley, *Red Hills of Florida*, 39.

59. DuVal, *Independence Lost*, 310.

60. J. Leitch Wright, *Creeks and Seminoles*, 86; Lockley, introduction, *Maroon Communities*, xx; Mulroy, *Freedom on the Border*, 9–10; Mulroy, *Seminole Freedmen*, 9; DuVal, *Independence Lost*, 248–49; Adams, *Who Belongs?*, 171–72.

61. Allison, *American Revolution*, 57; Merritt, "Native Peoples in the Revolutionary War," 242–44; Schmidt, *Native Americans and the American Revolution*, 25–6; DuVal, *Independence Lost*, 26, 29, 76, 81, 99.

62. Calloway, *American Revolution in Indian Country*, 26. See also Gordon, *South Carolina and the American Revolution*, 40; Schmidt, *Native Americans in the American Revolution*, 166.

63. Gary B. Nash, *Unknown American Revolution*, 262.

64. Speech of the Committee of Fincastle County, Virginia, to Ocanastota judge Friend, Atacullaculla and the Other Chiefs and Warriors of the Cherokee Nation, August 23, 1776, Davie Papers, Virginia Historical Society, Richmond.

65. The British understood this, with officials throughout the Native South expressing a determination to keep Indigenous people well supplied to ensure they remained "well disposed" to the British. See Davies, *Documents of the American Revolution*, 16:78, and Alfred Clarke to Governor Tonyn, May 1, 1781, Cornwallis Papers, PRO 30/11/6, National Archives of Great Britain.

66. Charles Hudson, *Catawba Nation*, 60; Merrell, *Indians' New World*, 195; Plane, "'Remarkable Elasticity of Character,'" 38.

67. Merrell, *Indians' New World*, 216–17; quote is at 217.

68. Calloway, *American Revolution in Indian Country*, 43; Gibbes, *Documentary History of the American Revolution*, 1:197.

69. Hamer, "John Stuart's Indian Policy," 351–66; Hatley, *Dividing Paths*, 229–30; Grenier, *First Way of War*, 159.

70. Thomas Brown to Cornwallis, n.d., PRO 30/11/347, National Archives of Great Britain.

71. Gordon, *South Carolina and the American Revolution*, 51–52; Abram, *Forging a Cherokee-American Alliance*, 14.

72. Mr. Hillsborough to Mr. Stuart, January 11, 1772, CO, Board of Trade and Secretaries of State, Folio 1, CO 5/73; Grace Steele Woodward, *Cherokees*, 85; Perdue, "Cherokee Planters," 113; McLoughlin, *Cherokee Renascence*, 3–4; Perdue, *Cherokee Women*, 104; Tortora, *Carolina in Crisis*, 3–4.

73. W. A. B. to John Murray, 4th Earl of Dunmore, Fol. 274, CO 23/15; Captain William Horton to Captain Ward, August 10, 1744, SP 42/27/106, National Archives of Great Britain; Willis, "Divide and Rule," 157–76; Braund, "Creek Indians, Blacks, and Slavery," 601–36; Saunt, *New Order of Things*, 57–59.

74. See for example Thomas Moodie to Emistescequo, September 6, 1768, Reel 2, August 16, 1754, to January 17, 1776, Colonial Records of Georgia, Georgia State Department of Archives and History.

75. On McGillivray, see DuVal, *Independence Lost*, 24–25. McGillivray was an astute diplomat. In the mid-1780s, McGillivray's distrust of the Americans had grown to such a degree that he courted support from the Spanish in hopes that they might provide the Creeks some protection from the Americans. See "Authorization of McGillivray's July 10, 1785 Memorial," Reel 2, Colonial Records of Georgia; Andres Atkinson to Juan Nepomuceno de Quesada, September 24, 1792, Reel 7, Panton, Leslie & Company Collection, John C. Pace Library, University of West Florida. However, by 1789 the prospect of war between Britain and Spain convinced him of the importance of signing a peace treaty with the nascent United States. See Kinnaird, *Spain in the Mississippi Valley*, 3:xxvii–xxviii.

76. Gibson, *Chickasaws*, 83; Calloway, *American Revolution in Indian Country*, 236; Corbitt and Corbitt, "Papers from the Spanish Archives," 110–42; DuVal, *Independence Lost*, 307.

77. Charles A. Weeks, *Paths to a Middle Ground*, 116.

78. Davies, *Documents of the American Revolution*, 15:96, 114; 17:178–79; Saunt, *New Order of Things*, 75, 81–82; Calloway, *American Revolution in Indian Country*, 236; Rindfleisch, "'Our Lands Are Our Life and Breath,'" 581–603.

79. Braund, *Deerskins and Duffels*, 57–58, chap. 9; Angela Pulley Hudson, *Creek Paths and Federal Roads*, 1–2; Michael P. Morris, *George Galphin*, chap. 6.

80. Saunt, "Age of Imperial Expansion," 77–91

81. Kinnaird, *Spain in the Mississippi Valley*, 2:18, 61–62, 323, 364, 383–84; O'Brien, *Choctaws in a Revolutionary Age*; DuVal, *Independence Lost*, 21, 90, 100, 115,

82. Major General John Campbell to Col. Brown, November 15, 1780, PRO 30/11/349, National Archives of Great Britain; Cushman, *History of the Choctaw, Chickasaw, and Natchez*, 299; Hurt, *Indian Frontier*, 20; O'Brien, *Choctaws in a Revolutionary Age*, 35.

83. Davies, *Documents of the American Revolution*, 17:28; Kidwell, *Choctaws and Missionaries in Mississippi*, 12.

84. O'Brien, "Choctaw Defense of Pensacola," 127.

85. Allevin et al. to Estevan Miro, March 9, 1783, Reel 1, Panton, Leslie & Company Collection, John C. Pace Library, University of West Florida; Kinnaird, *Spain in the Mississippi Valley*, 2:57, 105–7, 146; Akers, *Living in the Land of Death*; O'Brien, *Choctaws in a Revolutionary Age*, 68–70; Cushman, *History of the Choctaw, Chickasaw, and Natchez Indians*, 330; Calloway, *American Revolution in Indian Country*, 44.

86. Atkinson, *Splendid Land, Splendid People*, 38; DuVal, *Independence Lost*, 160–61; Inman, *Brothers and Friends*, 53; Kinnaird, *Spain in the Mississippi Valley*, 2:57.

87. Cegielski and Lieb, "*Hina' Falaa*, 'The Long Path,'" 24–54; quote is at 33.

88. Arrell M. Gibson, *Chickasaws*, 74; Calloway, *American Revolution in Indian Country*, 213–14, 220, 234–36, 238; Atkinson, *Splendid Land, Splendid People*,

23; DuVal, *Lost Independence*, 20. The British perceived the Chickasaws as being "well disposed" to the British but their neutrality was read as a reluctance to fight on Britain's behalf. See Davies, *Documents of the American Revolution*, 15:184 and 17:29.

89. Arrell M. Gibson, *Chickasaws*, 65, 73, 96; Atkinson, *Splendid Land, Splendid People*, 93, 99, 102; Calloway, *American Revolution in Indian Country*, 229; DuVal, *Independence Lost*, 153, 206, 239.

90. Calloway, *American Revolution in Indian Country*, 226–28; Atkinson, *Splendid Land, Splendid People*, 110.

91. Alexander Cameron to the Right Honorable Lord George Germain, July 18, 1780, CO, Board of Trade, Folio 206, CO 5/81, National Archives of Great Britain.

92. DuVal, *Independence Lost*, 240–45, 305.

93. Vaughan, *Early American Indian Documents*, 18:374–76; Arnow, *Seedtime on the Cumberland*, 326; DuVal, *Independence Lost*, 261.

94. David Taitt to Stuart, March 16, 1772, CO, Board of Trade, Folio 259, CO 5/73, National Archives of Great Britain; Cushman, *History of the Choctaw, Chickasaw, and Natchez Indians*, 53; *American Revolution in Indian Country*, 234, 238, 240–42; DuVal, *Independence Lost*, 244, 305–9.

95. Prucha, *Documents of United States Indian Policy*, 6–7; Grace Steele Woodward, *Cherokees*, 105; David W. Miller, *Taking of American Indian Lands*, 75–76.

96. Salisbury, "Native People and European Settlers," 483; Rosier, *Serving Their Country*, 4. The best and most complete analysis of President George Washington's Indian policy is Calloway, *The Indian World of George Washington*.

97. Jefferson, *Writings*, ed. Washington, 4:467.

98. Quoted in Dennis, "Red Jacket's Rhetoric," Stromberg, 21.

99. Herbert, "'To Treat with All Nations,'" 27.

100. J. Alling to John Leslie, October 2, 1790, Reel 6, Panton, Leslie & Company Collection, John C. Pace Library, University of West Florida.

101. See Dowd, *Spirited Resistance*.

102. Cave, "Delaware Prophet Neolin," 100; Kathleen DuVal, "Living in a Reordered World,'" 71.

103. DuVal, *Independence Lost*, 18.

104. Dowd, *Spirited Resistance*, 135; Jortner, *Gods of Prophetstown*, 29; Bellin, *Medicine Bundle*, 147.

105. Dowd, *Spirited Resistance*, 109; David Dixon, "'We Speak As One People,'" 59–60.

106. Dowd, *Spirited Resistance*, 68–70; Cave, *Prophets of the Great Spirit*, 37–39; Carpenter, *"Times Are Altered with Us,"* 190–92.

107. Dowd, *Spirited Resistance*, 52–54.

108. Grace Steele Woodward, *Cherokees*, 93–94; Hatley, *Dividing Path*, 227; Dowd, *Spirited Resistance*, 48–49, 53, 63.

109. Conley, *Cherokee Medicine Man*, 10.

110. See Calloway, *Victory with No Name*.

111. Willig, *Restoring the Chain of Friendship*, 213.

112. Dowd, *Spirited Resistance*, 169–83; Saunt, *New Order of Things*, 233–72.

CHAPTER SIX TRIBAL NATIONALISM, REMOVAL, AND DIASPORA

1. Saunt, *A New Order of Things*, 249–72; Davis, "'Remember Fort Mims,'" 611–36; Blackmon, *Creek War*, 15–18; Waselkov, *Conquering Spirit*, 117, 174.

2. Halbert and Ball, *Creek War of 1813 and 1814*, p. 169.

3. On the "eliminationist logic" of settler colonialism, see Wolfe, *Settler Colonialism*, 29; "Land, Labor, and Difference," 866–905; and "Settler Colonialism and the Elimination of the Native," 387–409; and also Veracini, *Settler Colonialism*, 13. On comparative British efforts to order the colonial world through the law, see Benton and Ford, *Rage for Order*.

4. Stephen B. Weeks, *Letters of Benjamin Hawkins*, 74, 175, 288; Caughey, *McGillivray of the Creeks*, 22–24; Perdue and Green, *Columbia Guide*, 83; Amos J. Wright, *McGillivray and McIntosh Traders*, 217.

5. *Niles' Weekly Register*, March 17, 1832, p. 42; Banner, *How the Indians Lost their Land*, 9, 203, 221; Lisa Ford, *Settler Sovereignty*, 3, 21, 191; Rosen, *American Indians and State Law*, 39.

6. Blunt, *American Annual Register*, 580; Peters, *Case of the Cherokee Nation*, 285; *American State Papers*, 6:1034.

7. J. Leitch Wright Jr., *Creeks and Seminoles*, 146–49.

8. Waselkov, *Conquering Spirit*, 41.

9. Davis, "'Remember Fort Mims,'" 615–19, 622; Waselkov, *Conquering Spirit*, 48.

10. Laxar, *Tecumseh and Brock*, 224–26.

11. Benn, *Iroquois in the War of 1812*, 22, 38, 52; Taylor, *Civil War of 1812*, 27, 167; Stagg, *War of 1812*, 5.

12. Piker, *Okfuskee*, 196; Thrower, "Casualties and Consequences of the Creek War," 10–29.

13. Calloway, *Pen and Ink Witchcraft*, 123–24; Summitt, *Sequoyah and the Invention of the Cherokee Alphabet*, 27; Gregory and Strickland, *Sam Houston with the Cherokees*, 9. For lesser known Cherokees, memories of the Battle of Horseshoe bend were passed down in oral narratives. See Smithers, *Cherokee Diaspora*, 255.

14. Robert Love to William Holland Thomas, October 29, 1822, Correspondence, 1814–1834, Thomas Papers, David M. Rubenstein Rare Book & Manuscript Library, Duke University.

15. Memorial to His Excellency, Gen Bustamente, Commander-in-Chief, &c., &c., July 2, 1827, Bollaert Papers, Newberry Library; McLoughlin, *Cherokee Renascence*, 264; Abram, *Forging a Cherokee-American Alliance*, 83–85; Smithers, *Cherokee Diaspora*, 52–53.

16. McLoughlin, *Cherokee Renascence*, chap. 16; Denson, *Demanding the Cherokee Nation*, 24.

17. Daniel Clark, "An Account of the Indian Tribes Inhabiting Louisiana," September 29, 1803, quoted in Edwin Clarence Carter and Bloom, *Territorial Papers*, 9:64.

18. Irwin, *Coming Down from Above*, 208; Zorgy, *Anetso*, 96; Smithers, *Cherokee Diaspora*, 75–76.

19. Such views were often expressed in romantic racialist terms, emphasizing the natural "nobility" of Native Southerners before contact with Europeans. See July 21, 1792, Benjamin Rush, Commonplace Book, and Journal, B R89c, American Philosophical Society; Benezet, *A Short Account*, 72; Evarts, *Essays on the Present Crisis*, 8, 21, 55; Worsley, *A View of the American Indians*, 143.

20. Nott, *Two Lectures*, 34; Jennison, *Cultivating Race*, 208; Mielke, *Moving Encounters*, 66.

21. Yarbrough, *Race and the Cherokee Nation*, 42–43. On the literary uses of "full-blood" and "half-breed" nomenclature in nineteenth-century literature, see Scheick, *The Half-Blood*; Harry J. Brown, *Injun Joe's Ghost*.

22. *Senate Journal, Florida*, 38; Weddle, *Changing Tides*, 254.

23. Arrell M. Gibson, *Chickasaws*, 113–14, 153–54; Hurt, *Indian Frontier*, 152.

24. Debo, *Rise and Fall of the Choctaw Republic*, 48–49; Mihesuah, *Choctaw Crime and Punishment*, 15; Osburn, *Choctaw Resurgence*, 10.

25. Hoxie, *Indian Country*, 49–50; Pitchlynn, *Gathering of Statesmen*, 5–6.

26. Ephraim Kirby to Thomas Jefferson, May 1, 1804, Ephraim Kirby Papers, 1763–1878, David M. Rubenstein Rare Book & Manuscript Library, Duke University. See also "Treaty with the Choctaw, 1830," in Kappler, *Indian Affairs*, 312; Akers, *Living in the Land of Death*, 4, 8, 23, 37; Carson, *Searching for the Bright Path*, 87–88; and David W. Miller, *Taking of American Indian Lands*, 148.

27. White, *Roots of Dependency*, 90–91; Guice, "Face to Face in Mississippi Territory," 158; Atkinson, *Splendid Land, Splendid People*, 177; Shell, *Evolution of the Alabama Agroecosystem*, 253; David W. Miller, *Taking of American Indian Lands*, 66–67; Angela Pulley Hudson, *Real Native Genius*, 17.

28. Rufus Ward, "Choctaw Farmsteads in Mississippi," 33–41; Carson, "Horses and the Economy," 495–513; Boulware, "'Skilful Jockies' and 'Good Sadlers,'" 68–95.

29. *Niles' Weekly Register*, March 22, 1817, p. 56; Carson, *Searching for the Bright Path*, 61, 64.

30. Notes on Cherokee History, Payne Papers, 209, Newberry Library.

31. Atkinson, *Splendid Land, Splendid People*, 24, 216, 220; Kidwell, *Choctaws and Missionaries*, 25–27.

32. Littlefield, *Africans and Seminoles*, 4.

33. Gifford, *Billy Bowlegs*; Porter, "Founder of the 'Seminole Nation,'" 362–84; Calloway, *American Revolution in Indian Country*, 249–50; Porter, *Black Seminoles*, 27–32; Weisman, *Like Beads on a String*, 9–10.

34. Rivers, *Rebels and Runaways*, 136; Hutchinson, "Osceola's Calicoes," 267–68; Hatch, *Osceola and the Great Seminole War*, 101. The best analysis of Osceola and the Second Seminole War is Monaco, *Second Seminole War*.

35. Nabhan, *Enduring Seeds*, 148–49; Littlefield, *Africans and Seminoles*, 17, 109–13.

36. Perdue, *Cherokee Women*, 61, 92, 116; Miles, "Circular Reasoning," 221–43. Ward rose to become a Beloved Woman among the Cherokees, counseling the white path of peace. See Donaldson, "'But We Are Your Mothers, You Are Our Sons,'" 35.

37. Reid, *Law of Blood*, 105; McLoughlin, *Cherokee Renascence*, 347–48; Perdue, *Cherokee Women*, 150; Miles, *Ties That Bind*, 229–30.

38. James McKay, "The Cherokee Nation Must be Free to Expel Black Freedmen," *The Guardian*, September 17, 2011, https://www.theguardian.com/commentisfree/2011/sep/17/cherokee-nation-black-freedmen.

39. Miles, *Ties That Bind*, 2, 14, 44, 57; Yarbrough, *Race and the Cherokee Nation*, 39–45.

40. On these issues see Yarbrough, *Race and the Cherokee Nation*; Miles, *House on Diamond Hill*; and Krauthamer, *Black Slaves, Indian Masters*.

41. *American State Papers*, 1:296–98; Caughey, *McGillivray of the Creeks*, 303; Ethridge, *Creek Country*, 161.

42. Zellar, *African Creeks*, 15, 39; Saunt, *Black, White, and Indian*, 10, 31–33, 43; Snyder, *Slavery in Indian Country*, 201; Miles, *House on Diamond Hill*, 72.

43. See Larry S. Watson, *Indian Removal Records*.

44. Thomas Jefferson to Benjamin Hawkins, February 18, 1803, *Writings*, edited by Merrill D. Peterson, 1115.

45. DeRosier, *Removal of the Choctaw Indians*, 26–28; Strickland, *Fire and the Spirits*, 51–2; McLoughlin, *Cherokee Renascence*, 130–31; Witgen, *Infinity of Nations*, 322, 365.

46. Calhoun, *Works*, 5:17–19; Michael D. Green, *Politics of Indian Removal*, 46. For a broader geographical analysis of removal politics, see Faragher, "'More Motley than Mackinaw,'" 320; Bowes, *Land Too Good for Indians*.

47. Prucha, *Documents*, 39–40; Satz, *American Indian Policy*, 6; Green, *Politics of Indian Removal*, 46; Haveman, *Rivers of Sand*, 6.

48. Andrew Jackson, *Papers*, 6:184; Andrew Jackson, *Papers*, 7:83–85; Hryniewicki, "Creek Treaty of Washington," 425–61; Prucha, *American Indian Treaties*, 149–50.

49. Georgia Controversy, March 3, 1827, in *Report of the Select Committee*, 10–11; Green, *Politics of Indian Removal*, 37, 107; Frank, *Creeks and Seminoles*, 98; Calloway, *White People, Indians, and Highlanders*, 193. See also Winn, *Triumph of the Ecunnau-Nuxulgee*.

50. Rockwell, *Indian Affairs*, 145–46. After his presidency, Adams viewed the topic of Indian removal as a Jacksonian conspiracy. See Lynn H. Parsons, "'A Perpetual Harrow upon My Feelings,'" 338.

51. *Journal of the House of Representatives*, 25; *Columbia Star*, June 19, 1830, p. 390.

52. Ryan, *Grammar of Good Intentions*, 28; Hershberger, "Mobilizing Women," 15–40. For the rationale behind Frelinghuysen's opposition to removal, see Evarts, *Essays*, and Frelinghuysen, *Speech*.

53. Norgen, *Cherokee Cases*, 80–83.

54. McKenney, *Sketches*, 427.

55. *Documents and Proceedings*, 37–42; Andrews, *From Revivals to Removal*, 194.

56. Harry Watson, *Liberty and Power*, 110.

57. Prucha, *Documents*, 52–53.

58. Quoted in Rogin, *Fathers and Children*, 241.

59. Kappler, *Indian Affairs*, 2:341–43.

60. Green, *Politics of Indian Removal*, 185. Haveman contends that in excess of 19,600 Creeks were relocated from all of their southeastern homelands. Haveman, *Rivers of Sand*, 299.

61. Jack, "Alabama and the Federal Government," 301–17; Ellisor, *Second Creek War*, 47–49.

62. Quotations are from Neah Micco and Tus-Ke-Neah-Haw to Lewis Cass, December 30, 1832, in *Correspondence*, 3:565. See also John Fowler to Robert L. Comb, December 29, 1819, in Edwin Clarence Carter and Bloom, *Territorial Papers*, 19:134; Hurt, *Indian Frontier*, 150.

63. Haveman, *Bending Their Own Way*, 83, 107, 248.

64. Kidwell, *Choctaws and Missionaries*, 119–20; Hurt, *Indian Frontier*, 142; Carson, *Searching for the Bright Path*, 87; Carson, "Mastering Language,'" 221.

65. Carson, *Searching for the Bright Path*, 119.

66. Perdue and Green, *Columbia Guide*, 84.

67. Kappler, *Indian Affairs*, 2:310–19.

68. Debo, *Rise and Fall*, 58.

69. Arrell M. Gibson, *Chickasaws*, 174, 257; Perdue and Green, *Columbia Guide*, 85; Atkinson, *Splendid Land, Splendid People*, 188, 209, 211, 225; St. Jean, *Remaining Chickasaw*, 9–10.

70. Arrell M. Gibson, *Chickasaws*, 142, 152, 172–74, 217; Barnett, *Mississippi's American Indians*, 204–8; St. Jean, *Remaining Chickasaw*, 9–13.

71. Kappler, *Indian Affairs*, 2:418–25; *Journal of the Senate*, 588; Barnett, *Mississippi's American Indians*, 205; Atkinson, *Splendid Land, Splendid People*, 233–34.

72. Davis, *Constitution and Laws*, 178.

73. Debo, *Road to Disappearance*, 102. For an overview of Chickasaw removal, see Paige, Bumpers, and Littlefield, *Chickasaw Removal*.

74. Foreman, *Indian Removal*, 216–17.

75. Debo, *Road to Disappearance*, 102; Krauthamer, *Black Slaves, Indian Masters*, 50; Gibson, *Chickasaws*, 189; St. Jean, *Remaining Chickasaw*, 32.

76. Denson, *Demanding the Cherokee Nation*, chap. 1.

77. Charles Hicks to Return J. Meigs, June 23, 1819, Correspondence and Miscellaneous Records, Records of the Cherokee Indian Agency in Tennessee, 1801–1835, M 208, RG 75, NARA.

78. On this point see Smithers, *Cherokee Diaspora*.

79. *Cherokee Phoenix*, March 20, 1828, p. 2; April 24, 1828, p. 3; May 11, 1828, p. 2.

80. *Vindication*, 8, Manuscripts Division, Library of Congress.

81. *Cherokee Phoenix*, July 21, 1828, p. 2; Boudinot, *Address to the Whites*; Perdue, *Cherokee Editor*, 92. On Boudinot and the *Cherokee Phoenix*, see Martin, "Cherokee Phoenix," 102–18; Malone, "*Cherokee Phoenix*," 163–88; Schneider, "Boudinot's Change," 151–77.

82. *Cherokee Phoenix*, March 13, 1828, p. 2

83. On this point, see David E. Wilkins and Lomawaima, *Uneven Ground*.

84. *The American Jurist and Law Magazine*, January, 1831, p. 225; Wirt, *Opinion*, 17; Ames, *State Documents*, 36; "An Act to Prevent the Exercise of Assumed and Arbitrary Power, By all Persons Under the Pretext of Authority from the Cherokee Indians . . .," in *Acts of the General Assembly of the State of Georgia*, 114–17; McLoughlin, *Cherokee Renascence*, 261; Vine Deloria Jr. and Lytle, *Nations Within*, chap. 2; Henry T. Malone, *Cherokees of the Old South*, 90; David Williams, *Georgia Gold Rush*; Smithers, *Cherokee Diaspora*, 17; Pratt, "Violence and the Competition for Sovereignty," 181–97. On Tassel's conviction, see Blunt, *American Annual Register*, 28; Garrison, *Legal Ideology*, 4; Lisa Ford, *Settler Sovereignty*, 189–91.

85. John Ridge to Hon. George Gilmer, n.d., John Ridge, ca. 1821–1835, Newberry Library.

86. *Niles' Weekly Register*, June 25, 1831, p. 298; *Examiner and Journal of Political Economy*, February 4, 1835, p. 210.

87. Jeremiah Evarts to "Dear Sir," January 16, 1830, Section A, Evarts Papers, David M. Rubenstein Rare Book & Manuscript Library, Duke University.

88. David E. Wilkins, *American Indian Sovereignty*, 368; Bruyneel, *Third Space*, 52; Lisa Ford, *Settler Sovereignty*, 191; Philip Weeks, *"Farewell, My Nation,"* 55.

89. McLoughlin, *Cherokee Renascence*, 443; Norgen, *Cherokee Cases*, 114, 145–49; Perdue and Green, *Cherokee Nation and the Trail of Tears*, 119.

90. Andrew Jackson, quoted in *Niles' Weekly Register*, April 4, 1835, p. 88.

91. Moulton, *John Ross*, 67; Wilkins, *Cherokee Tragedy*, 274; Garrison, *Legal Ideology*, 231; Calloway, *Pen and Ink Witchcraft*, 141.

92. To the Commissioners under the Cherokee Treaty of 1835, Correspondence, 1835–36, Thomas Papers, David M. Rubenstein Rare Book & Manuscript Library, Duke University; Grace Steele Woodward, *Cherokees*, 193; Moulton, *John Ross*, 73–75; Thornton, *Cherokees*, 78–79; Thurman Wilkins, *Cherokee Tragedy*, 4; Gaul, introduction, *To Marry an Indian*, ed. Gaul, 65.

93. John Ellis Wool to Head Quarters, January 11, 1837, Wool Papers, David M. Rubenstein Rare Book & Manuscript Library, Duke University; George R. Gilmer to Joel R. Poinsett, March 3, 1838, Records of the Cherokee Indian Agency, Cherokee Letters Received and Sent, Superintendency for Emigration of the Cherokees, Office of Indian Affairs, RG 75, NARA; Moulton, *John Ross*, 101; Royal, *Letters from Alabama*, 60; Grace Steele Woodward, *Cherokees*, 188–90.

94. Foreman, *Indian Removal*, 19; Frank, *Creeks and Southerners*, 101, 114; Monaco, *Second Seminole War*.

95. John L. Williams, *Territory of Florida*, 235–38; Mahon, *History of the Second*

Seminole War, chap. 3; Mulroy, *Seminole Freedmen*, 45; Baptist, *Creating an Old South*, 14; Hatch, *Osceola and the Great Seminole War*, 104, 141, 240.

96. Shire, *Threshold of Destiny*, 45; Edwin C. McReynolds, *Seminoles*, 144–45; Mahon, *History of the Second Seminole War*, chap. 6; Wickman, *Osceola's Legacy*, 91–92; Monaco, *Second Seminole War*.

97. Gibson, *Chickasaws*, 164; Perdue and Green, *Cherokee Nation and the Trail of Tears*, 154; Haveman, *Rivers of Sand*, 273.

98. Wallace, *Long, Bitter Trail*, 85–86.

99. DeRosier, *Removal of the Choctaw Indians*, 132.

100. Kidwell, "Struggle for Land and Identity in Mississippi," 64–93; Osburn, *Choctaw Resurgence*, chap. 1.

101. Kidwell, "Struggle for Land and Identity in Mississippi," 64.

102. Roberts, "Second Choctaw Removal," 94.

103. Smithers, *Cherokee Diaspora*, 182.

104. Thornton, *Cherokees*, 88; Finger, *Cherokee Americans*, 7; Stremlau, *Sustaining the Cherokee Family*, 34.

105. Doran, "Population Statistics," 492–515.

106. Mark E. Miller, *Claiming Tribal Identity*, 150–57; Haveman, *Rivers of Sand*, 268–69.

107. Perdue, "Legacy of Indian Removal," 3.

108. Lowery, *Lumbee Indians*, 59. On bureaucratic, or "paper," genocide, see Arica Coleman, *That the Blood Stay Pure*; Smithers, *Science, Sexuality, and Race*, 294–304.

EPILOGUE

1. Telephone interview, Chief Lynette Allston, July 17, 2017.

2. Telephone interview, Beverly Payne, July 24, 2017.

3. Telephone interview, Kelly Fayard, July 31, 2017.

4. Josh Moon, "Just Give Alabama Back to the Poarch Creeks, *Montgomery Advertiser*, August 25, 2016, http://www.montgomeryadvertiser.com/story/news /local/blogs/moonblog/2016/08/25/josh-moon-just-give-alabama-back-poarch -creeks/89337098/.

5. Poarch Creek Indians website, http://www.poarchneighbors.com/faces /sovereign/index.html.

6. Telephone interview, Chief Harold Hatcher, July 11, 2017.

7. McAuliffe, *Bloodland*; Smithers, "Beyond the 'Ecological Indian,'" 83–111; Grann, *Killers of the Flower Moon*.

8. Kennedy, "Native Americans, African Americans, and the Space that Is America," 196–217, esp. 200–201; Miles, *Tales from the Haunted South*, 16.

9. Historian James Taylor Carson has expressed reservations about the utility of diaspora as a framework of analysis in Native American history. See his "Who Was First and When?," 111–24, and "Ethnic Cleansing and the Trail of Tears."

10. A useful introduction to the study of diasporas is Kenny, *Diaspora*. Some important new conceptual insights on this topic can be found in Andrea Smith and Einstein, *Rebuilding Shattered Worlds*.

11. On this point, see Guyatt, *Bind Us Apart*. On race and the Enlightenment, see Eze, *Race and the Enlightenment*.

12. Thornton, "Cherokee Population Losses," 189–90.

13. Rozema, *Voices from the Trail of Tears*, 94.

14. Rozema, *Voices from the Trail of Tears*, 29, 31, 88, 94, 139; Wallace, *Long, Bitter Trail*, 43, 57, 93–94; Spence, *Dispossessing the Wilderness*, 15; Sturgis, *Trail of Tears*, 58; Neugin, "Memories of the Trail," 376; McCoy, *History of Baptist Indian Missions*, 373; Perdue and Green, *Cherokee Nation and Trail of Tears*, 137–39.

15. Hicks, quoted in Perdue, *Cherokee Removal*, 164–65.

16. McLoughlin, *After the Trail of Tears*, 252; Naylor, *African Cherokees*, 2; Haveman, *Bending Their Own Way*, 189, 204, 214.

17. Foreman, *Emigration of the Five Civilized Tribes*, 365–66. For the historical experiences of enslaved people on the Trail of Tears, see Krauthamer, *Black Slaves, Indian Masters*; Naylor, *African Cherokees*.

18. Foreman, *The Emigration of the Five Civilized Tribes*, 142; Zellar, *African Creeks*, 33–35; Chang, *Color of the Land*, 29; Lupold and French, *Bridging Deep South Rivers*, 61–62.

19. Akers, *Living in the Land of Death*, 64, 84, 121.

20. Gilbert, *Trail of Tears Across Missouri*, 3–4.

21. Sturm, *Blood Politics*, 65–66; Krauthamer, *Black Slaves, Indian Masters*, 93–95; Naylor, *African Cherokees*, 126; Haveman, *Rivers of Sand*, 266–67; Perdue and Green, *Columbia Guide*, 100–101.

22. Jason Baird Jackson, *Yuchi Ceremonial Life*, 34; Zellar, *African Creeks*, 98; Perdue and Green, *Columbia Guide*, 102; Haveman, *Rivers of Sand*, 122, 258; Lakomäki, *Gathering Together*, 191.

23. Conley, *Cherokee Nation*, 167; Miles, *Ties That Bind*, 181, 186; Stremlau, *Sustaining the Cherokee Family*, chap. 1; Smithers, *Cherokee Diaspora*, 136.

24. Debo, *Rise and Fall of the Choctaw Republic*, 76; St. Jean, *Remaining Chickasaw*, 16–17; Krauthamer, *Black Slaves, Indian Masters*, 6, 9.

25. Naylor, *African Cherokees*, 126, 134; Krauthamer, *Black Slaves, Indian Masters*, 93, 98–99.

26. Pitchlynn, "Inaugural Address," 2, Huntington Library, San Marino, Calif.

27. Minda G. Hardin, interview, March 25, 1937, Indian Pioneer Papers, Western History Collection, University of Oklahoma, Norman.

28. Fayard, "'We've Always Known Who We Are,'" 1.

29. Perdue, "Southern Indians and Jim Crow," 54–90; Melanie Benson Taylor, *Reconstructing the Native South*, 87. For more on this point, see Adams, *Who Belongs?*

30. Plateau Region as unofficial refuge for Cherokee, interview with Ken Wills, Coal River Folklife Collection, American Folklore Center, Library of Congress; Spencer, *Special Report*, 3; Finger, *Eastern Band of Cherokees*, 14, 31, 176; Finger,

Cherokee Americans, 256; Mark E. Miller, *Claiming Tribal Identity*; Fayard, "'We've Always Known Who We Are.'"

31. See Osburn, *Choctaw Resurgence in Mississippi*; Finger, *Cherokee Americans*; Fayard, "'We've Always Known Who We Are'"; McReynolds, *Seminoles*; J. Leitch Wright, *Creeks and Seminoles*; Hobson, McAdams, and Walkiewicz, *People Who Stayed*; Lowery, *Lumbee Indians in the Jim Crow South*; Perdue, "Legacy of Indian Removal," 3–36.

32. For more, see Bates, *We Will Always Be Here*.

BIBLIOGRAPHY

ARCHIVAL SOURCES

American Folklore Center. Library of Congress, Washington, D.C.
Coal River Folklife Collection.

American Philosophical Society, Philadelphia.
Barton, Benjamin Smith, Papers.
Rush, Benjamin. Commonplace Book, 1792–1813, and Journal [1800].
Speck, Frank G., Papers.

Bodleian Library, Oxford University, Oxford, England.
North Family Papers.

David M. Rubenstein Rare Book & Manuscript Library, Duke University, Durham, N.C.
Evarts, Jeremiah, Papers.
Kirby, Ephraim, Papers, 1763–1878.
Thomas, William Holland, Papers.
Wool, John Ellis, Papers.

Georgia State Department of Archives and History, Atlanta.
Colonial Records of Georgia.

Huntington Library, San Marino, Calif.
Loudoun Papers: Americana, 1510–1839.
Pitchlynn, Peter P. "The Inaugural Address of Gov. Pitchlynn," 1863.
Vaudreuil Papers, 1698–1788.

John C. Pace Library, University of West Florida, Pensacola.
Panton, Leslie & Company Collection, 1739–1847.

Manuscripts Division. Library of Congress, Washington, D.C.
East Florida Records, 1737–1858.
A Vindication of the Cherokee Claims, Addressed to the Town Meeting in Philadelphia, on the 11th of January, 1830.

National Archives of Great Britain, London.
 Colonial Office (hereafter CO). Board of Trade and Secretaries of State: American
  and West Indians, Original Correspondence, Indian Affairs, Surveys, Etc.,
  1766–1767. CO 5/67.
 CO. Board of Trade and Secretaries of State: American and West Indians, Original
  Correspondence, Indian Affairs, Surveys, Etc., 1771–1772. CO 5/73.
 CO. Board of Trade and Secretaries of State: American and West Indians, Original
  Correspondence, Indian Affairs, Surveys, Etc., 1779–1780. CO 5/81.
 CO. Colonial Office and Predecessors: Bahamas, Original Correspondence. CO
  23/15.
 CO. Colonies, General: Original Correspondence, Secretary of State. CO 323/17.
 CO. South Carolina, Journal of Council, February 1752–November 1752. CO
  5/467.
 Public Record Office (PRO). Cornwallis, Charles, Papers. PRO 30/11/6.
 State Papers (SP). Secretary of State, Report from the Upper Creek Nation that a
  Great Body of Spaniards Was Expected in Florida that Summer, August 10,
  1744. SP 42/27/106.

National Archives of Scotland, Edinburgh.
 Documents Relating to Royal Scots, 1684–1855. RH 2/4/561.

National Archives Record Administration (NARA), Washington, D.C.
 Records of the Cherokee Indian Agency in Tennessee, 1801–1835. Cherokee
  Letters Received and Sent, January 1, 1835–January 26, 1839, Superintendency
  for Emigration of the Cherokees. Record Group 75.

Newberry Library, Chicago.
 Bollaert, William, Papers. VAULT Ayer MS 89.
 Payne, John Howard, Papers, 1794–1841. Ayer MS 689.
 Ridge, John, ca. 1821–1835. Box Ayer MS 761.

South Caroliniana Library, University of South Carolina, Columbia.
 Glen, James, Papers.

Southern Historical Collection, University of North Carolina, Chapel Hill.
 Quarles, James Perrin, Jr., Papers.
 Wills, William Henry, Papers.

Virginia Historical Society, Richmond.
 Davie, Preston, Papers, 1750–1967. MSS 1 D2856 d7–9.

Western History Collection, University of Oklahoma, Norman.
 Indian Pioneer Papers.

William L. Clements Library, Manuscripts Division, University of Michigan, Ann
Arbor.
 Lyttelton, William Henry, Papers, 1730–1806.
 Shelburne Papers.

BOOKS AND ARTICLES

Abram, Susan M. *Forging a Cherokee-American Alliance in the Creek War: From Creation to Betrayal.* Tuscaloosa: University of Alabama Press, 2015.

Acosta, José de. *Natural and Moral History of the Indies.* Edited by Jane E. Mangan. Durham, N.C.: Duke University Press, 2002

"An Act to Prevent the Exercise of Assumed and Arbitrary Power, by all Persons under Pretext of Authority from the Cherokee Indians." In *Acts of the General Assembly of the State of Georgia, Passed in Milledgeville at an Annual Session in November and December, 1829,* pp. 114–17. Milledgeville, Ga.: Camak and Ragand, 1830.

Adair, James. *The History of the American Indians.* Edited by Kathryn E. Holland Braund. Tuscaloosa: University of Alabama Press, 2005.

———. *The History of the American Indians.* Edited by Samuel C. Williams. 1775. Reprint, Johnson City, Tenn.: Watauga, 1930.

Adams, Mikaëla M. *Who Belongs? Race, Resources, and Tribal Citizenship in the Native South.* New York: Oxford University Press, 2016.

Adovasio, J. M., with Jake Page. *The First Americans: In Pursuit of Archeology's Greatest Mystery.* New York: Modern Library Paperbacks, 2003.

Akers, Donna. *Living in the Land of Death: The Choctaw Nation, 1830–1860.* East Lansing: Michigan State University Press, 2004.

Allison, Robert. *The American Revolution: A Concise History.* New York: Oxford University Press, 2011.

Alvord, Clarence Walworth, and Lee Bidgood. *The First Explorations of the Trans-Allegheny Region by the Virginians, 1650–1674.* Cleveland, Ohio: Arthur H. Clark, 1912.

American State Papers: Indian Affairs. Vol. 1. Washington, D.C.: Gales and Seaton, 1832.

American State Papers: Military Affairs. Vol. 6. Washington, D.C.: Gales and Seaton, 1860.

Ames, Herman V., ed. *State Documents on Federal Relations: The States and the United States.* Clark, N.J.: Lawbook Exchange, 2006.

Anderson, Chris, and Jean M. O'Brien, eds. *Sources and Methods in Indigenous Studies.* London: Routledge, 2017.

Anderson, David G. *Chiefdoms: Political Change in the Late Prehistoric Southeast.* Tuscaloosa: University of Alabama Press, 1994.

Anderson, Fred. *Crucible of War: The Seven Years' War and the Fate of Empire in British North America, 1754–1766.* New York: Random House, 2000.

———. *The War That Made America: A Short History of the French and Indian War.* New York: Viking, 2005.

Anderson, Gary Clayton. *The Indian Southwest, 1580–1830: Ethnogenesis and Reinvention.* Norman: University of Oklahoma Press, 1999.

Andrew, John A., III. *From Revivals to Removal: Jeremiah Evarts, the Cherokee Nation, and the Search for the Soul of America.* Athens: University of Georgia Press, 1992.

Arnold, Morris. *The Rumble of a Distant Drum: The Quapaws and Old World Newcomers, 1673–1804.* Fayetteville: University of Arkansas Press, 2000.

Arnow, Harriette S. *Seedtime on the Cumberland*. Lincoln: University of Nebraska Press, 1960.

Aron, Paul D. *Mysteries in History: From Prehistory to the Present*. Santa Barbara, Calif. ABC-CLIO, 2006.

Atkinson, James R. "The De Soto Expedition through North Mississippi in 1540–41." *Mississippi Archaeology* 22, no. 1 (1987): 67–73.

———. *Splendid Land, Splendid People: The Chickasaw Indians to Removal*. Tuscaloosa: University of Alabama Press, 2004.

Atleo, Richard E. (Emeek). *Tsawalk: A Nuu-chah-nulth Worldview*. Vancouver: University of British Columbia Press, 2004.

Axtell, James. *The Indians' New South: Cultural Change in the Colonial Southeast*. Baton Rouge: Louisiana State University Press, 1997.

———. *Natives and Newcomers: The Cultural Origins of North America*. New York: Oxford University Press, 2001.

Banner, Stuart. *How the Indians Lost Their Land: Law and Power on the Frontier*. Cambridge, Mass.: Harvard University Press, 2009.

Baptist, Edward E. *Creating an Old South: Middle Florida's Plantation Frontier before the Civil War*. Chapel Hill: University of North Carolina Press, 2002.

Barnett, James F., Jr. *Mississippi's American Indians*. Jackson: University of Mississippi Press, 2012.

———. *The Natchez Indians: A History to 1735*. Jackson: University Press of Mississippi, 2007.

Barr, Juliana. *Peace Came in the Form of a Woman: Indians and Spaniards in the Texas Borderlands*. Chapel Hill: University of North Carolina Press, 2007.

Barrett, Elinore. *The Spanish Colonial Settlement Landscapes of New Mexico, 1598–1680*. Albuquerque: University of New Mexico Press, 2012.

Bartram, William. *Travels of William Bartram: Naturalist Edition*. Edited by Francis Harper. Athens: University of Georgia Press, 1998.

———. *Travels through North and South Carolina, Georgia, East and West Florida, the Cherokee Country, the Extensive Territories of the Muscogulges or Creek Confederacy, and the Country of Chactaws*. Dublin, Ireland: J. Moore, W. Jones, R. McAllister, and J. Rice, 1794.

Bates, Denise E., ed. *We Will Always Be Here: Native Peoples on Living and Thriving in the South*. Gainesville: University Press of Florida, 2016.

Baugh, Daniel. *The Global Seven Years War, 1754–1763*. New York: Routledge, 2011.

Beck, Robin. *Chiefdoms, Collapse, and Coalescence in the Early American South*. New York: Cambridge University Press, 2013.

Beck, Robin A., Jr. "Catawba Coalescence and the Shattering of the Carolina Piedmont, 1540–1675." In Ethridge and Shuck-Hall, *Mapping the Mississippian Shatter Zone*, 115–41.

———. "Consolidation and Hierarchy: Chiefdom Variability in the Mississippian Southeast." *American Antiquity* 68, no. 4 (October 2003): 641–61.

Bellin, Joshua D. *Medicine Bundle: Indian Sacred Performance and American Literature, 1824–1932*. Philadelphia: University of Pennsylvania Press, 2008.

Benezet, Anthony. *A Short Account of that Part of Africa Inhabited by the Negroes, with Respect to the Fertility of the Country, the Good Disposition of Many of the Natives, and the Manner by Which the Slave Trade is Carried On.* Philadelphia: W. Dunlap, 1762.

Benn, Carl. *The Iroquois in the War of 1812.* Toronto: University of Toronto Press, 2004.

Bennett, Deb. *Conquerors: The Roots of New World Horsemanship.* Solvang, Calif.: Amigo, 1998.

Bense, Judith Ann. *Archaeology of the Southeastern United States: Paleoindian to World War I.* San Diego, Calif.: Academic Press, 1994.

Benton, Lauren, and Lisa Ford. *Rage for Order: The British Empire and the Origins of International Law, 1800–1850.* Cambridge, Mass.: Harvard University Press, 2016.

Blackmon, Richard. *The Creek War, 1813–1814.* Washington, D.C.: Center of Military History, 2014.

Blanck, Emily. *Tyrannicide: Forging an American Law of Slavery in Revolutionary South Carolina and Massachusetts.* Athens: University of Georgia Press, 2014.

Blitz, John H. "Adoption of the Bow in Prehistoric North America." *North American Archaeologist* 9, no. 2 (1988): 123–45.

———. *Ancient Chiefdoms of the Tombigbee.* Tuscaloosa: University of Alabama Press, 1993.

———. "Mississippian Chiefdoms and the Fission-Fusion Process." *American Antiquity* 64, no 4 (October 1999): 577–92.

Blitz, John H., and Karl G. Lorenz. *The Chattahoochee Chiefdoms.* Tuscaloosa: University of Alabama Press, 2006.

Block, Sharon. *Rape and Sexual Power in Early America.* Chapel Hill: University of North Carolina Press, 2006.

Bloustein, Elise A. *Deerskin Diplomacy: Trade between the Cherokees and South Carolina in the Eighteenth Century.* AB honors thesis, Harvard University, 1975.

Blu, Karen I. *The Lumbee Problem: The Making of an American Indian People.* Lincoln: University of Nebraska Press, 1980.

Blunt, Joseph, ed. *The American Annual Register; for the Year 1829–30.* Vol. 5. Boston: Gray and Bowen, 1832.

Boback, John M. "Indian Warfare, Household Competency, and the Settlement of the Western Virginia Frontier, 1749–1794." Ph.D. diss., West Virginia University, 2007.

Boles, John B., ed. *A Companion to the American South.* Malden, Mass.: Blackwell, 2012.

Bolton, Herbert E. *The Hasinais: Southern Caddoans As Seen by the Earliest Europeans.* Norman: University of Oklahoma Press, 1987.

Bond, Bradley G., ed. *French Colonial Louisiana and the Atlantic World.* Baton Rouge: Louisiana State University Press, 2005.

———. *Mississippi: A Documentary History.* Jackson: University Press of Mississippi, 2003.

Bonvillain, Nancy. *Native Nations: Cultures and Histories of Native North America.* 2nd ed. Lanham, Md.: Rowman & Littlefield, 2017.

Bossy, Denise I. "Indian Slavery in Southeastern Indian and British Societies, 1670–1730." In Gallay, *Indian Slavery*, 219–39.

———. "The South's Other Slavery: Recent Research on Indian Slavery." *Native South* 9 (2016): 27–53.

Boudinot, Elias. *An Address to the Whites, Delivered in the First Presbyterian Church, On the 26th of May, 1826*. Philadelphia: William F. Geddes, 1826.

Boulware, Tyler. *Deconstructing the Cherokee Nation: Town, Region, and Nation among Eighteenth-Century Cherokees*. Gainesville: University Press of Florida, 2015.

———. "The Effects of the Seven Years' War on the Cherokee Nation." *Early American Studies* 5, no. 2 (Fall 2007): 395–426.

———. "'Our Mad Young Men': Authority and Violence in Cherokee Country." In *Blood in the Hills: A History of Violence in Appalachia*, edited by Bruce Stewart, 80–98. Knoxville: University Press of Kentucky, 2012.

———. "'Skilful Jockies' and 'Good Sadlers': Native Americans and Horses in the Southeastern Borderlands." In Frank and Crothers, *Borderland Narratives*, 68–95.

Bousman, C. Britt, and Eric Oksanen. "The Protoarchaic in Central Texas and Surrounding Areas." In *From the Pleistocene to the Holocene: Human Organization and Cultural Transformations in Prehistoric North America*, edited by C. Britt Bousman and Bradley J. Vierra, 197–232. College Station: Texas A&M University Press, 2012.

Bowes, John. *Land Too Good for Indians: Northern Indian Removal*. Norman: University of Oklahoma Press, 2016.

Bowne, Eric E. *Mound Sites of the Ancient South: A Guide to the Mississippian Chiefdoms*. Athens: University of Georgia Press, 2013.

———. "The Rise and Fall of the Westo Indians." *Early Georgia* 28, no. 1 (2000): 56–78.

———. *The Westo Indians: Slave Traders of the Early Colonial South*. Tuscaloosa: University of Alabama Press, 2005.

Boyce, Douglas W. "'As the Wind Scatters the Smoke': The Tuscaroras in the Eighteenth Century." In *Beyond the Covenant Chain: The Iroquois and their Neighbors in Indian North America, 1600–1800*, edited by Daniel K. Richter and James H. Merrell, 151–63. University Park: Pennsylvania State University Press, 2003.

Boyd, Mark F. "Fort San Luis: Documents Describing the Tragic End of the Mission Era." In *Here They Once Stood: The Tragic End of the Apalachee Missions*, edited by Mark F. Boyd, Hale G. Smith, and John W. Griffin, 1–19. 1959. Reprint, Gainesville: University Press of Florida, 1999.

Boyd, Mark F., and José Navarro Latorre. "Spanish Interest in British Florida, and in the Progress of the American Revolution: Relations with the Spanish Faction of Creek Indians." *Florida Historical Quarterly* 32, no. 2 (October 1953): 92–130.

Bradley, Bruce, and Dennis Stanford. "The Solutrean-Clovis Connection: Reply to Straus, Meltzer and Goebel." *World Archeology* 38, no. 4 (2006): 704–14.

Bragdon, Kathleen J. *The Columbia Guide to American Indians of the Northeast*. New York: Columbia University Press, 2001.

Braund, Kathryn E. Holland. "The Creek Indians, Blacks, and Slavery." *Journal of Southern History* 57, no. 4 (November 1991): 601–36.

———. *Deerskins and Duffels: Creek Indian Trade with Anglo-America, 1685–1815*. Lincoln: University of Nebraska Press, 1993.

Brescia, William, Jr. "Choctaw Oral Tradition Relating to Tribal Origin." In Reeves, *Choctaw before Removal*, 3–16.

Brill, James W. "The Technology of Violence and Cultural Evolution in the Santa Barbara Channel Region." In Allen and Jones, *Violence and Warfare among Hunter-Gatherers*, edited by Mark W. Allen and Terry L. Jones, 314–32. London: Routledge, 2014.

Brodhead, J. R., and E. B. O'Callaghan, eds. *Documents Relative to the Colonial History of the State of New-York*. 15 vols. Albany, N.Y.: Weed, Parsons, 1853–1887.

Brooks, James F. *Captives and Cousins: Slavery, Kinship, and Community in the Southwest Borderlands*. Chapel Hill: University of North Carolina Press, 2002.

Brown, Douglas Summers. *The Catawba Indians: The People of the River*. Columbia: University of South Carolina Press, 1966.

Brown, Harry J. *Injun Joe's Ghost: The Indian Mixed-Blood in American Writing*. Columbia: University of Missouri Press, 2004.

Brown, Ian W., and Vincas P. Steponaitis. "The Grand Village of the Natchez Indians Was Indeed Grand: A Reconstruction of the Fatherland Site Landscape." In Waselkov and Smith, *Forging Southeastern Identities: Social Archaeology, Ethnohistory, and Folklore of the Mississippian to Early Historic South*, edited by Gregory A. Waselkov and Marvin T. Smith, 182–204. Tuscaloosa: University of Alabama Press, 2017.

Brown, Richard F., ed. *Coastal Encounters: The Transformation of the Gulf South in the Eighteenth Century*. Lincoln: University of Nebraska Press, 2007.

Browne, J. "Projectile Points." *American Antiquity* 5 (1940): 209–13.

Bruyneel, Kevin. *The Third Space of Sovereignty: The Postcolonial Politics of U.S.–Indigenous Relations*. Minneapolis: University of Minnesota Press, 2007.

Buffalo Tiger and Harry A. Kersey Jr. *Buffalo Tiger: A Life in the Everglades*. Lincoln: University of Nebraska Press, 2002.

Burns, William E. *Science and Technology in Colonial America*. Westport, Conn.: Greenwood, 2005.

Busbee, Westley F., Jr., *Mississippi: A History*. 2nd ed., Malden, Mass: John Wiley and Sons, 2015.

Bushnell, Amy Turner. "Patricio de Hinachuba: Defender of the Word of God, The Crown of the King, and the Little Children of Ivitachuco." *American Indian Culture and Research Journal* 30, no. 3 (1979): 1–21.

Calhoun, John C. *The Works of John C. Calhoun*. Edited by Richard K. Crallé. 10 vols. New York: D. Appleton, 1851–1864.

Calloway, Colin G. *The American Revolution in Indian Country: Crisis and Diversity in Native American Communities*. New York: Cambridge University Press, 1995.

———. *The Indian World of George Washington*. New York: Oxford University Press, 2018.

———. *New Worlds for All: Indians, Europeans, and the Remaking of Early America*. Baltimore: Johns Hopkins University Press, 1998.

———. *Pen and Ink Witchcraft: Treaties and Treaty Making in American Indian History.* New York: Oxford University Press, 2013.

———. *The Scratch of a Pen: 1763 and the Transformation of North America.* New York: Oxford University Press, 2007.

———. *The Victory with No Name: The Native American Defeat of the First American Army.* New York: Oxford University Press, 2015.

———. *White People, Indians, and Highlanders: Tribal Peoples and Colonial Encounters in Scotland and America.* New York: Oxford University Press, 2008.

Cambron, James W., and Spencer A. Waters. "Petroglyphs and Pictographs in the Tennessee Valley and Surrounding Area." *Journal of Alabama Archaeology* 5, no. 2 (1959): 27–51.

Cameron, Catherine M. *Captives: How Stolen People Changed the World.* Lincoln: University of Nebraska Press, 2016.

Camuto, Christopher. *Another Country: Journeying toward the Cherokee Mountains.* Athens: University of Georgia Press, 2000.

Capron, Louis. *The Medicine Bundles of the Florida Seminole and the Green Corn Dance.* Washington, D.C.: U.S. Government Printing Office, 1953.

Carlisle, Rodney P., and J. Geoffrey Golson. *Native America from Prehistory to First Contact.* Santa Barbara, Calif.: ABC-CLIO, 2007.

Carpenter, Roger M. *"Times Are Altered with Us": American Indians from First Contact to the New Republic.* Malden, Mass.: John Wiley and Sons, 2015.

Carson, James Taylor. "Dollars Never Fail to Melt Their Hearts: Native Women and the Market Revolution." In *Neither Lady nor Slave: Working Women of the Old South,* edited by Susanna Delfino and Michele Gillespie, 15–33. Chapel Hill: University of North Carolina Press, 2002.

———. "Ethnic Cleansing and the Trail of Tears: Cherokee Pasts, Places, and Identities." *Southern Spaces.* July 12, 2017. Review of *The Cherokee Diaspora: An Indigenous History of Migration, Resettlement, and Identity,* by Gregory D. Smithers. https://southernspaces.org/2017/ethnic-cleansing-and-trail-tears-cherokee-pasts-places-and-identities.

———. "Greenwood LeFlore: Southern Creole, Choctaw Chief." In O'Brien, *Pre-Removal Choctaw History,* 221–36.

———. "Horses and the Economy and Culture of the Choctaw Indians, 1690–1840." *Ethnohistory* 42, no. 3 (Summer 1995): 495–513.

———. "Mastering Language: Liberty, Slavery, and Native Resistance in the Early Nineteenth-Century South." In Smithers and Newman, *Native Diasporas,* 209–34.

———. "Native Americans, the Market Revolution, and Culture Change: The Choctaw Cattle Economy, 1690–1830." In O'Brien, *Pre-Removal Choctaw History,* 183–99.

———. "Sacred Circles and Dangerous People: Native American Cosmology and the French Settlement of Louisiana." In Bond, *French Colonial Louisiana,* 65–82.

———. *Searching for the Bright Path: The Mississippi Choctaws from Prehistory to Removal.* Lincoln: University of Nebraska Press, 1999.

———. "Who Was First and When? The Diasporic Implications of Indigeneity." In

Between Dispersion and Belonging: Global Approaches to Diaspora in Practice, edited by Amitava Chowdhury and Donald Harman Akenson, 111–24. Montreal: McGill-Queen's University Press, 2016.

Carter, Cecile Elkins. *Caddo Indians: Where We Come From.* Norman: University of Oklahoma Press, 1995.

Carter, Edwin Clarence, and John Porter Bloom, eds. *The Territorial Papers of the United States.* 28 vols. Washington, D.C.: U.S. Government Printing Office, 1934–1975.

Cashin, Edward J. *Guardians of the Valley: Chickasaws in Colonia South Carolina and Georgia.* Columbia: University of South Carolina Press, 2009.

———. *Governor Henry Ellis and the Transformation of British North America.* Athens: University of Georgia Press, 1994.

———. *Lachlan McGillvray, Indian Trader: The Shaping of the Southern Colonial Frontier.* Athens: University of Georgia Press, 1992.

———. "Oglethorpe's Contest for the Backcountry, 1733–1749." In *Oglethorpe in Perspective: Georgia's Founder after Two Hundred Years,* edited by Phinizy Spalding and Harvey H. Jackson, 99–111. Tuscaloosa: University of Alabama Press, 1989.

Caughey, John W. *McGillivray of the Creeks.* 1938. Reprint, Columbia: University of South Carolina Press, 2007.

Cave, Alfred A. "The Delaware Prophet Neolin: A Reappraisal." In *The American Indian: Past and Present,* edited by Roger L. Nicols, 96–114. 6th ed. Norman: University of Oklahoma Press, 2008.

———. *Prophets of the Great Spirit: Native American Revitalization Movements in Eastern North America.* Lincoln: University of Nebraska Press, 2006.

Cayton, Andrew W., and Fredrika J. Teute, eds. *Contact Points: American Frontiers from the Mohawk Valley to the Mississippi, 1750–1830.* Chapel Hill: University of North Carolina Press, 1998.

Cegielski, Wendy, and Brad R. Lieb. "'Hina' Falaa, 'The Long Path': An Analysis of Chickasaw Settlement Using GIS in Northeast Mississippi, 1650–1840." *Native South* 4 (2011): 24–54.

Chacon, Richard J., and Ruben G. Mendoza, eds. *North American Indigenous Warfare and Ritual Violence.* Tucson: University of Arizona Press, 2007.

Chang, David A. *The Color of the Land: Race, Nation, and the Politics of Land Ownership in Oklahoma, 1832–1929.* Chapel Hill: University of North Carolina Press, 2010.

Chappell, Sally A. Kitt. *Cahokia: Mirror of the Cosmos.* Chicago: University of Chicago Press, 2002.

Civitello, Linda. *Cuisine and Culture: A History of Food and People.* Hoboken, N.J.: John Wiley & Sons, 2008.

Clark, Daniel. "An Account of the Indian Tribes Inhabiting Louisiana," September 29, 1803. Quoted in Edwin Clarence Carter and Bloom, *Territorial Papers,* 9:64.

Clark, Walter. ed., *State Records of North Carolina.* Vol. 11. *1776–1777,* with supplement, *1730–1776.* Winston, N.C.: M. I. and J. C. Stewart, 1895.

Clayton, Lawrence A., Vernon J. Knight Jr., and Edward C. Moore, eds. *The De Soto*

Chronicles: The Expedition of Hernando de Soto to North America in 1539–1543.
2 vols. Tuscaloosa: University of Alabama Press, 1993.

Cobb, Amanda J. *Listening to our Grandmothers' Stories: The Bloomfield Academy for Chickasaw Females, 1852–1949.* Lincoln: University of Nebraska Press, 2000.

Cobb, Charles R. "Mississippian Chiefdoms: How Complex?" *Annual Review of Anthropology* 32 (2003): 63–84.

Coe, Joffre. *The Formative Cultures of the Carolina Piedmont.* Philadelphia: American Philosophical Society, 1964.

———. *Town Creek Indian Mound: A Native American Legacy.* Chapel Hill: University of North Carolina Press, 1995.

Coleman, Arica L. *That the Blood Stay Pure: African Americans, Native Americans, and the Predicament of Race and Identity in Virginia.* Bloomington: Indiana University Press, 2013.

Coleman, Kenneth. *A History of Georgia.* 1977. Reprint, Athens: University of Georgia Press, 1991.

Confer, Clarissa W. *Daily Life in Pre-Columbian Native America.* Westport, Conn.: Greenwood, 2008.

Conley, Robert J. *Cherokee Medicine Man: The Life and Work of a Modern-Day Healer.* Norman: University of Oklahoma Press, 2005.

———. *The Cherokee Nation: A History.* Albuquerque: University of New Mexico Press, 2005.

———. *Cherokee Thoughts: Honest and Uncensored.* Norman: University of Oklahoma Press, 2008.

Cooper, Thomas, ed. *The Statutes at Large of South Carolina: Acts, 1685–1716.* Vol. 2. Columbia, S.C.: A. S. Johnston, 1827.

Corbitt, Duvon C., and Roberta D. Corbitt, eds. and trans. "Papers from the Spanish Archives." *East Tennessee Historical Society Publications* 9 (1937): 110–42.

Corkran, David H. *The Cherokee Frontier: Conflict and Survival, 1740-62.* Norman: University of Oklahoma Press, 1962.

———. *The Creek Frontier, 1540–1783.* Norman: University of Oklahoma Press, 1967.

Correspondence on the Subject of the Emigration of Indians, between the 30th November, 1831, and 27th December, 1833. Vol. 3. Washington, D.C.: Duff Green, 1835.

Covington, James W. "Apalachee Indians Move West." *Florida Anthropologist* 17 (1964): 221–25.

———. "Migration of the Seminoles into Florida, 1700–1820." *Florida Historical Quarterly* 46, no. 4 (April 1968): 340–57.

———. "Relations between the Eastern Timucuan Indians and the French and Spanish." In Charles Hudson, *Four Centuries of Southern Indians,* 11–27.

Crane, Jeff. *The Environment in American History: Nature and the Formation of the United States.* New York: Routledge, 2015.

Crane, Verner. *The Southern Frontier, 1670–1732.* 1929. Reprint, Tuscaloosa: University of Alabama Press, 2004.

Crawford, Michael. *The Origins of Native Americans: Evidence from Anthropological Genetics.* New York: Cambridge University Press, 1998.

Cronon, William. "A Place for Stories: Nature, History, and Narrative." *Journal of American History* 78, no. 4 (March 1992): 1347–76.

Croom, Edward M., Jr. "Herbal Medicine among the Lumbee Indians." In *Herbal and Magical Medicine: Traditional Healing Today*, edited by James K. Kirkland, Holly F. Matthews, Charles W. Sullivan III, and Karen Baldwin, 137–69. Durham, N.C.: Duke University Press, 1992.

Crosby, Alfred W., Jr. *The Columbian Exchange: Biological and Cultural Consequences of 1492*. 30th anniversary ed. Westport, Conn.: Praeger, 2003.

Cushman, H. B. *History of the Choctaw, Chickasaw, and Natchez Indians*. Edited by Angie Debo. Norman: University of Oklahoma Press, 1999.

Dalan, Rinita A. "The Construction of Mississippian Cahokia." In *Cahokia: Domination and Ideology in the Mississippian World*, edited by Timothy R. Pauketat and Thomas E. Emerson, 89–102. Lincoln: University of Nebraska Press, 1997.

Danley, Mark H., and Patrick J. Speelman, eds. *The Seven Years' War: Global Views*. Leiden, Netherlands: Brill, 2012.

Davies, K. G., ed. *Documents of the American Revolution, 1770–1783*. 21 vols. Dublin: Irish University Press, 1972–1981.

Davis, Karl. "'Remember Fort Mims:' Reinterpreting the Origins of the Creek War." *Journal of the Early Republic* 22, no. 4 (Winter 2002): 611–36.

Deagan, Kathleen A. "Spanish-Indian Interaction in Sixteenth-Century Florida and Hispaniola." In *Cultures in Contact: The European Impact on Native Cultural Interactions in Eastern North America, A.D. 1000–1800*, edited by W. W. Fitzhugh, 281–318. Washington, D.C.: Smithsonian Institution Press, 1987.

Debo, Angie. *The Rise and Fall of the Choctaw Republic*. 2nd ed. Norman: University of Oklahoma Press, 1961.

———. *The Road to Disappearance: A History of the Creek Indians*. Norman: University of Oklahoma Press, 1941.

Delcourt, Paul A., and Hazel R. Delcourt. *Prehistoric Native Americans and Ecological Change: Human Ecosystems in Eastern North America since the Pleistocene*. New York: Cambridge University Press, 2004.

Deloria, Philip J. "Historiography." In Philip J. Deloria and Salisbury, *Companion to American Indian History*, 6–24.

———. "What Is the Middle Ground, Anyway?" *William and Mary Quarterly* 63 (January 2006): 81–96.

Deloria, Philip J., and Neal Salisbury, eds. *A Companion to American Indian History*. Malden, Mass.: Blackwell, 2001.

Deloria, Vine, Jr. "American Indians in Historical Perspective." In Wunder, *Native American Law and Colonialism*, 123–34.

———. *Red Earth, White Lies: Native Americans and the Myth of Scientific Fact*. Golden, Colo.: Fulcrum, 1995.

Deloria, Vine, Jr., and Clifford M. Lytle. *The Nations Within: The Past and Future of American Indian Sovereignty*. New York: Pantheon Books, 1984.

DeMallie, Raymond J. "Tutelo and Neighboring Groups." In Fogelson, *Handbook*, 14:286–300.

Dennis, Matthew. "Red Jacket's Rhetoric: Postcolonial Persuasions on the Native Frontiers of the Early American Republic." In *American Indian Rhetorics of Survivance: Word Medicine, Word Magic,* edited by Ernest Stromberg, 15–33. Pittsburgh: University of Pittsburgh Press, 2006.

Denson, Andrew. *Demanding the Cherokee Nation: Indian Autonomy and American Culture, 1830–1900.* Lincoln: University of Nebraska Press, 2004.

DeRosier, Arthur H., Jr. *The Removal of the Choctaw Indians.* Knoxville: University of Tennessee Press, 1970.

DeVorsey, Louis, Jr. "Indian Boundaries in Colonial Georgia." *Georgia Historical Quarterly* 54, no. 1 (Spring 1970): 63–78.

Diaz-Granados, Carol, and James R. Duncan. *The Petroglyphs and Pictographs of Missouri.* Tuscaloosa: University of Alabama Press, 2000.

Dickson, D. Bruce. "The Yanomamo of the Mississippi Valley? Some Reflections on Larson (1972), Gibson (1974), and Mississippian Period Warfare in the Southeastern United States." *American Antiquity* 46 (1974), 75–133.

Dixon, David. "'We Speak as One People': Native Unity and the Pontiac Indian Uprising." In *The Boundaries Between Us: Natives and Newcomers along the Frontiers of the Old Northwest Territory, 1750–1850,* edited by Daniel P. Barr, 44–65. Kent, Ohio: Kent State University Press, 2006.

Dixon, E. James. *Bones, Boats, and Bison: Archeology and the First Colonization of Western North America.* Albuquerque: University of New Mexico Press, 2000.

Documents and Proceedings Relating to the Formation of a Board in the City of New York for the Emigration, Preservation, and Improvement of the Aborigines of America, July 22, 1829. New York: Vanderpool and Cole, 1829

Donaldson, Laura E. "'But We Are Your Mothers, You Are Our Sons': Gender, Sovereignty, and the Nation in Early Cherokee Women's Writing." In *Indigenous Women and Feminism: Politics, Activism, Culture,* edited by Cheryl Suzack, Shari M. Huhndorf, Jeanne Perreault, and Jean Barman, 43–55. Vancouver: University of British Columbia Press, 2010.

Doolen, Andy. *Territories of Empire: U.S. Writing from the Louisiana Purchase to Mexican Independence.* New York: Oxford University Press, 2014.

Doran, Michael F. "Population Statistics of Nineteenth Century Indian Territory." *Chronicles of Oklahoma* 53 (1975): 492–515.

Dowd, Gregory Evans. "The Panic of 1751: The Significance of Rumors on the South Carolina-Cherokee Frontier." *William and Mary Quarterly,* 3rd ser., 53, no. 3 (July 1996): 527–60.

———. *A Spirited Resistance: The North American Indian Struggle for Unity, 1745–1815.* Baltimore: Johns Hopkins University Press, 1993.

———. *War under Heaven: Pontiac, the Indian Nations, and the British Empire.* Baltimore: Johns Hopkins University Press, 2002.

Downes, Randolph C. "Creek-American Relations, 1782–1790." *Georgia Historical Quarterly* 21, no. 2 (June 1937): 142–84.

Drake, Samuel. *The Book of the Indians; Or, Biography and History of the Indians of*

North America, from its First Discovery to the Year 1841. 9th ed. Boston: Benjamin B. Mussey, 1845.

Driver, Harold E. *Indians of North America.* Chicago: University of Chicago Press, 1969.

Dubcovsky, Alejandra. "'All of Us Will Have to Pay for These Activities': Colonial and Native Narratives of the 1704 Attack on Ayubale." *Native South* 10 (2017): 1–18.

———. "Defying Indian Slavery: Apalachee Voices and Spanish Sources in the Eighteenth Century Southeast." *William and Mary Quarterly* 75, no. 2 (April 2018): 295–322.

———. *Informed Power: Communication in the Early American South.* Cambridge, Mass.: Harvard University Press, 2016.

Dubin, Lois Sherr. *North American Indian Jewelry and Adornment: From Prehistory to the Present.* New York: Harry N. Abrams, 1999.

Dunaway, Wilma A. "Incorporation as an Interactive Process: Cherokee Resistance to Expansion of the Capitalist World-System, 1560–1763." *Sociological Inquiry* 60, no. 1 (January 1990): 455–70.

———. *Women, Work, and Family in the Antebellum Mountain South.* New York: Cambridge University Press, 2008.

Duncan, Barbara R. *Living Stories of the Cherokee.* Chapel Hill: University of North Carolina Press, 1998.

Duran, Bonnie, Eduardo Duran, and Maria Yellow Horse Brave Heart. "Native Americans and the Trauma of History." In Thornton, *Studying Native America,* 60–76.

DuVal, Kathleen. *Independence Lost: Lives on the Edge of the American Revolution.* New York: Random House, 2015.

———. "Living in a Reordered World, 1680–1763." In Hoxie, *Oxford Handbook,* 71.

———. "The Mississippian Peoples' Worldview." In *Geography and Ethnography: Perceptions of the World in Pre-Modern Societies,* edited by Kurt A. Raaflaub and Richard J. A. Talbert, 89–107. Malden, Mass.: Wiley-Blackwell, 2010.

———. *The Native Ground: Indians and Colonists in the Heart of Empire.* Philadelphia: University of Pennsylvania Press, 2006.

Dye, David H. "Snaring Life from the Stars and the Sun: Mississippian Tattooing and the Enduring Cycle of Life and Death." In *Drawing with Great Needles: Ancient Tattoo Traditions of North America,* edited by Aaron Deter-Wolf and Carol Diaz-Granados, 21–251. Austin: University of Texas Press, 2013.

———. "Warfare in the Sixteenth-Century Southeast: The de Soto Expedition in the Interior." In Thomas, *Columbian Consequences,* 211–22.

Earle, Timothy K., ed. *Chiefdoms: Power, Economy, and Ideology.* New York: Cambridge University Press, 1993.

———. "The Evolution of Chiefdoms." In Earle, *Chiefdoms,* 1–15.

———. "Property Rights and the Evolution of Chiefdoms." In Earle, *Chiefdoms,* 71–99.

Ellerbe, Jenny, and Diana M. Greenlee. *Poverty Point: Revealing the Forgotten City.* Baton Rouge: Louisiana State University Press, 2015.

Ellisor, John T. *The Second Creek War: Interethnic Conflict and Collusion on a Collapsing Frontier*. Lincoln: University of Nebraska Press, 2010.

Emerson, Ellen R. *Indian Myths; Or, Legends, Traditions, and Symbols of the Aborigines of America*. Boston: James R. Osgood, 1884.

Emerson, Thomas E. *Cahokia and the Archaeology of Power*. Tuscaloosa: University of Alabama Press, 1997.

Engelbrecht, William E. "New York Iroquois Political Development." In *Archaeology of the Iroquois: Selected Readings and Research Sources*, edited by Jordan E. Kerber, 219–33. Syracuse, N.Y.: Syracuse University Press, 2007.

Erdoes, Richard, and Alfonso Aritz, eds. *American Indian Myths and Legends*. New York: Pantheon, 1988.

Erlandson, Jon, and Todd J. Braje. "Foundations for the Far West: Paleoindian Cultures on the Western Fringe of North America." In Pauketat, *Oxford Handbook*, 149–59.

Ethridge, Robbie. "Contact Era Studies and the Southeastern Indians." In *Native and Spanish New Worlds: Sixteenth-Century Entradas in the American Southwest and Southeast*, edited by Clay Mathews, Jeffrey M. Mitchem, and Charles M. Haecker, 63–77. Tucson: Arizona State University Press, 2013.

———. *Creek Country: The Creek Indians and Their World*. Chapel Hill: University of North Carolina Press, 2003.

———. "The Emergence of the Colonial South: Colonial Indian Slaving, the Fall of the Precontact Mississippian World, and the Emergence of a New Social Geography." In *Native American Adoption, Captivity, and Slavery in Changing Contexts*, edited by Max Carocci and Stephanie Pratt, 47–64. New York: Palgrave Macmillan, 2012.

———. "The European Invasion and the Transformation of Tennessee, 1540–1715." In Ray, *Before the Volunteer State*, 3–34.

———. *From Chicaza to Chickasaw: The European Invasion and the Transformation of the Mississippian World, 1540–1715*. Chapel Hill: University of North Carolina Press, 2010.

———. "Introduction: Mapping the Mississippian Shatter Zone." In Ethridge and Shuck-Hall, *Mapping the Mississippian Shatter Zone*, 1–62.

Ethridge, Robbie, and Charles Hudson. "The Early Historic Transformation of the Southeastern Indians." In *Cultural Diversity in the U.S. South: Anthropological Contributions to a Region in Transition*, edited by Carole E. Hill and Patricia D. Beaver, 34–50. Athens: University of Georgia Press, 1998.

———, eds. *The Transformation of the Southeastern Indians, 1540–1760*. Jackson: University of Mississippi Press, 2002.

Ethridge, Robbie, and Sheri M. Shuck-Hall, eds. *Mapping the Mississippian Shatter Zone: The Colonial Indian Slave Trade and Regional Instability in the American South*. Lincoln: University of Nebraska Press, 2009.

Evarts, Jeremiah [William Penn]. *Essays on the Present Crisis in the Condition of the American Indians*. Boston: Perkins and Marvin, 1829.

Everett, C. S., and Marvin Richardson. "Ethnicity Affirmed: The Haliwa-Saponi and the Dance, Culture, and Meaning of North Carolina Powwows." In *Signifying Serpents and Mardi Gras Runners: Representing Identity in Selected Souths,* edited by R. Celeste Ray and Luke E. Lassiter, 51–71. Athens: University of Georgia Press, 2003.

Ewen, Alexander. *The Bering Strait Theory.* Chap. 1. Washington, D.C.: National Council of American Indians Embassy of Tribal Nations, 2017. Indian Country Books. Indian Country Today Media Network website. https://indiancountrymedianetwork.com/books/indian-origins-the-bering-strait-theory/.

Eze, Emmanuel C. ed. *Race and the Enlightenment: A Reader.* Malden, Mass.: Wiley-Blackwell, 1997.

Faiman-Silva, Sandra. *Choctaws at the Crossroads: The Political Economy of Class and Culture in the Oklahoma Timber Region.* Lincoln: University of Nebraska Press, 1997.

Faragher, John Mack. "'More Motley than Mackinaw': From Ethnic Mixing to Ethnic Cleansing on the Frontier of the Lower Missouri, 1783–1833." In Cayton and Teute, *Contact Points,* 304–26.

Fayard, Kelly. "'We've Always Known Who We Are': Belonging in the Poarch Band of Creek Indians." Ph.D. diss., University of Michigan, 2011.

Fenn, Elizabeth A., and Peter H. Wood. *Natives and Newcomers: The Way We Lived in North Carolina before 1770.* Chapel Hill: University of North Carolina Press, 1983.

Fenton, William N. *The Great Law and the Longhouse: A Political History of the Iroquois Confederacy.* Norman: University of Oklahoma Press, 1988.

Fiedel, Stuart J. *Prehistory of the Americas.* 2nd ed. New York: Cambridge University Press, 1992.

Finger, John R. *Cherokee Americans: The Eastern Band of Cherokees in the Twentieth Century.* Lincoln: University of Nebraska Press, 1991.

———. *The Eastern Band of Cherokees, 1819–1900.* Knoxville: University of Tennessee Press, 1984.

Fitts, Mary Elizabeth. *Fit for War: Sustenance and Order in the Mid-Eighteenth-Century Catawba Nation.* Gainesville: University Press of Florida, 2017.

———. "Mapping Catawba Coalescence." *North Carolina Archaeology* 55 (2006): 1–59.

Fitts, Mary E., and Charles L. Heath. "'Indians Refusing to Carry Burdens': Understanding the Success of Catawba Political, Military, and Settlement Strategies in Colonial Carolina." In Ethridge and Shuck-Hall, *Mapping the Mississippian Shatter Zone,* 142–62.

Fixico, Donald L., ed. *Rethinking American Indian* History. Albuquerque: University of New Mexico Press, 1997.

———. *"That's What They Used to Say": Reflections on American Indian Oral Traditions.* Norman: University of Oklahoma Press, 2017.

Fladmark, Knut R. "Feasibility of the Northwest Coast as a Migration Route." In *Early Man in America: From a Circum-Pacific Perspective,* edited by Alan L. Bryan, 119–28. University of Alberta Department of Anthropology Occasional Papers, no. 1. Edmonton: University of Alberta Department of Anthropology, 1978.

———. "Routes: Alternative Migration Corridors for Early Man in North America." *American Antiquity* 44, no. 1 (January 1979): 55–69.

———. "Times and Places: Environmental Correlates of Mid-to-Late Wisconsinan Human Population Expansion in North America." In *Early Man in the New World,* edited by Richard Shutler Jr., 13–43. Beverly Hills, Calif.: Sage, 1983.

Fogelson, Ray, ed. *Handbook of North American Indians: Southeast.* Vol. 14. Washington, D.C.: Smithsonian Institution, 2004.

———. "Who Were the Aní-Kutáni? An Excursion into Cherokee Historical Thought." *Ethnohistory* 31, no. 4 (Autumn 1984): 255–63.

Forbes, Jack. *The American Discovery of Europe.* Urbana: University of Illinois Press, 2007.

Ford, Ben, ed. *The Archaeology of Maritime Landscapes: When the Land Meets the Sea.* New York: Springer, 2011.

———. "The Shoreline As a Bridge, Not a Boundary: Cognitive Maritime Landscapes of Lake Ontario." In Ford, *Archaeology of Maritime Landscapes,* 63–80.

Ford, Lisa. *Settler Sovereignty: Jurisdiction and Indigenous People in America and Australia, 1788–1836.* Cambridge, Mass.: Harvard University Press, 2010.

Ford, Richard I. "Human Disturbance and Biodiversity: A Case Study from Northern New Mexico." In Minnis and Elisens, *Biodiversity and Native America,* 207–22.

Foreman, Grant. *Indian Removal: Emigration of the Five Civilized Tribes.* Norman: University of Oklahoma Press, 1932.

Fortescue, J. W., ed. *Calendar of State Papers, Colonial Series, America and West Indies, 1681–1685.* London: Her Majesty's Stationery Office, 1898.

Foster, H. Thomas, II. "The Identification and Significance of Apalachicola for the Origins of the Creek Indians in the Southeastern United States." *Southeastern Archaeology* 36, no. 1 (2017): 1–13.

Foster, H. Thomas, II, with Mary Theresa Bonhage-Freund and Lisa D. O'Steen. *Archaeology of the Lower Muskogee Creek Indians, 1715–1836.* Tuscaloosa: University of Alabama Press, 2007.

Foster, William C. *Climate and Culture Change in North America, AD 900–1600.* Austin: University of Texas Press, 2012.

———. *Historic Native Peoples of Texas.* Austin: University of Texas Press, 2008.

Frank, Andrew K. *Creeks and Southerners: Biculturalism on the Early American Frontier.* Indians of the Southeast Series. Lincoln: University of Nebraska Press, 2005.

———. "Red, Black, and Seminole: Community Convergence on the Florida Borderlands, 1780–1840." In Frank and Crothers, *Borderland Narratives,* 46–67.

———. *The Routledge Historical Atlas of the American South.* New York: Routledge, 1999.

Frank, Andrew K., and A. Glenn Crothers. *Borderland Narratives: Negotiation and Accommodation in America's Contested Spaces, 1500–1850.* Gainesville: University Press of Florida, 2017.

Frelinghuysen, Theodore. *Speech of Mr. Frelinghuysen, of New Jersey, Delivered in the Senate of the United States, April 6, 1830.* Washington, D.C.: Office of the National Journal, 1830.

Gaillardet, Frédéric, and James L. Shepherd III. *Sketches of Early Texas and Louisiana.* Austin: University of Texas Press, 1966.

Gallay, Alan, ed. *Colonial Wars of North America, 1512–1763: An Encyclopedia.* New York: Routledge, 1996.

———. *The Formation of the Planter Elite: Jonathan Bryan and the Southeastern Colonial Frontier.* Athens: University of Georgia Press, 1989.

———. *The Indian Slave Trade: The Rise of the English Empire, 1670–1717.* New Haven, Conn.: Yale University Press, 2002.

———, ed. *Indian Slavery in Colonial America.* Lincoln: University of Nebraska Press, 2009.

Galloway, Patricia, ed. "Choctaw Factionalism and Civil War, 1746–1750." In Reeves, *Choctaw before Removal,* 120–56.

———. "Choctaw Factionalism and Civil War, 1746–1750." In O'Brien, *Pre-Removal Choctaw History,* 70–102.

———. *Choctaw Genesis, 1500–1700.* Lincoln: University of Nebraska Press, 1995.

———, trans. "Henri de Tonti du village des Chacta, 1702: The Beginning of the French Alliance." In Galloway, *La Salle and His Legacy,* 146–75.

———, ed. *The Hernando de Soto Expedition: History, Historiography, and "Discovery" in the Southeast.* Lincoln: University of Nebraska Press, 1997.

———. *La Salle and His Legacy: Frenchmen and Indians in the Lower Mississippi Valley.* Jackson: University Press of Mississippi, 1982.

———. *Practicing Ethnohistory: Mining Archives, Hearing Testimony, Constructing Narrative.* Lincoln: University of Nebraska Press, 2006.

Garrison, Tim Alan. *The Legal Ideology of Removal: The Southern Judiciary and the Sovereignty of Native American Nations.* Athens: University of Georgia Press, 2002.

Garrison, Tim Alan, and Greg O'Brien, eds. *The Native South: New Histories and Enduring Legacies.* Lincoln: University of Nebraska Press, 2017.

Gatschet, Albert S. *A Migration Legend of the Creek Indians.* Philadelphia: D.G. Brinton, 1884.

Gaul, Theresa Strouth, ed. *To Marry an Indian: The Marriage of Harriet Gold and Elias Boudinot in Letters, 1823–1839.* Chapel Hill: University of North Carolina Press, 2005.

Gibbes, R. W. *Documentary History of the American Revolution.* 3 vols. New York: D. Appleton, 1853–1857.

Gibson, Abraham. *Feral Animals in the American South: An Evolutionary History.* New York: Cambridge University Press, 2016.

Gibson, Arrell M. *The Chickasaws.* Norman: University of Oklahoma Press, 1971.

Gibson, Jon L. *The Ancient Mounds of Poverty Point: Place of Rings.* Gainesville: University Press of Florida, 2001.

Gifford, John C. *Billy Bowlegs and the Seminole War.* Coconut Grove, Fla.: Triangle, 1925.

Gilbert, Joan. *The Trail of Tears Across Missouri.* Columbia: University of Missouri Press, 1996.

Girard, Jeffrey S., Timothy K. Perttula, and Mary Beth Trubitt. *Caddo Connections:*

Cultural Interactions within and Beyond the Caddo World. Lanham, Md.: Rowman and Littlefield, 2014.

Glezakos, Stavroula. "Words Gone Sour?" In *Reference and Referring*, edited by William P. Kabasenche, Michael O'Rourke, and Matthew H. Slater, 385–404. Cambridge, Mass.: MIT Press, 2012.

Gordon, John W. *South Carolina and the American Revolution: A Battlefield History*. Columbia: University of South Carolina Press, 2003.

Grady, Timothy P. *Anglo-Spanish Rivalry in Colonial South-East America, 1650–1725*. Abingdon, England: Pickering & Chatto, 2010.

Grann, David. *Killers of the Flower Moon: The Osage Murders and the Birth of the FBI*. New York: Doubleday, 2016.

Grantham, Bill. *Creation Myths and Legends of the Creek Indians*. Gainesville: University Press of Florida, 2002.

Green, Michael D. *The Politics of Indian Removal: Creek Government and Society in Crisis*. Lincoln: University of Nebraska Press, 1982.

Gregory Jack D., and Rennard Strickland. *Sam Houston with the Cherokees, 1829–1833*. Norman: University of Oklahoma Press, 1996.

Grenier, John. *The First Way of War: American War Making on the Frontier, 1607–1814*. New York: Cambridge University Press, 2005.

Gruhn, Ruth. "Linguistic Evidence in Support of the Coastal Route of Earliest Entry into the New World." *Man* 23, no. 1 (March 1988): 77–100.

———. "The Pacific Coast Route of Initial Entry: An Overview." In *Method and Theory for Investigating the Peopling of the Americas,* edited by Robson Bonnichsen and D. Gentry Steele, 249–56. Corvallis: Oregon State University, 1994.

Guice, John D. W. "Face to Face in Mississippi Territory, 1798–1817." In Reeves, *Choctaw before Removal*, Reeves, 157–80.

Gutiérrez, Ramón A. *When Jesus Came, the Corn Mothers Went Away: Marriage, Sexuality, and Power in New Mexico, 1500–1846*. Stanford, Calif.: Stanford University Press, 1991.

Guyatt, Nicholas. *Bind Us Apart: How Enlightened Americans Invented Racial Segregation*. New York: Basic Books, 2016.

Hahn, Steven C. "The Cussita Migration Legend: History, Ideology, and the Politics of Mythmaking." In Pluckhahn and Ethridge, *Light on the Path*, 57–93.

———. *The Invention of the Creek Nation, 1670–1763*. Lincoln: University of Nebraska Press, 2004.

Halbert, Henry S. "A Choctaw Migration Legend." *American Antiquarian and Oriental Journal* 16 (1894): 215–16.

Halbert, Henry S., and T. H. Ball. *The Creek War of 1813 and 1814*. 1895. Reprint, Tuscaloosa: University of Alabama Press, 1995.

Hall, Joseph M., Jr. *Zamumo's Gifts: Indian-European Exchange in the Colonial Southeast*. Philadelphia: University of Pennsylvania Press, 2009.

Hall, Robert L. "Cahokia Identity and Interaction Models of Cahokia Mississippian." In *Cahokia and the Hinterlands: Middle Mississippian Cultures of the Midwest,* edited by Thomas E. Emerson and R. Barry Lewis, 3–34. Bloomington: University of Illinois Press, 2000.

Hally, David J. *King: The Social Archaeology of a Late Mississippian Town in Northwestern Georgia*. Tuscaloosa: University of Alabama Press, 2008.

———. "Platform-Mound Construction and the Instability of Mississippian Chiefdoms." In *Political Structure and Change in the Prehistoric Southeastern United States*, edited by John F. Scarry, 92–127. Gainesville: University Press of Florida, 1996.

Hally, David J., Marvin T. Smith, and James B. Langford Jr. "The Archaeological Reality of de Soto's Coosa." In Thomas, *Columbian Consequences*, 121–38.

Hämäläinen, Pekka. *The Comanche Empire*. New Haven, Conn.: Yale University Press, 2008.

———. "The Shapes of Power: Indians, Europeans, and North American Worlds from the Seventeenth to the Nineteenth Century." In *Contested Spaces of Early America*, edited by Juliana Barr and Edward Countryman, 31–68. Philadelphia: University of Pennsylvania Press, 2014.

Hamer, Philip M. "John Stuart's Indian Policy during the Early Months of the American Revolution." *Mississippi Valley Historical Review* 17, no. 3 (December 1930): 351–66.

Hann, John H. *The Native American World Beyond Apalachee: West Florida and the Chattahoochee Valley*. Gainesville: University Press of Florida, 2006.

Hanna, Charles A. *The Wilderness Trail; Or, The Ventures and Adventures of the Pennsylvania Traders on the Allegheny Path*. 2 vols. New York: G. P. Putnam's Sons, 1911

Harmon, Alexandra. *Rich Indians: Native People and the Problem of Wealth in American History*. Chapel Hill: University of North Carolina, 2010.

Harrell, Sara G. *Tomo-Chi-Chi: The Story of an American Indian*. Minneapolis, Minn.: Dillon, 1977.

Hatch, Thom. *Osceola and the Great Seminole War: A Struggle for Justice and Freedom*. New York: St. Martin's, 2012.

Hatley, Tom. "Cherokee Women Farmers Hold Their Ground." In Waselkov, Wood, and Hatley, *Powhatan's Mantle*, 305–35.

———. *The Dividing Paths: Cherokees and South Carolinians through the Revolutionary Era*. New York: Oxford University Press, 1993.

Haveman, Christopher D., ed. *Bending Their Own Way: Creek Indian Removal Documents*. Lincoln: University of Nebraska Press, 2018.

———. *Rivers of Sand: Creek Indian Emigration, Relocation, and Ethnic Cleansing in the American South*. Lincoln: University of Nebraska Press, 2016.

Heard, J. Norman. *Handbook of the American Frontier: Four Centuries of Indian-White Relationships: The Southeastern Woodlands*. Metuchen, N.J.: Scarecrow, 1987

Hendrix, M. Patrick. *Down and Dirty: Archaeology of the South Carolina Lowcountry*. Charleston, S.C.: History Press, 2006.

Herbert, Jason. "'To Treat with All Nations': Invoking Authority in the Chickasaw Nation, 1783–1795." *Ohio Valley History* 18, no. 1 (Spring 2018): 27–44.

Herrera, Carlos R. *Juan Bautista de Anza: The King's Governor in New Mexico.* Norman: University of Oklahoma Press, 2014.

Hershberger, Mary. "Mobilizing Women, Anticipating Abolition: The Struggle against Indian Removal in the 1830s." *Journal of American History* 86, no. 1 (June 1999): 15–40.

Hill, Jonathan D., ed. *History, Power, and Identity: Ethnogenesis in the Americas, 1492–1992.* Iowa City: University of Iowa Press, 1996.

Hill, Susan M. *The Clay We Are Made Of: Haudenosaunee Land Tenure on the Grand River.* Winnipeg: University of Manitoba Press, 2017.

Hixson, Walter L. *American Settler Colonialism: A History.* New York: Palgrave Macmillan, 2013.

Hobson, Geary, Janet McAdams, and Kathryn Walkiewicz, eds. *The People Who Stayed: Southeastern Indian Writing after Removal.* Norman: University of Oklahoma Press, 2010.

Hoffman, Paul E. *Florida's Frontiers.* Bloomington: Indiana University Press, 2002.

Hogner, Dorothy C. *Our American Horse.* 1944. Reprint, Dover, 2015.

Hoig, Stan. *The Cherokees and Their Chiefs: In the Wake of Empire.* Fayetteville: University of Arkansas Press, 1998.

Homer, Davis A., ed. *Constitution and Laws of the Chickasaw Nation Together with the Treaties of 1832, 1833, 1834, 1837, 1852, 1855, and 1866.* Parsons, Kans.: Foley Railway Printing Company, 1899.

Homes, Charles E. "The Beringian and Transitional Periods in Alaska: Technology of the East Beringian Tradition as Viewed from Swan Point." In *From the Yenisei to the Yukon: Interpreting Lithic Assemblage Variability in Late Pleistocene/Early Holocene Beringia,* edited by Ted Goebel and Ian Buvit, 179–91. College Station: Texas A&M University Press, 2011.

Hopkins, Donald R. *The Greatest Killer: Smallpox in History.* Chicago: University of Chicago Press, 2002.

Horn, Rebecca. "Indigenous Identities in Mesoamerica after the Spanish Conquest." In Smithers and Newman, *Native Diasporas,* 31–78.

Hoxie, Frederick E., ed. *Oxford Handbook of American Indian History.* New York: Oxford University Press, 2016.

———. *This Indian Country: American Indian Activists and the Place They Made.* New York: Penguin, 2013.

Hranicky, William Jack. *Prehistoric Projectile Points Found Along the Atlantic Coastal Plain.* 3rd ed. Boca Raton, Fla.: Universal, 2011.

Hryniewicki, Richard J. "The Creek Treaty of Washington, 1826." *Georgia Historical Quarterly* 48 (December 1964): 425–41.

Hudson, Angela Pulley. *Creek Paths and Federal Roads: Indians, Settlers, and Slaves and the Making of the American South.* Chapel Hill: University of North Carolina Press, 2010.

———. *Real Native Genius: How an Ex-Slave and a White Mormon Became Famous Indians.* Chapel Hill: University of North Carolina Press, 2015.

Hudson, Charles. *The Catawba Nation.* Athens: University of Georgia Press, 1970.

————, ed. *Four Centuries of Southern Indians.* Athens: University of Georgia Press, 1975.

————. *Knights of Spain, Warriors of the Sun: Hernando de Soto and the South's Ancient Chiefdoms.* Athens: University of Georgia Press, 1997.

————. *The Southeastern Indians.* 1976. Reprint, Knoxville: University of Tennessee Press, 1999.

Hurt, R. Douglas, *The Indian Frontier, 1763–1846.* Albuquerque: University of New Mexico Press, 2002.

Hutchinson, Elizabeth. "Osceola's Calicoes." In Johnston and Frank, *Global Trade and Visual Arts in Federal New England,* 267–87.

Ingram, Daniel. *Indians and British Outposts in Eighteenth-Century America.* Gainesville: University Press of Florida, 2014.

Inman, Natalie R. *Brothers and Friends: Kinship in Early America.* Athens: University of Georgia Press, 2017.

Innes, Pamela Joan, Linda Alexander, and Bertha Tilkens. *Beginning Creek.* Norman: University of Oklahoma Press, 2004.

Irwin, Lee. *Coming Down from Above: Prophecy, Resistance, and Renewal in Native American Religions.* Norman: University of Oklahoma Press, 2008.

Iseminger, William. *Cahokia Mounds: America's First City.* Charleston, S.C.: History Press, 2010.

Ivers, Larry E. *This Torrent of Indians: War on the Southern Frontier, 1715–1728.* Columbia: University of South Carolina Press, 2016.

Jack, J. H. "Alabama and the Federal Government: The Creek Indian Controversy." *Mississippi Valley Historical Review* 3, no. 3 (1916): 301–14.

Jackson, Andrew. *The Papers of Andrew Jackson.* Edited by Daniel Feller, Harold D. Moser, Laura-Eve Moss, and Thomas Coens. 10 vols. Knoxville: University of Tennessee Press, 1980–2017.

Jackson, Jason Baird. "Introduction: On Studying Yuchi History." In Jason Baird Jackson, *Yuchi Indian Histories,* xiii–xxxiv.

————. *Yuchi Ceremonial Life: Performance, Meaning, and Tradition in a Contemporary American Indian Community.* Lincoln: University of Nebraska Press, 2005.

————. *Yuchi Folklore: Cultural Expression in a Southeastern Native American Community.* Norman: University of Oklahoma Press, 2013.

————, ed. *Yuchi Indian Histories Before the Removal Era.* Lincoln: University of Nebraska Press, 2012.

Jacobs, Wilbur R., ed. *The Appalachian Indian Frontier: The Edmond Atkin Report and Plan of 1755.* Lincoln: University of Nebraska Press, 1967.

Jefferson, Thomas. *Writings: Autobiography; A Summary View of the Rights of British America; Notes on the State of Virginia; Public Papers; Addresses; Messages, and Replies; Miscellany; Letters.* Edited by Merrill D. Peterson. New York: Library of America, 1984.

————. *The Writings of Thomas Jefferson.* Edited by H. A. Washington. 9 vols. New York: John C. Riker, 1853–1855.

Jenkins, Ned J. "Tracing the Origins of the Early Creeks, 1050–1700 CE." In Ethridge and Shuck-Hall, *Mapping the Mississippian Shatter Zone*, 188–249.

Jennison, Watson W. *Cultivating Race: The Expansion of Slavery in Georgia, 1750–1860*. Knoxville: University Press of Kentucky, 2012.

Johansen, Bruce E. *The Native Peoples of North America: A History*. New Brunswick, N.J.: Rutgers University Press, 2006.

Johansen, Bruce E., and Barry M. Pritzker, eds. *Encyclopedia of American Indian History*. 2 vols. Santa Barbara, Calif.: ABC-CLIO, 2008.

Johnson, Carolyn Ross. *Cherokee Women in Crisis: Trail of Tears, Civil War, and Allotment, 1838–1907*. Tuscaloosa: University of Alabama Press, 2003.

Johnston, Patricia, and Caroline Frank, eds. *Global Trade and Visual Arts in Federal New England*. Durham: University of New Hampshire Press, 2014.

Jones, David E. *Native North American Armor, Shields, and Fortifications*. Austin: University of Texas Press, 2004.

Jortner, Adam. *The Gods of Prophetstown: The Battle of Tippecanoe and the Holy War for the American Frontier*. New York: Oxford University Press, 2012.

Journal of the House of Representatives, Begun and Held at the City of Washington, December 7, 1829. Washington, D.C.: Duff Green, 1829.

Journal of the Senate of the United States of America: Being the First Session of the Twenty-Fourth Congress, Begun and Held at the City of Washington, December 7, 1835. Washington, D.C.: Gales and Seaton, 1835.

Juricek, John T. *Colonial Georgia and the Creeks: Anglo-Indian Diplomacy on the Southern Frontier, 1733–1763*. Gainesville: University Press of Florida, 2010.

Juster, Susan. *Sacred Violence in Early America*. Philadelphia: University of Pennsylvania Press, 2016.

Kang, Gay E. "Exogamy and Peace Relations of Social Units: A Cross-Cultural Test." *Ethnology* 18 (1979): 85–99.

Kappler, Charles J., ed. *Indian Affairs: Laws and Treaties*. 2 vols. Washington, D.C.: Government Printing Office, 1904.

Kehoe, Alice Beck. *North America Before the European Invasions*. 2nd ed. Abingdon, England: Routledge, 2017.

Kelly, John E. "The Emergence of Mississippian Culture in the American Bottom Region." In *The Mississippian Emergence*, edited by Bruce D. Smith, 113–52. Tuscaloosa: University of Alabama Press, 1990.

Kelton, Paul. *Cherokee Medicine, Colonial Germs: An Indigenous Nation's Fight against Smallpox, 1518–1824*. Norman: University of Oklahoma Press, 2015.

———. *Epidemics and Enslavement: Biological Catastrophe in the Native Southeast, 1492–1715*. Lincoln: University of Nebraska Press, 2007.

———. "The Great Southeastern Smallpox Epidemic, 1696–1700: The Region's First Major Epidemic?" In Ethridge and Hudson, *Transformation of the Southeastern Indians, 1540–1760*, 21–37.

Kennedy, Virginia. "Native Americans, African Americans, and the Space that Is America: Indian Presence in the Fiction of Toni Morrison." In *Crossing Waters, Crossing Worlds: The African Diaspora in Indian Country*, edited by Tiya Miles and Sharon P. Holland, 196–217. Durham, N.C.: Duke University Press, 2006.

Kenny, Kevin. *Diaspora: A Very Short Introduction*. New York: Oxford University Press, 2013.

Kersey, Harry A., Jr. "Those Left Behind: The Seminole Indians of Florida." In *Southeastern Indians Since the Removal Era*, edited by Walter L. Williams, 174–90. Athens: University of Georgia Press, 1979.

Kessell, John L. *Spain in the Southwest: A Narrative History of Colonial New Mexico, Arizona, Texas, and California*. Norman: University of Oklahoma Press, 2002.

Kidd, Colin. *The Forging of Races: Race and Scripture in the Protestant Atlantic World, 1600–2000*. New York: Cambridge University Press, 2006.

Kidwell, Clara Sue. *Choctaws and Missionaries in Mississippi, 1818–1918*. Norman: University of Oklahoma Press, 1995.

———. "The Struggle for Land and Identity in Mississippi, 1830–1918." In Samuel J. Wells and Tubby, *After Removal*, 64–93.

King, Adam. *Etowah: The Political History of a Chiefdom Capital*. Tuscaloosa: University of Alabama Press, 2003.

Kinnaird, Lawrence, ed. *Spain in the Mississippi Valley, 1765–1794: The Revolutionary Period, 1765–1781*. 3 vols. Washington, D.C.: U.S. Government Printing Office, 1949.

Kitchen, Andrew, Michael M. Miyamoto, and Connie Mulligan. "A Three-Stage Colonization Model for the Peopling of the Americas." *PLOS One* 3, no. 2 (2008): e1596.

Klotter, James C., and Freda C. Klotter. *A Concise History of Kentucky*. Lexington: University Press of Kentucky, 2008.

Knecht, Heidi, ed., *Projectile Technology*. New York: Plenum Press, 1997

Knight, Vernon J., Jr., and Vince P. Steponaitis, eds. *Archaeology of the Moundville Chiefdom: Chronology, Content, Contest*. Tuscaloosa: University of Alabama Press, 1998.

Kowalewski, Stephen A. "Coalescent Societies." In Pluckhahn and Ethridge, *Light on the Path*, 94–122.

———. "Large-Scale Ecology in Aboriginal Eastern North America." In *Native American Interactions: Multiscalar Analyses and Interpretations in the Eastern Woodlands*, edited by Michael S. Nassaney and Kenneth E. Sassaman, 147–73. Knoxville: University of Tennessee Press, 1995.

Kraut, Alan M. *Silent Travelers: Germs, Genes, and the Immigrant Menace*. Baltimore: Johns Hopkins University Press, 1994.

Krauthamer, Barbara. *Black Slaves, Indian Masters: Slavery, Emancipation, and Citizenship in the Native American South*. Chapel Hill: University of North Carolina Press, 2013.

Kroeber, Alfred L. *Cultural and Natural Areas of Native North America*. Berkeley: University of California Press, 1939.

Krupp, E. C. *Echoes of the Ancient Skies: The Astronomy of Lost Civilizations*. New York: Harper & Row, 1983.

Kulikoff, Allan. *From British Peasants to Colonial American Farmers*. Chapel Hill: University of North Carolina Press, 2000.

Labaree, L. W., ed. *Royal Instructions to British Colonial Governors, 1670–1776.* 2 vols. New York: Octagon Books, 1967.

Lakomäki, Sami. *Gathering Together: The Shawnee People through Diaspora and Nationhood, 1600–1870.* New Haven, Conn.: Yale University Press, 2014.

Lamana, Gonzalo. *Domination without Dominance: Inca-Spanish Encounters in Early Colonial Peru.* Durham, N.C.: Duke University Press, 2008.

Lambert, Valerie. *Choctaw Nation: A Story of American Indian Resurgence.* Lincoln: University of Nebraska Press, 2007.

Landers, Jane G. *Atlantic Creoles in the Age of Revolutions.* Cambridge, Mass.: Harvard University Press, 2010.

———. "A Nation Divided? Blood Seminoles and Black Seminoles on the Florida Frontier." In Richard F. Brown, *Coastal Encounters,* 99–116.

Lankford, George E. "The Great Serpent in Eastern North America." In Reilly and Garber, *Ancient Objects and Sacred Realms,* 107–35

———. *Native American Legends of the Southeast: Tales from the Natchez, Caddo, Biloxi, Chickasaw, and Other Nations.* Tuscaloosa: University of Alabama Press, 2011.

———. "Some Cosmological Motifs in the Southeastern Ceremonial Complex." In Reilly and Garber, *Ancient Objects and Sacred Realms,* 8–38.

Larson, Clark S. *Bioarchaeology of Spanish Florida: The Impact of Colonialism.* Gainesville: University Press of Florida, 2001.

Laubin, Reginald, and Gladys Laubin. *American Indian Archery.* Norman: University of Oklahoma Press, 1980.

La Vere, David. *The Caddo Chiefdoms: Caddo Economics and Politics, 700–1835.* Lincoln: University of Nebraska Press, 1998.

———. *The Tuscarora War: Indians, Settlers, and the Fight for the Carolina Colonies.* Chapel Hill: University of North Carolina Press, 2013.

Lawson, John. *A New Voyage to Carolina.* Edited by Hugh T. Lefler. Chapel Hill: University of North Carolina Press, 1967.

Laxar, James. *Tecumseh and Brock: The War of 1812.* Toronto: House of Anansi Press, 2012.

Leach, Douglas Edward. "Colonial Indian Wars." In Washburn, *History of Indian-White Relations,* 128–43.

Lederer, John. *The Discoveries of John Lederer, in Three Several Marches from Virginia, to the West of Carolina, and other Parts of the Continent: Begun in March 1669, and ended in September 1670.* Translated by William Talbot. London: J. C. for Samuel Heyrick, at Grays-Inne-Gate in Holborn, 1672.

Lee, Susan Pendleton. *New Primary History of the United States.* Rev. ed. Richmond, Va.: B. F. Johnson, 1899.

Lee, Wayne E. *Barbarians and Brothers: Anglo-American Warfare, 1500–1865.* New York: Oxford University Press, 2011.

———. "Fortify, Fight, or Flee: Tuscarora and Cherokee Defensive Warfare and Military Culture Adaptation." *Journal of Military History* 68, no. 3 (July 2004): 713–70.

————. "Peace Chiefs and Blood Revenge: Patterns of Restraint in Native American Warfare, 1500–1800." *Journal of Military History* 71, no. 3 (July 2007): 701–41.

Leeming, David Adams. *Creation Myths of the World*. Vol 1, parts 1–2. Santa Barbara, Calif.: ABC-CLIO, 1994.

————. *The Oxford Companion to World Mythology*. New York: Oxford University Press, 2005.

Leeming, David Adams, and Jake Page. *The Mythology of Native North America*. Norman: University of Oklahoma Press, 1998.

LeMaster, Michelle. *Brothers Born of One Mother: British-Native American Relations in the Colonial Southeast*. Charlottesville: University of Virginia Press, 2012.

Lenman, Bruce. *Britain's Colonial Wars, 1688–1783*. New York: Routledge, 2014.

Lerch, Patricia Barker. *Waccamaw Legacy: Contemporary Indians Fight for Survival*. Tuscaloosa: University of Alabama Press, 2004.

Lewis, David, Jr., and Ann T. Jordan. *Creek Indian Medicine Ways: The Enduring Power of Mvskoke Religion*. Albuquerque: University of New Mexico Press, 2002.

Littlefield, Daniel F., Jr. *Africans and Seminoles: From Removal to Emancipation*. Jackson: University Press of Mississippi, 2001.

Lockhart, James. *Nahuas and Spaniards: Postconquest Central Mexican History and Philology*. Stanford, Calif.: Stanford University Press, 1991.

Lockley, Timothy James, ed. *Maroon Communities in South Carolina: A Documentary Record*. Columbia: University of South Carolina Press, 2009.

Lowery, Malinda Maynor. *Lumbee Indians in the Jim Crow South: Race, Identity, and the Making of a Nation*. Chapel Hill: University of North Carolina Press, 2010.

Lupold, John S., and Thomas L. French, Jr. *Bridging Deep South Rivers: The Life and Legend of Horace King*. Athens: University of Georgia Press, 2004.

Lynott, M. J. "Identification of Attribute Variability in Emergent Mississippian and Mississippian Arrow Points from Southeastern Missouri." *Midcontinental Journal of Archaeology* 16 (1991): 189–211.

Lyon, Eugene. *The Enterprise of Florida: Pedro Menéndez de Avilés and the Spanish Conquest of 1565–1568*. Gainesville: University Press of Florida, 1983.

Madsden, David B. "Colonization of the Americas before the Last Glacial Maximum: Issues and Problems." In Madsden, *Entering America*, 1–26.

————. *Entering America: Northeast Asia and Beringia before the Last Glacial Maximum*. Salt Lake City: University of Utah Press, 2004.

Mahon, John K. *History of the Second Seminole War, 1835–1842*. Rev. ed. Gainesville: University Press of Florida, 1985.

Mails, Thomas E. *The Cherokee People: The Story of the Cherokees from Earliest Origins to Contemporary Times*. Tulsa, Okla.: Council Oaks Books, 1992.

Malone, Henry T. "The *Cherokee Phoenix*: Supreme Expression of Cherokee Nationalism." *Georgia Historical Quarterly* 34, no 3 (September 1950): 163–88.

————. *Cherokees of the Old South: A People in Transition*. 1956. Reprint, Athens: University of Georgia Press, 2010.

Malone, Patrick M. *The Skulking Way of War: Technology and Tactics among the New England Indians*. Lanham, Md.: Madison Books, 2000.

Mapp, Paul. "French Geographic Conceptions of the Unexplored West and the Louisiana Cession of 1762." In Bond, *French Colonial Louisiana*, 134–74.

Marcoux, Jon B. "Cherokee Households and Communities in the English Contact Period, 1670–1740." Ph.D. diss., University of North Carolina, Chapel Hill, 2008.

Martin, Paul S. *The Last 10,000 Years: A Fossil Pollen Record of the American Southwest.* Tucson: University of Arizona Press, 1963.

Martin, Robert G. "The Cherokee Phoenix: Pioneer of Indian Journalism." *Chronicles of Oklahoma* 25 (Summer 1947): 102–18.

———. *Twilight of the Mammoths: Ice Age Extinctions and the Rewilding of America.* Berkeley: University of California Press, 2003.

Martire d'Anghiera, Pietro. *De Orbe Novo: The Eight Decades of Peter Martyr D'Anghera.* Translated by Francis Augustus MacNutt. 2 vols. New York: G. P. Putnam's Sons, 1912.

Martínez, María Elena. *Genealogical Fictions: Limpieza de Sangre, Religion, and Gender in Colonial Mexico.* Stanford, Calif.: Stanford University Press, 2008.

Mason, Carol I. *The Archaeology of Ocmulgee Old Fields, Macon, Georgia.* Tuscaloosa: University of Alabama Press, 2005.

Mason, Otis Tufton. *North American Bows, Arrows, and Quivers.* Publication No. 962. From *Annual Report of the Board of Regents of the Smithsonian Institution . . . to July, 1893.* Washington, D.C.: Government Printing Office, 1894.

McAuliffe, Dennis, Jr. *Bloodland: A Family Story of Oil, Greed and Murder on the Osage Reservation.* San Francisco: Council Oaks Books, 1999.

McCandless, Peter. *Slavery, Disease, and Suffering in the Southern Lowcountry.* New York: Cambridge University Press, 2011.

McClinton, Rowena. "Cherokee and Christian Expressions of Spirituality through First Parents: Eve and Selu." In Garrison and O'Brien, *Native South*, 70–83.

McConnell, Michael N. *A Country Between: The Upper Ohio Valley and its Peoples, 1724–1774.* Lincoln: University of Nebraska Press, 1992.

McCoy, Isaac. *History of Baptist Indian Missions: Embracing Remarks of the Aboriginal Tribes; Their Settlement within the Indian Territory, and Their Future Prospects.* Washington, D.C.: William M. Morrison, 1840.

McDonnell, Michael A. *Masters of Empire: Great Lakes Indians and the Making of America.* New York: Hill and Wang, 2015.

McDowell, William L., Jr., ed. *Documents Relating to Indian Affairs, 1754–1765.* Colonial Records of South Carolina, Series 2. 3 vols. Columbia: University of South Carolina Press, 1970.

———, ed. *Journals of the Commissioners of the Indian Trade.* Colonial Records of South Carolina. Columbia: South Carolina Archives Department, 1955.

McElrath, Dale L., Thomas E. Emerson, and Andrew C. Fortier, eds. *Late Woodland Societies: Tradition and Transformation across the Midcontinent.* Lincoln: University of Nebraska Press, 2000.

———. "Social Evolution or Social Response? A Fresh Look at the 'Good Gray Cultures' after Four Decades of Midwest Research." In McElrath, Emerson, and Fortier, *Late Woodland Societies*, 3–36.

McGrath, Ann. *Illicit Love: Interracial Sex and Marriage in the United States and Australia.* Lincoln: University of Nebraska Press, 2015.

McIlwain, Charles H. *An Abridgement to the Indian Affairs, Contained in Four Folio Volumes, Transacted in the Colony of New York, from the Year 1678 to the Year 1751.* Cambridge, Mass.: Harvard University Press, 1915.

McKenney, Thomas L. *Sketches of a Tour to the Lakes, of the Character and Customs of the Chippeway Indians, and of Incidents Connected with the Treaty of Fond du Lac.* Baltimore, Md.: Fielding Lucas, Jr., 1827.

McLoughlin, William G. *After the Trail of Tears: The Cherokees' Struggle for Sovereignty, 1839–1880.* Chapel Hill: University of North Carolina Press, 1993.

———. *Cherokee Renascence in the New Republic.* Princeton, N.J.: Princeton University Press, 1986.

———. *The Cherokees and Christianity: Essays on Acculturation and Cultural Persistence.* Edited by Walter H. Conser Jr. Athens: University of Georgia Press, 1994.

McManamon, Francis P. *Archaeology in America: An Encyclopedia.* Westport, Conn.: Greenwood, 2009.

McNeese, Tim, ed. *Myths of Native America.* New York: Four Walls Eight Windows, 1999.

McNiven, Ian J., and Lynette Russell. *Appropriated Pasts: Indigenous Peoples and the Colonial Culture of Archaeology.* Lanham, Md.: AltaMira, 2005.

McReynolds, Edwin C. *The Seminoles.* Norman: University of Oklahoma Press, 1957.

McReynolds, Theresa E. "Catawba Population Dynamics during the Eighteenth and Nineteenth Centuries." *North Carolina Archaeology* 53 (October 2004): 42–59.

Mehrer, Mark W. *Cahokia's Countryside: Household Archaeology, Settlement Patterns, and Social Power.* DeKalb: Northern Illinois University Press, 1995.

Meltzer, David J. *First Peoples in a New World: Colonizing Ice Age America.* Berkeley: University of California Press, 2009.

Merrell, James H. *The Indians' New World: Catawbas and Their Neighbors from European Contact through the Era of Removal.* Chapel Hill: University of North Carolina Press, 1989.

———. *Into the American Woods: Negotiators on the Pennsylvania Frontier.* New York: W. W. Norton, 1999.

Merritt, Jane T. "Native Peoples in the Revolutionary War." In *The Oxford Handbook of the American Revolution,* edited by Edward G. Gray and Jane Kamensky, 234–49. New York: Oxford University Press, 2013.

Meyers, Maureen. "From Refugees to Slave Traders: The Transformation of the Westo Indians." In Ethridge and Shuck-Hall, *Mapping the Mississippian Shatter Zone,* 81–103.

Mielke, Laura L. *Moving Encounters: Sympathy and the Indian Question in Antebellum Literature.* Amherst: University of Massachusetts Press, 2008.

Mihesuah, Devon Abbott. *Choctaw Crime and Punishment, 1884–1907.* Norman: University of Oklahoma Press, 2009.

Milanich, Jerald T. *The Timucua.* Cambridge, Mass.: Blackwell, 1996.

Miles, Tiya. "'Circular Reasoning': Recentering Cherokee Women in the Antiremoval

Campaigns." *American Quarterly* 61, no. 2 (June 2009): 221–43.

———. *The House on Diamond Hill: A Cherokee Plantation Story*. Chapel Hill: University of North Carolina Press, 2010.

———. *Tales from the Haunted South: Dark Tourism and Memories of Slavery from the Civil War Era*. Chapel Hill: University of North Carolina Press, 2015.

———. *Ties That Bind: The Story of an Afro-Cherokee Family in Slavery and Freedom*. Berkeley: University of California Press, 2005.

Miller, Carl F. "Reevaluation of the Eastern Siouan Problem, with Particular Emphasis on the Virginia Branches—The Occaneechi, the Saponi, and the Tutelo." Smithsonian Institution Bureau of American Ethnology Bulletin 164. *Anthropological Papers* 52 (1957): 115–211.

Miller, David W. *The Taking of American Indian Lands in the Southeast: A History of Territorial Cessions and Forced Relocations, 1607–1840*. Jefferson, N.C.: McFarland, 2011

Miller, Mark E. *Claiming Tribal Identity: The Five Tribes and the Politics of Federal Acknowledgment*. Norman: University of Oklahoma Press, 2013.

Milne, George Edward. *Natchez Country: Indians, Colonists, and the Landscapes of Race in French Louisiana*. Athens: University of Georgia Press, 2015.

———. "Picking up the Pieces: Natchez Coalescence in the Shatter Zone." In Ethridge and Shuck-Hall, *Mapping the Mississippian Shatter* Zone, 388–417.

Milner, George R. The Moundbuilders: *Ancient Peoples of Eastern North America*. New York: Thames and Hudson, 2010.

———. "Warfare, Population, and Food Production in Prehistoric Eastern North America." In Chacon and Mendoza, *North American Indigenous Warfare*, 182–201.

Minnis, Paul E. *People and Plants in Ancient North America*. Washington, D.C.: Smithsonian Institution Press, 2003.

Minnis, Paul E., and Wayne J. Elisens, eds. *Biodiversity and Native America*. Norman: University of Oklahoma Press, 2000.

Mithen, Steven. *After the Ice: A Global Human History, 20,000–5,000 BC*. Cambridge, Mass.: Harvard University Press, 2003.

Monaco, C. S. *The Second Seminole War and the Limits of American Aggression*. Baltimore: Johns Hopkins University Press, 2018.

Mooney, James. *James Mooney's History, Myths, and Sacred Formulas of the Cherokees*. Fairview, N.C.: Bright Mountain Books, 1992.

———. *Myths of the Cherokee*. New York: Dover, 1995.

Moore, David G. *Catawba Valley Mississippian: Ceramics, Chronology, and Catawba Indians*. Tuscaloosa: University of Alabama Press, 2002.

Moore, Peter N. *World of Toil and Strife: Community Transformation in Backcountry South Carolina, 1750–1805*. Columbia: University of South Carolina Press, 2007.

Morris, Craig. "Signs of Division, Symbols of Unity: Arts in the Inka Empire." In *Circa 1492: Art in the Age of Exploration,* edited by Jay A. Levenson, 521–28. New Haven, Conn.: Yale University Press, 1991.

Morris, Michael P. *The Bringing of Wonder: Trade and the Indians of the Southeast,*

1700–1878. Westport, Conn.: Greenwood, 1999.

———. *George Galphin and the Transformation of the Georgia-South Carolina Backcountry*. Lanham, Md.: Lexington Books, 2015.

Mould, Tom. "'Chahta Siyah Ókih': Ethnicity in the Oral Tradition of the Mississippi Band of Choctaw Indians." In *Ethnic Heritage in Mississippi: The Twentieth Century*, edited by Shana Walton and Barbara Carpenter, 219–60. Jackson: University of Mississippi Press, 2012.

———. *Choctaw Tales*. Jackson: University of Mississippi Press, 2004.

Moulton, Gary E. *John Ross, Cherokee Chief*. Athens: University of Georgia Press, 1978

Mulcahy, Matthew. *Hubs of Empire: The Southeastern Lowcountry and British Caribbean*. Baltimore: Johns Hopkins University Press, 2014.

Mulkeam, Lois. *George Mercer Papers: Relations to the Ohio Company of Virginia*. Pittsburgh: University of Pittsburgh Press, 1954.

Muller, Jon. *Mississippian Political Economy*. New York: Plenum, 1997.

Mulroy, Kevin. *Freedom on the Border: The Seminole Maroons in Florida, the Indian Territory, Coahuila, and Texas*. Lubbock: Texas Tech University Press, 1993.

———. *The Seminole Freedmen: A History*. Norman: University of Oklahoma Press, 2007.

Nabhan, Gary P. *Enduring Seeds: Native American Agriculture and Wild Plant Conservation*. Tucson: University of Arizona Press, 1989.

Nash, Alice. "'None of the Women Were Abused': Indigenous Contexts for the Treatment of Women Captives in the Northeast." In *Sex Without Consent: Rape and Sexual Coercion in America*, edited by Merrill D. Smith, 10–26. New York: New York University Press, 2002.

Nash, Gary B. *The Unknown American Revolution: The Unruly Birth of Democracy and the Struggle to Create America*. New York: Penguin Books, 2005.

Nass, John P., Jr., and Richard W. Yerkes. "Social Differentiation in Mississippian and Fort Ancient Societies." In *Mississippian Communities and Households*, edited by Daniel Rogers and Bruce D. Smith 58–80. Tuscaloosa: University of Alabama Press, 1995.

Naylor, Celia E. *African Cherokees in Indian Territory: From Chattel to Citizens*. Chapel Hill: University of North Carolina Press, 2008.

Nelson, Jon. *Quetico: Near to Nature's Heart*. Toronto: Dunburn, 2009.

Neugin, Rebecca. "Memories of the Trail." *Journal of Cherokee Studies* 3 (1978): 176.

Nichols, David A. *Engines of Diplomacy: Indian Trading Factories and the Negotiation of American Empire*. Chapel Hill: University of North Carolina Press, 2016.

Norgen, Jill. *The Cherokee Cases: Two Landmark Federal Decisions in the Fight for Sovereignty*. Norman: University of Oklahoma Press, 2004.

Norton, John. *The Journal of Major John Norton, 1816*. Edited by Carl F. Klinck and James J. Talman. Toronto: Champlain Society, 1970.

Nott, Josiah. *Two Lectures on the Natural History of the Caucasian and Negro Races*. Mobile, Ala.: Dade and Thompson, 1844.

Oatis, Steven J. *A Colonial Complex: South Carolina's Frontiers in the Era of the Yamasee War, 1680–1730*. Lincoln: University of Nebraska Press, 2004.

Oberg, Kalervo. "Types of Social Structure among the Lowland Tribes of South and Central America." *American Anthropologist* 57, no. 3 (1955): 472–87.

O'Brien, Greg. "The Choctaw Defense of Pensacola in the American Revolution." In O'Brien, *Pre-Removal Choctaw History*, 123–47.

———. *Choctaws in a Revolutionary Age, 1750–1830*. Lincoln: University of Nebraska Press, 2005.

———. "The Coming of Age of Choctaw History." In O'Brien, *Pre-Removal Choctaw History*, 3–25.

———, ed. *Pre-Removal Choctaw History: Exploring New Paths*. Norman: University of Oklahoma Press, 2008.

———. "Protecting Trade through War: Choctaw Elites and British Occupation of the Floridas." In O'Brien, *Pre-Removal Choctaw History*, 103–22.

———. "Quieting the Ghosts: How the Choctaws and Chickasaws Stopped Fighting." In Garrison and O'Brien, *Native South*, 47–69.

———. "Supplying Our Wants: Choctaws and Chickasaws Reassess the Trade Relationship with Britain, 1771–72." In Richard F. Brown, *Coastal Encounters*, 59–80.

O'Hara, Kieran D. *Cave Art and Climate Change*. Bloomington, Ind.: Archway, 2014.

Oliphant, John. *Peace and War on the Anglo-Cherokee Frontier, 1756–1763*. Baton Rouge: Louisiana State University Press, 2001.

Olsen, Brad. *Sacred Places, North America: 108 Destinations*. 2nd ed. San Francisco, Consortium of Collective Consciousness, 2008.

O'Neill, Dan. *The Mystery of the Bering Land Bridge*. Cambridge, Mass.: Westview, 2004.

Onofrio, Jan. *Dictionary of Indian Tribes of the Americas*. 3 vols. Newport Beach, Calif.: American Indian Publishers, 1993.

Osburn, Katherine M. B. *Choctaw Resurgence in Mississippi: Race, Class, and Nation Building in the Jim Crow South, 1830–1977*. Lincoln: University of Nebraska Press, 2014.

Owens, Robert M. *Red Dreams, White Nightmares: Pan-Indian Alliances in the Anglo-American Mind, 1763–1815*. Norman: University of Oklahoma Press, 2015.

Padget, Cindy D. "The Lost Indians of the Lost Colony: A Critical Legal Study of the Lumbee Indians of North Carolina." *American Indian Law Review* 21, no. 2 (1997): 391–424.

Pagden, Anthony. *The Fall of Natural Man: The American Indian and the Origins of Comparative Ethnology*. New York: Cambridge University Press, 1982.

Paige, Amanda L., Fuller L. Bumpers, and Daniel F. Littlefield Jr. *Chickasaw Removal*. Ada, Okla.: Chickasaw Press, 2010.

Paisley, Clifton. *The Red Hills of Florida, 1528–1865*. Tuscaloosa: University of Alabama Press, 1989.

Parsons, Lynn H. "'A Perpetual Harrow upon My Feelings': John Quincy Adams and the American Indian." In Vaughan, *New England Encounters*, 324–58.

Pauketat, Timothy R. *The Archaeology of Downtown Cahokia: The Tract 15A and Dunham Tract Excavations*. Urbana: University of Illinois Press, 1998.

———. *The Ascent of Chiefs: Cahokia and Mississippian Politics in Native North America*. Tuscaloosa: University of Alabama Press, 1994.

————, ed. *The Oxford Handbook of North American Archaeology*. New York: Oxford University Press, 2011.

————. "Politicization and Community in the Pre-Columbian Mississippi Valley." In *The Archaeology of Communities: A New World Perspective*, edited by Marcello A. Canuto and Jason Yaeger, 16–43. New York: Routledge, 2000.

Paulett, Robert. *An Empire of Small Places: Mapping the Southeastern Anglo–Indian Trade, 1732–1795*. Athens: University of Georgia Press, 2012.

Perdue, Theda, ed. *Cherokee Editor: The Writings of Elias Boudinot*. Athens: University of Georgia Press, 1996.

————. "Cherokee Planters: The Development of Plantation Slavery Before Removal." In *The Cherokee Indian Nation: A Troubled History*, edited by Duane H. King, 110–28. *The Cherokee Indian Nation*: Knoxville: University of Tennessee Press, 1979.

————, ed. *The Cherokee Removal: A Brief History with Documents*. 3rd ed. Boston: Bedford/St. Martin's, 2016.

————. *Cherokee Women: Gender and Culture Change, 1700–1835*. Lincoln: University of Nebraska Press, 1998.

————. "The Legacy of Indian Removal." *Journal of Southern History* 78, no. 1 (February 2012): 3–36.

————. *Slavery and the Evolution of Cherokee Society, 1540–1866*. Knoxville: University of Tennessee Press, 1979.

————. "Southern Indians and Jim Crow." In *The Folly of Jim Crow: Rethinking the Segregated South*, edited by Stephanie Cole and Natalie J. Ring, 54–90. College Station: Texas A&M University Press, 2012.

————. "Writing the Ethnohistory of Native Women." In Fixico, *Rethinking American Indian History*, 73–86.

Perdue, Theda, and Michael D. Green. *The Cherokee Nation and the Trail of Tears*. New York: Viking, 2007.

————. *The Columbia Guide to American Indians of the Southeast*. New York: Columbia University Press, 2001.

Perego, Ugo A., et al. "Distinctive Paleo-Indian Migration Routes from Beringia Marked by Two Rare mtDNA Haplogroups." *Current Biology* 19, no. 1 (January 13, 2009): 1–8.

Perttula, Timothy K. *"The Caddo Nation": Archaeological and Ethnohistoric Perspectives*. Austin: University of Texas Press, 1997.

————. "Social Changes among the Caddo Indians in the 16th and 17th Centuries." In Ethridge and Hudson, *Transformation of the Southeastern Indians*, 249–70.

Pesantubbee, Michelene E. *Choctaw Women in a Chaotic World: The Clash of Cultures in the Colonial Southeast*. Albuquerque: University of New Mexico Press, 2005.

Peterken, George F. *Natural Woodland: Ecology and Conservation in Northern Temperate Regions*. New York: Cambridge University Press, 1996.

Peters, Richard. *The Case of the Cherokee Nation against the State of Georgia, Argued and Determined at the Supreme Court of the United States, January Term, 1831*. Philadelphia: John Grigg, 1831.

Peterson, Harold L. *Arms and Armor in Colonial America, 1525–1783*. 1956. Reprint, Dover, 2000.

Piker, Joshua A. *The Four Deaths of Acorn Whistler: Telling Stories in Colonial America*. Cambridge, Mass.: Harvard University Press, 2013.

———. *Okfuskee: A Creek Indian Town in Colonial America*. Cambridge, Mass.: Harvard University Press, 2004.

Pitchlynn, Peter P. *A Gathering of Statesmen: Records of the Choctaw Council Meetings, 1826–1828*. Edited and translated by Marcia Haag and Henry Willis. Norman: University of Oklahoma Press, 2013.

Plane, Mark R. "Catawba Ethnicity: Identity and Adaptation on the English Colonial Landscape." *North Carolina Archaeology* 53 (October 2004): 60–79.

———. "Catawba Militarism: An Ethnohistorical and Archaeological Overview." *North Carolina Archaeology* 53 (October 2004): 80–120.

———. "'Remarkable Elasticity of Character': Colonial Discourse, the Market Economy, and Catawba Itinerancy, 1770–1820." In *American Indians and the Market Economy, 1775–1850,* edited by Lance Greene and Mark R. Plane, 33–52. Tuscaloosa: University of Alabama Press, 2010.

Pluckhahn, Thomas J., and Robbie Ethridge, eds. *The Light on the Path: The Anthropology and History of the Southeastern Indians*. Tuscaloosa: University of Alabama Press, 2006.

Porter, Kenneth W. *The Black Seminoles: History of a Freedom-Seeking People*. Gainesville: University Press of Florida, 1996.

———. "The Founder of the 'Seminole Nation': Secoffee or Cowkeeper." *Florida Historical Quarterly* 27, no. 4 (April 1949): 362–84.

Potter-Deimel, Raeschelle J. "A Wounded Eagle Soars over the Hills of Mississippi! A Choctaw Story." In *Challenges of Native American Studies: Essays in Celebration of the Twenty-Fifth American Indian Workshop,* edited by Barbara Saunders and Lea Zuyderhoudt, 323–34. Leuven, Belgium: Leuven University Press, 2004.

Powell, Joseph. *The First Americans: Race, Evolution, and the Origin of Native Americans*. New York: Cambridge University Press, 2005.

Powell, William S. *North Carolina Through Four Centuries*. Chapel Hill: University of North Carolina Press, 1989.

Power, Susan C. *Early Art of the Southeastern Indians: Feathered Serpents and Winged Beings*. Athens: University of Georgia Press, 2004.

Pratt, Adam J. "Violence and the Competition for Sovereignty in Cherokee Country, 1829–1835." *American Nineteenth Century History* 17, no. 2 (June 2016): 181–97.

Preston, David L. *The Texture of Contact: European and Indian Settler Communities on the Frontiers of Iroquoia, 1667–1783*. Lincoln: University of Nebraska Press, 2009.

Pritzker, Barry. *A Native American Encyclopedia: History, Culture, and Peoples*. New York: Oxford University Press, 2000.

Prucha, Francis Paul. *American Indian Treaties: The History of a Political Anomaly*. Berkeley: University of California Press, 1994.

———, ed. *Documents of United States Indian Policy*. 3rd ed. Lincoln: University of Nebraska Press, 2000.

Raab, James W. *Spain, Britain and the American Revolution in Florida, 1763–1783.* Jefferson, N.C.: McFarland, 2008.

Ragavan, Maanasa, et al. "Upper Palaeolithic Siberian Genome Reveals Dual Ancestry of Native Americans." *Nature* 505 (January 2, 2014): 87–91.

Ramsey, William L. *The Yamasee War: A Study of Culture, Economy, and Conflict in the Colonial South.* Lincoln: University of Nebraska Press, 2008.

Ray, Kristofer, ed. *Before the Volunteer State: New Thoughts on Early Tennessee, 1540–1800.* Knoxville: University of Tennessee Press, 2014.

———. "Constructing a Discourse of Indigenous Slavery, Freedom and Sovereignty." *Native South* 10 (2017): 19–39.

———. "Introduction: Understanding the Tennessee Corridor." In Ray, *Before the Volunteer State,* ix–x.

Ready, Milton. *The Tar Heel State: A History of North Carolina.* Columbia: University of South Carolina Press, 2005.

Rees, Mark A., and Patrick C. Livingood, eds. *Plaquemine Archaeology.* Tuscaloosa: University of Alabama Press, 2007.

Reeves, Carolyn Keller, ed. *The Choctaw before Removal.* Jackson: University Press of Mississippi, 1985.

Reff, Daniel T. *Disease, Depopulation, and Cultural Change in Northwestern New Spain.* Salt Lake City: University of Utah Press, 1991.

Regnier, Amanda L. *Reconstructing Tuscalusa's Chiefdom: Pottery Styles and the Social Composition of Late Mississippian Communities along the Alabama River.* Tuscaloosa: University of Alabama Press, 2014.

Reich, David, et al. "Reconstructing Native American Population History." *Nature* 488 (August 16, 2012): 370–74.

Reid, John P. *A Law of Blood: The Primitive Law of the Cherokee Nation.* New York: New York University Press, 1970.

Reilly, F. Kent, and James F. Garber, eds. *Ancient Objects and Sacred Realms: Interpretations of Mississippian Iconography.* Austin: University of Texas Press, 2007.

Report of the Select Committee of the House of Representatives, to Which Were Referred the Messages of the President U.S., of the 5th and 8th February, and 2d March, 1827. Washington, D.C.: Gales and Seaton, 1827.

Reséndez, Andrés. *The Other Slavery: The Uncovered Story of Indian Enslavement in America.* Boston: Houghton Mifflin Harcourt, 2016.

Restall, Matthew. *Seven Myths of the Spanish Conquest.* Oxford, England: Oxford University Press, 2003.

Reynolds, William R., Jr. *The Cherokee Struggle to Maintain Identity in the 17th and 18th Centuries.* Jefferson, N.C.: McFarland, 2015.

Richter, Daniel K. *Before the Revolution: Americas Ancient Pasts.* Cambridge, Mass.: Harvard University Press, 2011.

———. *The Ordeal of the Longhouse: The Peoples of the Iroquois League in the Era of European Colonization.* Chapel Hill: University of North Carolina Press, 1992.

Rindfleisch, Bryan. "'Our Lands Are Our Life and Breath': Coweta, Cusseta, and the

Struggle for Creek Territory and Sovereignty during the American Revolution."
Ethnohistory 60, no. 4 (2013): 581–603.

———. "The 'Owner of the Town Ground, Who Overrules All When on the Spot':
Escotachaby of Coweta and the Politics of Personal Networking in Creek Country,
1740–1780." *Native South* 9 (2016); 54–88.

Rivers, Larry E. *Rebels and Runaways: Slave Resistance in Nineteenth-Century Florida.*
Urbana: University of Illinois Press, 2012.

Roberts, Charles. "The Second Choctaw Removal, 1903." In Samuel J. Wells and
Tubby, *After Removal,* 94–111.

Rockwell, Stephen J. *Indian Affairs and the Administrative State in the Nineteenth
Century.* New York: Cambridge University Press, 2010.

Rodning, Christopher B. *Center Places and Cherokee Towns: Archaeological Perspectives
on Native American Architecture and Landscape in the Southern Appalachians.*
Tuscaloosa: University of Alabama Press, 2015.

———. "Reconstructing the Coalescence of Cherokee Communities in Southern
Appalachia." In Ethridge and Hudson, *Transformation of the Southeastern Indians,*
155–76.

Rodning, Christopher B., and Jayur M. Mehta. "Resilience and Persistent Places
in the Mississippi River Delta of Southeastern Louisiana." In *Beyond Collapse:
Archaeological Perspectives on Resilience, Revitalization, and Transformation in
Complex Societies,* edited by Ronald K Faulseit, 342–79. Carbondale: Southern
Illinois University Press, 2016.

Rogers, Richard A. "Glacial Geography and Native North American Languages."
Quaternary Research 23, no. 1 (January 1985): 130–37.

Rogin, Michael P. *Fathers and Children: Andrew Jackson and the Subjugation of the
American Indian.* New York: Alfred A. Knopf, 1975.

Roper, L. H. *Conceiving Carolina: Proprietors, Planters, and Plots, 1662–1729.* New
York: Palgrave Macmillan, 2004.

Rosen, Deborah A. *American Indians and State Law: Sovereignty, Race, and Citizenship, 1790–1880.* Lincoln: University of Nebraska Press, 2007.

———. *Border Law: The First Seminole War and American Nationhood.* Cambridge,
Mass.: Harvard University Press, 2015.

Rosier, Paul C. *Serving Their Country: American Indian Politics and Patriotism in
the Twentieth Century.* Cambridge, Mass.: Harvard University Press, 2009.

Rowland, Dunbar, and Albert Godfrey Sanders, eds. *Mississippi Provincial Archives:
French Dominion, 1701–1743.* 3 vols. Jackson: Press of the Mississippi Department
of Archives and History, 1927–1932.

Royall, Anne N. *Letters from Alabama on Various Subjects.* Washington, D.C.,
1830.

Rozema, Vicki, ed. *Cherokee Voices: Early Accounts of Cherokee Life in the East.* Winston-Salem, N.C.: John F. Blair, 2002.

———, ed. *Voices from the Trail of Tears.* Winston-Salem, N.C.: John F. Blair, 2003.

Rushforth, Brett. *Bonds of Alliance: Indigenous and Atlantic Slaveries in New France.*
Chapel Hill: University of North Carolina Press, 2012.

Ryan, Susan M. *The Grammar of Good Intentions: Race and the Antebellum Culture of Benevolence.* Ithaca, N.Y.: Cornell University Press, 2004.

Sabo, George, III. "The Terán Map and Caddo Cosmology." In *The Archaeology of the Caddo,* edited by Timothy K. Perttula and Chester P. Walker, 431–47. Lincoln: University of Nebraska Press, 2012.

Sahlins, Marshall. "Poor Man, Rich Man, Big-Man, Chief: Political Types in Melanesia and Polynesia." *Comparative Studies in Society and History* 5, no. 3 (April 1963): 285–303.

———. *Social Stratification in Polynesia.* Seattle: University of Washington Press, 1958.

Salafia, Matthew. *Slavery's Borderland: Freedom and Bondage along the Ohio River.* Philadelphia: University of Pennsylvania Press, 2013.

Salisbury, Neal. "Native People and European Settlers in Eastern North America, 1600–1783." In *The Cambridge History of the Native Peoples of the Americas: Volume I, North America,* edited by Bruce G. Trigger and Wilcomb E. Washburn, 399–460. New York: Cambridge University Press, 1996.

Sattler, Richard A. "Remnants, Renegades, and Runaways: Seminole Ethnogenesis Reconsidered." In *History, Power, and Identity: Ethnogenesis in the Americas, 1492–1992,* edited by Jonathan D. Hill, 36–69. Iowa City: University of Iowa Press, 1996.

Satz, Ronald N. *American Indian Policy in the Jacksonian Era.* Norman: University of Oklahoma Press, 1975.

Saunders, Joe W. "Middle Archaic and Watson Brake." In *Archaeology of Louisiana,* edited by Chip McGimsey, 63–76. Baton Rouge: Louisiana State University Press, 2010.

Saunders, William L., ed. *The Colonial Records of North Carolina.* Vol. 2. *1713–1728.* Raleigh: P. M. Hale, 1886.

Saunt, Claudio. "The Age of Imperial Expansion, 1763–1821." In Hoxie, *Oxford Handbook,* 77–91.

———. *Black, White, and Indian: Race and the Unmaking of an American Family.* New York: Oxford University Press, 2005.

———. "'Domestick . . . Quiet being broke': Gender Conflict among Creek Indians in the Eighteenth Century." In Cayton and Teute, *Contact Points,* 151–74.

———. *A New Order of Things: Property, Power, and the Transformation of the Creek Indians, 1733–1816.* New York: Cambridge University Press, 1999.

Sayre, Gordon M. *The Indian Chief as Tragic Hero: Native Resistance and the Literatures of America, from Moctezuma to Tecumseh.* Chapel Hill: University of North Carolina Press, 2005.

Scarry, C. Margaret. "Domestic Life on the Northwest Riverbank at Moundville." In Knight and Steponaitis, *Archaeology of the Moundville Chiefdom,* 63–101.

Schaafsma, Polly. "Head Trophies and Scalping." In *The Taking and Displaying of Human Body Parts as Trophies by Amerindians,* edited by Richard J. Chacon and David H. Sye, 90–123. New York: Springer, 2007.

Scheick, William J. *The Half-Blood: A Cultural Symbol in 19th-Century American Fiction.* Knoxville: University of Kentucky Press, 1979.

Schlotterbeck, John. *Daily Life in the Colonial South.* Santa Barbara, Calif.: ABC-CLIO, 2013.

Schmidt, Ethan A. *Native Americans in the American Revolution: How the War Divided, Devastated, and Transformed the Early American Indian World.* Santa Barbara, Calif.: Praeger, 2014.

Schmitz, Kamille R. "A Review of Bioarchaeological Thought on the Peopling of the New World." In *Settlement of the American Continents: A Multidisciplinary Approach to Human Biogeography,* edited by Michael C. Barton, Geoffrey A. Clark, David R. Yesner, and Georges A. Pearson, 64–75. Tucson: University of Arizona Press, 2004.

Schneider, Bethany. "Boudinot's Change: Boudinot, Emerson, and Ross on Cherokee Removal." *ELH* 75 (2008): 151–77.

Scudder, Horace E. *A History of the United States of America.* Philadelphia: J. H. Butler, 1884.

Searcy, Margaret Zehmer. "Choctaw Subsistence, 1540–1830: Hunting, Fishing, Farming, and Gathering." In Reeves, *Choctaw before Removal,* 32–54.

Seck, Ibrahuma. "The Relationship between St. Louis of Senegal, Its Hinterlands, and Colonial Louisiana." In Bond, *French Colonial Louisiana,* 265–90.

Senate Journal. Journal of the Proceedings of the Senate of the First General Assembly of the State of Florida, at its First Session, Begun and Held in the City of Tallahassee, on Monday, June 23, 1845. Tallahassee: Office of the Florida Sentinel, 1845.

Shaffer, Lynda N., and Thomas Reilly. *Native Americans Before 1492: Moundbuilding Realms of the Mississippian Woodlands.* New York: Routledge, 1992.

Shea, John J. "The Solutrean-Clovis Connection: Another Look." *Evolutionary Anthropology* 21 (2012): 293–95.

Shell, Eddie W. *Evolution of the Alabama Agroecosystem: Always Keeping Up, but Never Catching Up.* Montgomery, Ala.: New South Press, 2011.

Shipp, Barnard. *The History of Hernando de Soto and Florida; or Records of the Events of Fifty-Six Years, from 151 to 1568.* Philadelphia: Robert M. Lindsay, 1881.

Shire, Laurel Clark. *The Threshold of Manifest Destiny: Gender and National Expansion in Florida.* Philadelphia: University of Pennsylvania Press, 2016.

Shoemaker, Nancy. *A Strange Likeness: Becoming Red and White in Eighteenth-Century North America.* New York: Oxford University Press, 2006.

———. "Wonder and Repulsion: North American Indians in Eighteenth-Century." In *Europe Observed: Multiple Gazes in Early Modern Encounters,* edited by Kumkum Chatterjee and Clement Hawes, 173–93. Lewisburg, Pa.: Bucknell University Press, 2008.

Shuck-Hall, Sheri Marie. "Alabama and Coushatta Diaspora and Coalescence in the Mississippian Shatter Zone." In Ethridge and Shuck-Hall, *Mapping the Mississippian Shatter Zone,* 250–71.

——— *Journey to the West: The Alabama and Coushatta Indians.* Norman: University of Oklahoma Press, 2008.

Sider, Gerald M. *Living Indian Histories: Lumbee and Tuscarora People in North Carolina.* New York: Cambridge University Press, 1993.

———. *Lumbee Indian Histories: Race, Ethnicity, and Indian Identity in the Southern United States.* New York: Cambridge University Press, 1993.

Silverberg, Robert. *The Mound Builders.* Athens: Ohio University Press, 1968.

Silverman, David J. *Thundersticks: Firearms and the Violent Transformation of Native America.* Cambridge, Mass.: Harvard University Press, 2016.

Simek, J. F., A. Cressler, N. P. Herrmann, and S. C. Sherwood. "Sacred Landscapes of the South-Eastern USA: Prehistoric Rock and Cave Art in Tennessee." *Antiquity* 87, no. 336 (2013): 430–46.

Slotkin, Richard. *Regeneration through Violence: The Mythology of the American Frontier, 1600–1860.* Norman: University of Oklahoma Press, 2000.

Smith, Andrea, and Anna Einstein. *Rebuilding Shattered Worlds: Creating Community by Voicing the Past.* Lincoln: University of Nebraska Press, 2016.

Smith, Dean H. *Modern Tribal Development: Paths to Self-Sufficiency and Cultural Integrity in Indian Country.* Walnut Creek, Calif.: AltaMira, 2000.

Smith, F. Todd. *From Dominance to Disappearance: The Indians of Texas and the Near Southwest, 1786–1859.* Lincoln: University of Nebraska Press, 2005.

———. *Louisiana and the Gulf South Frontier, 1500–1821.* Baton Rouge: Louisiana State University Press, 2014.

Smith, Marvin T. "Aboriginal Depopulation in the Postcontact Southeast." In *The Forgotten Centuries: Indians and Europeans in the American South, 1521–1704*, edited by Charles Hudson and Carmen Chaves Tesser, 257–75. Athens: University of Georgia Press, 1994.

———. "Aboriginal Population Movements in the Early Historic Period Interior Southeast." In Waselkov, Wood, and Hatley, *Powhatan's Mantle*, 43–56.

———. *Archaeology of Aboriginal Culture Change in the Southeast: Depopulation during the Early Historic Period.* Gainesville: University of Florida Press, 1987.

Smith, Scott C. *Landscape and Politics in the Ancient Andes: Biographies of Place at Khonkho Wankane.* Albuquerque: University of New Mexico Press, 2016.

Smithers, Gregory D. "Beyond the 'Ecological Indian': Environmental Politics and Traditional Ecological Knowledge in Modern North America." *Environmental History* 20, no. 1 (January 2015): 83–111.

———. *The Cherokee Diaspora: An Indigenous History of Migration, Resettlement, and Identity.* New Haven, Conn.: Yale University Press, 2015.

———. "'Our Hands and Hearts Are Joined Together': Friendship, Colonialism, and the Cherokee People in Early America." *Journal of Social History* 50, no. 4 (Summer 2017): 609–29.

———. *Science, Sexuality, and Race in the United States and Australia, 1780–1940.* Rev. ed. Lincoln: University of Nebraska Press, 2017.

Smithers, Gregory D., and Brooke N. Newman, eds. *Native Diasporas: Indigenous Identities and Settler Colonialism in the Americas.* Lincoln: University of Nebraska Press, 2014.

Snow, Dean R. *Archaeology of Native North America.* Abingdon, England: Routledge, 2016.

———. "Iroquois-Huron Warfare." In Chacon and Mendoza, *North American Indigenous Warfare*, 149–59.

Snyder, Christina. *Slavery in Indian Country: The Changing Face of Captivity in Early America*. Cambridge, Mass.: Harvard University Press, 2010.

———. "The South." In Hoxie, *Oxford Handbook*, 315–33.

Spear, Jennifer. *Race, Sex, and Social Order in Early New Orleans*. Baltimore: Johns Hopkins University Press, 2009.

Speck, Frank G. *Ceremonial Songs of the Creek and Yuchi Indians*. Philadelphia: University Museum, 1909–1911.

Spence, Mark David. *Dispossessing the Wilderness: Indian Removal and the Making of National Parks*. New York: Oxford University Press, 1999.

Spencer, Lucien A. *Special Report of the Florida Seminole Agency*. Washington, D.C.: Government Printing Office, 1921.

Stagg, J. C. A. *The War of 1812: Conflict for a Continent*. New York: Cambridge University Press, 2012.

Stanford, Dennis J., and Bruce A. Bradley. *Across Atlantic Ice: The Origins of America's Clovis Culture*. Berkeley: University of California Press, 2012.

Stannard, David E. *American Holocaust: Columbus and the Conquest of the New World*. New York: Oxford University Press, 1992.

Starkey, Armstrong. *European and Native American Warfare, 1675–1815*. London: UCL Press, 1998.

———. "European-Native American Warfare in North America." In *War in the Early Modern World, 1450–1815*, edited by Jeremy Black, 237–62. London: Routledge, 1999.

Steponaitis, Vincas P. "Contrasting Patterns of Mississippian Development." In Earle, *Chiefdoms*, 193–228.

Stern, Jessica Y. *The Lives in Objects: Native Americans, British Colonists, and Cultures of Labor and Exchange in the Southeast*. Chapel Hill: University of North Carolina Press, 2017.

Stevenson, Brenda E. *What is Slavery?* New York: Polity, 2015.

Stick, David, ed. *An Outer Banks Reader*. New York: University of North Carolina Press, 1998.

St. Jean, Wendy. *Remaining Chickasaw in Indian Territory, 1830s–1907*. Tuscaloosa: University of Alabama Press, 2011. Stockel, H. Henrietta. *The Lightning Stick: Arrows, Wounds, and Indian Legends*. Reno: University of Nevada Press, 1995.

Stodder, Ann L. W., Debra L. Martin, Alan H. Goodman, and Daniel T. Reff. "Cultural Longevity and Biological Stress in the American Southwest." In *The Backbone of History: Health and Nutrition in the Western Hemisphere*, edited by Richard H. Steckel and Jerome C. Rose, 481–505. New York: Cambridge University Press, 2002.

Stookey, Lorena Laura. *Thematic Guide to World Mythology*. Westport, Conn.: Greenwood, 2004.

Straus, Lawrence Guy, David J. Meltzer, and Ted Goebel. "Ice Age Atlantis? Exploring the Solutrean-Clovis 'Connection.'" *World Archeology* 37, no. 4 (2005): 507–32.

Stremlau, Rose. *Sustaining the Cherokee Family: Kinship and the Allotment of an Indian Nation*. Chapel Hill: University of North Carolina Press, 2011.

Strickland, Rennard. *Fire and the Spirits: Cherokee Law from Clan to Court*. Norman: University of Oklahoma Press, 1975.

Strong, Pauline Turner. "Transforming Outsiders: Captivity, Adoption, and Slavery Reconsidered." In Philip J. Deloria and Salisbury, *Companion to American Indian History*, 339–56.

Stubbs, John D., Jr. "The Chickasaw Contact with the La Salle Expedition." In Galloway, *La Salle and His Legacy*, 41–48.

Sturgis, Amy H. *The Trail of Tears and Indian Removal.* Westport, Conn.: Greenwood, 2007.

Sturm, Circe. *Blood Politics: Race, Culture, and Identity in the Cherokee Nation of Oklahoma.* Berkeley: University of California Press, 2002.

Sturtevant, William C. "Creek into Seminole: North American Indians in Historical Perspective." In *North American Indians in Historical Perspective,* edited by E. B. Leacock and N. O. Lurie, 92–128. New York: Random House, 2004.

———. "The Medicine Bundles and Busks of the Florida Seminole." *Florida Anthropologist* 7 (1954), 31–70.

———. "Spanish-Indian Relations in Southeastern North America." *Ethnohistory* 9, no. 1 (Winter 1962): 41–94.

Summerhayes, Colin P. *Earth's Climate Evolution.* Hoboken, N.J.: John Wiley & Sons, Ltd., 2015

Summitt, April R. *Sequoyah and the Invention of the Cherokee Alphabet.* Santa Barbara, Calif.: ABC-CLIO, 2012.

Swanton, John R. *Chickasaw Society and Religion.* Foreword by Greg O'Brien. Lincoln: University of Nebraska Press, 2006.

———. *Early History of the Creek Indians and their Neighbors.* 1922. Reprint, Gainesville: University Press of Florida, 1998.

———. *Final Report of the United States De Soto Expedition Commission.* 1939. Reprint, Washington, D.C.: Smithsonian institution Press, 1985.

———. *The Indian Tribes of North America.* Baltimore: Genealogical Publishing, 1952.

———. *The Indians of the Southeastern United States.* 1946. Reprint, Washington, D.C.: Smithsonian Institution Press, 1979.

———. *Myths and Tales of the Southeastern Indians.* Introduction by George E. Lankford. 1929. Reprint, Norman: University of Oklahoma Press, 1995.

———. *Source Material for the Social and Ceremonial Life of the Choctaw Indians.* 1931. Reprint, Tuscaloosa: University of Alabama Press, 2001.

Sweet, Julie Anne. *Negotiating for Georgia: British-Creek Relations in the Trustee Era, 1733–1752.* Athens: University of Georgia Press, 2005.

Tamm, Erika, et al. "Beringian Standstill and Spread of Native American Founders." *PLOS One* 2, no 9 (September 5, 2007): e829.

Taylor, Alan. *American Colonies: The Settling of North America.* New York: Penguin Books, 2001.

———. *American Revolutions: A Continental History, 1750–1804.* New York: W. W. Norton, 2016.

———. *The Civil War of 1812: American Citizens, British Subjects, Irish Rebels and Indian Allies.* New York: Alfred A. Knopf, 2010.

Taylor, Melanie Benson. *Reconstructing the Native South: American Indian Literature and the Lost Cause.* Athens: University of Georgia Press, 2012.

Temple, Sarah Gober, and Kenneth L. Coleman. *Georgia Journeys*. Athens: University of Georgia Press, 1961.

Thomas, David Hurst, ed. *Columbian Consequences*. Washington, D.C.: Smithsonian Institution Press, 1990.

Thornton, Russell. *American Indian Holocaust and Survival: A Population History since 1492*. Norman: University of Oklahoma Press, 1987.

———. "Cherokee Population Losses during the Trail of Tears: A New Perspective and a New Estimate." *Ethnohistory* 31, no. 4 (1984): 289–300.

———. *The Cherokees: A Population History*. Lincoln: University of Nebraska Press, 1992.

———, ed. *Studying Native America: Problems and Prospects*. Madison: University of Wisconsin Press, 1998.

Thrasher, Christopher D. *Fight Sports and American Masculinity: Salvation in Violence from 1607 to the Present*. Jefferson, N.C.: McFarland, 2015.

Thrower, Robert G. "Casualties and Consequences of the Creek War: A Modern Creek Perspective." In *Tohopeka: Rethinking the Creek War and the War of 1812*, edited by Kathryn E. Holland Braun, 10–29. Tuscaloosa: University of Alabama Press, 2012.

Thrush, Coll. *Indigenous London: Native Travelers at the Heart of Empire*. New Haven, Conn.: Yale University Press, 2016.

Tortora, Daniel J. *Carolina in Crisis: Cherokees, Colonists, and Slaves in the American Southeast, 1756–1763*. Chapel Hill: University of North Carolina Press, 2015.

Trigger, Bruce G. *Children of Aataentsic: A History of the Huron People to 1660*. Kingston, Ont., Canada: McGill-Queen's University Press, 1976.

———. "Inequality and Communication in Early Civilization." *Anthropologica* 18 (1976): 27–52.

Tuan, Yi-Fu. *Space and Place: The Perspective of Experience*. Minneapolis: University of Minnesota Press, 1977.

Tucker, Spencer C., ed. *The Encyclopedia of North American Indian Wars, 1607–1890: A Political, Social, and Military History*. 2 vols. Santa Barbara, Calif.: ABC-CLIO, 2011, 2015.

Tucker, Toba Pato. *Haudenosaunee: Portraits of the Firekeepers, the Onondaga Nation*. Syracuse, N.Y.: Syracuse University Press, 1999.

Tuniz, Claudio, Richard Gillespie, and Cheryl Jones. *The Bone Reader: Science and Politics in Human Origins Research*. London: Routledge, 2009.

Tuttle, Edmund B. *The Boy's Book about Indians*. Philadelphia: J. B. Lippincott, 1873.

Usner, Daniel H., Jr. "American Indians on the Cotton Frontier: Changing Economic Relations with the Citizens and Slaves in the Mississippi Territory." *Journal of American History* 72, no. 2 (September 1985): 297–317.

———. *Indians, Settlers, and Slaves in a Frontier Exchange Economy: The Lower Mississippi Valley before 1783*. Chapel Hill: University of North Carolina Press, 1992.

Vaughan, Alden T., ed. *Early American Indian Documents*. 20 vols. Vol. 8, *New Jersey Treaties, 1683–1713*, edited by Barbara Graymont. Vol. 9, *New York and New Jersey Treaties, 1714–1753*, edited by Barbara Graymont. Vol. 13, *North and South*

Carolina Treaties, 1654–1756, edited by W. Stitt Robinson. Vol 18, *Revolution and Confederation,* edited by Colin G. Calloway. Bethesda, Md.: University Publications of America, 2004.

———. *New England Encounters: Indians and Euroamericans, ca. 1600–1850.* Boston: Northeastern University Press, 1999.

———. *Transatlantic Encounters: American Indians in Britain, 1500–1776.* New York: Cambridge University Press, 2006.

Vavilov, N. I. *Origins and Geography of Cultivated Plants.* Translated by Doris Love. New York: Cambridge University Press, 1987.

Veracini, Lorenzo. *Settler Colonialism: A Theoretical Overview.* London: Palgrave Macmillan, 2011.

Wallace, Anthony F. C. *The Long, Bitter Trail: Andrew Jackson and the Indians.* New York: Hill and Wang, 1993.

———. *Tuscarora: A History.* Albany, N.Y.: State University of New York Press, 2012.

Walthall, John A. *Prehistoric Indians of the Southeast: Archaeology of Alabama and the Middle South.* Tuscaloosa: University of Alabama Press, 1980.

Ward, Matthew C. *Breaking the Backcountry: Seven Years War in Virginia and Pennsylvania, 1754–1765.* Pittsburgh: University of Pittsburgh Press, 2003.

Ward, H. Trawick, and R. Stephen Davis Jr. *Time Before History: The Archaeology of North Carolina.* Chapel Hill: University of North Carolina Press, 1999.

Ward, Rufus. "Choctaw Farmsteads in Mississippi, 1830." In Samuel J. Wells and Tubby, *After Removal,* 33–41.

Warren, Stephen. "Reconsidering Coalescence: Yuchi and Shawnee Survival Strategies in the Colonial Southeast." In Jason Baird Jackson, *Yuchi Indian Histories,* 151–88.

———. *Worlds the Shawnee Made: Migration and Violence in Early America.* Chapel Hill: University of North Carolina Press, 2014.

Waselkov, Gregory A. *A Conquering Spirit: Fort Mims and the Redstick War of 1813–1814.* Tuscaloosa: University of Alabama Press, 2006.

Waselkov, Gregory A., and Kathryn E. Holland Braund, eds. *William Bartram on the Southeastern Indians.* Lincoln: University of Nebraska Press, 1995.

Waselkov, Gregory A., Peter H. Wood, and Tom Hatley, eds. *Powhatan's Mantle: Indians in the Colonial Southeast.* Rev. and expanded ed. Lincoln: University of Nebraska Press, 2006.

Washburn, Wilcomb E. *History of Indian-White Relations.* Vol. 4, *Handbook of the North American Indians,* edited by William C. Sturtevant. Washington, D.C.: Government Printing Office, 1989.

Wasserman, Adam. *A People's History of Florida, 1513–1876: How Africans, Seminoles, Women, and Lower Class Whites Shaped the Sunshine State.* 3rd ed. Sarasota, Fla.: A. Wasserman, 2010.

Watson, Harry. *Liberty and Power: The Politics of Jacksonian America.* New York: Hill & Wang, 1990.

Watson, Kelly L. *Insatiable Appetites: Imperial Encounters with Cannibals in the North Atlantic World.* New York: New York University Press, 2015.

Watson, Larry S., ed. *Indian Removal Records: Senate Document 512, 23 Cong., 1 Sess.* Vol. 4. Yuma, Ariz.: HISTREE, 1987.

Weatherford, Jack. *Native Roots: How the Indians Enriched America.* New York: Fawcett, 1991.

Weaver, Jace. *Other Words: American Indian Literature, Law, and Culture.* Norman: University of Oklahoma Press, 2001.

———. *The Red Atlantic: American Indigenes and the Making of the Modern World, 1000–1927.* Chapel Hill: University of North Carolina Press, 2014.

Webb, Clarence H. *The Poverty Point Culture.* Baton Rouge: School of Geosciences, Louisiana State University, 1982.

Weber, David J. *Spanish Frontier in North America.* New Haven, Conn.: Yale University Press, 2009.

Weddle, Robert S. *Changing Tides: Twilight and Dawn in the Spanish Sea, 1763–1803.* College Station: Texas A&M Press, 1995.

Weeks, Charles A. *Paths to a Middle Ground: The Diplomacy of Natchez, Boukfouka, Nogales, and San Fernando de las Barrancas.* Tuscaloosa: University of Alabama Press, 2005.

Weeks, Philip. *"Farewell, My Nation": American Indians and the United States in the Nineteenth Century.* 3rd ed. Malden, Mass.: John Wiley & Sons, 2016.

Weeks, Stephen B. *Letters of Benjamin Hawkins, 1796–1804.* Vol. 9. Savannah: Georgia Historical Society, 1916.

Weer, Paul. "The Muskhogean Indians." *Proceedings of the Indiana Academy of Science* 48 (1938): 19–22.

Weidensaul, Scott. *The First Frontier: The Forgotten History of Struggle, Savagery, and Endurance in Early America.* Boston: Houghton Mifflin Harcourt, 2012.

Weisman, Brent R. *Like Beads on a String: A Culture History of the Seminole Indians in North Peninsular Florida.* Tuscaloosa: University of Alabama Press, 1989.

Welch, Paul D. *Moundville's Economy.* Tuscaloosa: University of Alabama Press, 1991.

———. "Outlying Sites with the Moundville Chiefdom." In Knight and Steponaitis, *Archaeology of the Moundville Chiefdom,* 133–66.

Wells, Mary Ann. *Native Land: Mississippi, 1540–1798.* Jackson: University Press of Mississippi, 1994.

———. *Searching for Red Eagle: A Personal Journey into the Spirit World of Native America.* Jackson: University Press of Mississippi, 1998.

Wells, Samuel J., and Roseanna Tubby, eds. *After Removal: The Choctaw in Mississippi.* Jackson: University Press of Mississippi, 1986.

West, Frederick Hadleigh. "Late Paleolithic Cultures in Alaska." In *Early Native Americans: Prehistoric Demography, Economy, and Technology,* edited by David L. Browman, 161–87. The Hague: Mouton, 1980.

White, Richard. *The Roots of Dependency: Subsistence, Environment, and Social Change among the Choctaws, Pawnees, and Navajos.* Lincoln: University of Nebraska Press, 1983.

Wickman, Patricia Riles. *Osceola's Legacy.* Rev. ed. Tuscaloosa: University of Alabama Press, 2006.

Widmer, Randolph J. *Evolution of Calusa: A Nonagricultural Chiefdom of the Southwest Florida Coast.* Tuscaloosa: University of Alabama Press, 1988.

Wildcat, Daniel R. *Red Alert: Saving the Planet with Indigenous Knowledge.* Golden, Colo.: Fulcrum, 2009.

Wilkins, David E. *American Indian Sovereignty and the U.S. Supreme Court: The Masking of Justice.* Austin: University of Texas Press, 1997.

Wilkins, David E., and K. Tsianina Lomawaima. *Uneven Ground: American Indian Sovereignty and Federal Law.* Norman: University of Oklahoma Press, 2001.

Wilkins, Thurman. *Cherokee Tragedy: The Ridge Family and the Decimation of a People.* Norman: University of Oklahoma Press, 1986.

"William Burnet." *The American Quarterly Register* 13 (1841): 290–92.

Williams, David. *The Georgia Gold Rush: Twenty-Niners, Cherokees, and Gold Fever.* Columbia: University of South Carolina Press, 1994.

Williams, John L., ed. *The Territory of Florida; Or, Sketches of the Topography, Civil and Natural History, of the Country, the Climate, and the Indian Tribes, from the First Discovery to the Present Time.* New York: A. T. Goodrich, 1837.

Williams, Robert A., Jr. *Linking Arms Together: American Indian Treaty Visions of Law and Peace, 1600–1800.* New York: Routledge, 1999.

Williams, Samuel Cole. *Early Travels in the Tennessee Country, 1540–1800.* Johnson City, Tenn.: Watauga, 1928.

Willig, Timothy D. *Restoring the Chain of Friendship: British Policy and the Indians of the Great Lakes, 1783–1815.* Lincoln: University of Nebraska Press, 2008.

Willis, William S. "Divide and Rule: Red, White, and Black in the Southeast." *Journal of Negro History* 48, no. 3 (July 1963): 157–76.

Wilson, Gregory D. *The Archaeology of Everyday at Life at Early Moundville.* Tuscaloosa: University of Alabama Press, 2008.

Winn, William W. *The Triumph of the Ecunnau-Nuxulgee: Land Speculators, George M. Troup, State Rights, and the Removal of the Creek Indians from Georgia and Alabama, 1825–38.* Macon, Ga.: Mercer University Press, 2015.

Wirt, William. *Opinion on the Right of the State of Georgia to Extend Her Laws over the Cherokee Nation.* New Echota, Cherokee Nation: Cherokee Phoenix, 1830.

Witgie, Michael. *An Infinity of Nations: How the Native New World Shaped Early North America.* Philadelphia: University of Pennsylvania Press, 2012.

Witthoft, John. "Notes on a Cherokee Migration Story." Communicated by W. N. Fenton. *Journal of the Washington Academy of Sciences* 37, no. 9 (1947): 304–5.

Wolfe, Patrick. "Land, Labor, and Difference: Elementary Structures of Race." *American Historical Review* 106, no. 3 (June 2001): 866–905.

———. "Settler Colonialism and the Elimination of the Native." *Journal of Genocide Research* 8, no. 4 (2006): 387–409.

———. *Settler Colonialism and the Transformation of Anthropology: The Politics and Poetics of an Ethnographic Event.* London: Cassell, 1999.

Womack, Craig S. *Red on Red: Native American Literary Separatism.* Minneapolis: University of Minnesota Press, 1999.

Wood, Peter H. "The Changing Population of the Colonial South: An Overview by Race and Region, 1685–1790." In Waselkov, Wood, and Hatley, *Powhatan's Mantle*, 57–132.

Woodward, Buck. "Indian Land Sales and Allotment in Antebellum Virginia: Trustees, Tribal Agency, and the Nottoway Reservation." *American Nineteenth Century History* 17, no. 2 (June 2016): 161–81.

Woodward, Grace Steele. *The Cherokees*. Norman: University of Oklahoma Press, 1963.

Woodward, Susan L., and Jerry N. McDonald. *Indian Mounds of the Middle Ohio Valley: A Guide to Mounds and Earthworks of the Adena, Hopewell, Cole, and Fort Ancient People*. Lincoln: University of Nebraska Press, 2002.

Worsley, Israel. *A View of the American Indians: Their General Character, Customs, Language, Public Festivals, Religious Rites, and Traditions*. London: R. Hunter, 1828.

Worth, John E. *The Struggle for the Georgia Coast*. Tuscaloosa: University of Alabama Press, 2007.

———. *The Timucuan Chiefdoms of Spanish Florida: Assimilation*. Gainesville: University of Florida Press, 1998.

Wright, Amos J. *The McGillivray and McIntosh Traders: On the Old Southwest Frontier, 1716–1815*. Montgomery, Ala.: New South Books, 2007.

Wright, J. Leitch, Jr. *Creeks and Seminoles: The Destruction and Regeneration of the Muscogulge People*. Lincoln: University of Nebraska Press, 1986.

———. *The Only Land They Knew: American Indians in the Old South*. Lincoln: University of Nebraska Press, 1999.

Wunder, John R., ed. *Native American Law and Colonialism, before 1776 to 1903*. New York: Garland, 1996.

———. *Native American Sovereignty*. New York: Garland, 1999.

Yarbrough, Fay A. *Race and the Cherokee Nation: Sovereignty in the Nineteenth Century*. Philadelphia: University of Pennsylvania Press, 2008.

Young, Biloine Whiting, and Melvin L. Fowler. *Cahokia: The Great Native American Metropolis*. Bloomington: University of Illinois Press, 2000.

A Young Gentleman. *A New Voyage to Georgia*. London: Printed for J. Wilford, 1737.

Ywahoo, Dhyani. *Voices of Our Ancestors: Cherokee Teachings from the Wisdom Fire*. Boston: Shambala, 1987.

Zellar, Gary. *African Creeks: Estelvste and the Creek Nation*. Norman: University of Oklahoma Press, 2007.

Zimmerman, Larry J. "Archaeology." In *A Companion to the Anthropology of American Indians*, edited by Thomas Biolsi, 526–41. Blackwell, 2004.

Zorgy, Michael J. *Anetso, the Cherokee Ball Game: At the Center of Ceremony and Identity*. Chapel Hill: University of North Carolina Press, 2010.

INDEX

Lightning Source UK Ltd.
Milton Keynes UK
UKHW040714290319
340140UK00001B/55/P

9 780806 162287